DEA...

BEAUTY

Based on the life of Ouida Keeton

By:

Marcelle Harwell

&

Teresa Holloway

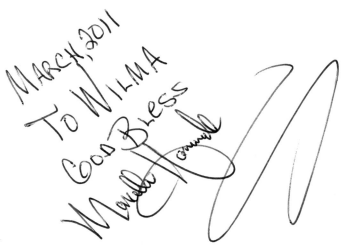

MARCH 2011
TO WILMA
GOOD BLESS

1

PREFACE

I was a young woman of twenty when my Grandmother told me the tragic story of a beautiful woman whose mother tried to keep her from the man she loved. They lived here in our hometown of Laurel, Mississippi, the year was 1935.

The tale of woe was so disturbing that I never forgot it. Occasionally, I would think of her as I passed the dilapidated old house where she once lived, where the horrid deed took place. Now torn down, and a vegetable market in its place, the memory of her still comes to mind. This year I thought of her again and I decided it was time someone told her story, the life of Ouida Keeton, a bright and beautiful young woman, who murdered her mother in a most gruesome way. I hope I can portray her with as near the truth as possible. I have researched and studied everything I could about her and her family; documents, newspapers, trial transcripts, medical records from Whitfield Mental Hospital and talking with older residents of our town. The story I will tell here is based on what I believe would be Ouida's own thoughts of her life as a child to her last moments as she lay dying in the hospital at Whitfield Insane Asylum in 1973. The people and things she loved, her dreams of happiness and finally her insanity and murder of her mother.

The murder trial of Ouida Keeton was the most sensational case in the history of Mississippi.

ACKNOWLEDGEMENTS

First, I want to thank my maternal grandmother, Dorothy Pope, for her inspiration to write this book. I probably would have never known about Ouida Keeton without her deep interest in the murder case.

My mother's sister, Sue Rigdon, for helping me with some of the details that she remembered as a young girl.

The invaluable help from the ladies at Bart Gavin's Office of the Circuit Clerk in Jones County, Joyce Bush and Jennifer Walker, who took out special time for me, in searching for court records that had been lost somewhere in the mountain of old records.

In addition, a special thanks for the help of Larry Ishee, Chancery Clerk of Jones County and ladies in his staff.

I also want to express my gratitude to Shelia Hicks, at the Mississippi State Hospital at Whitfield, Mississippi, for her kindness and valuable time. Also Judge David Lyons for his help and invaluable time. You are a special friend.

Many thanks to Debra Blackledge and her mother, Dorothy A. Jones, for the material I used in my book. I appreciate your help very much.

Thank you, Jimmy Bass, who tried his best to find pictures for my book. You have always been so kind to me. You are one of Laurel's treasures.

Finally, I would like to thank, Regina Bartran Dixon, my sweet niece, for all of her technical advice on Ouida Keeton's condition. She has a Masters Degree in psychology and counseling and is a licensed mental health counselor.

3

CHAPTER I

As the early morning sun, shinning in my eyes woke me up to the sweet smell of Jasmine outside the French doors to my room. I lay in my soft feather bed thinking of what I would do today, the cool breeze softly caressed my face. I pulled the covers up higher to my chin to postpone the certainty that I would have to get out of my cozy warm bed. As I rose from my bed of sweet dreams, I put my feet on the cool wood floor and walked across the room to my washstand. As I look in the mirror I see a sleepy-eyed young girl named Ouida, with long tosseled curls of deep brown hair, big brown eyes and freckles, that I so hated. I washed my face from the basin on the washstand and toweled it dry. Now, I am freshened enough to face a new day. I put on my robe and walked out onto the wide gallery.

The rising sun is peeking thru the beautiful live oaks that frame the house, casting shadows across the lawn. As the sun rises higher, it completely shades the old house with their huge branches. Our lovely old family home built in 1821, is a raised Louisiana cottage; it is not a plantation anymore, because we only own six acres of land now. At one time before the devastation of the Civil War, our home was a plantation with twelve hundred acres. We live near the Village of Angie, Louisiana, a sleepy little village with an old country store, a hardware store, a post office, city hall and a few other small businesses. We are not far from Pearl River. There is also a sawmill near the river.

Copy of petition from Mrs. Daisy Keeton's Estate on file in the Office of the Chancery Clerk , Jones County.

In 1900, Ma gave birth to a son; she named him John, after Pa. He was born two years before me and was a very special child. John was a beautiful little boy, with black curly hair and a face like an angel. My memory of him is still clear. Ma loved John more than any of us, but I can understand why, because he was so sweet and loving. I loved him very much too. We played together all the time.

One beautiful summer day we went down to Pearl River, near our house to have a picnic on the sandbar. We couldn't swim in the water that day because the water was up and the currents strong. Louisa, our maid, and Pa were with us, Ma didn't like the water so she stayed home. We ate our picnic lunch then me, Earl and John went exploring. We walked along the rivers edge picking up mussels. John suddenly saw a baby raccoon and chased after him. As he climbed a high bank trying to catch the little raccoon, the sand under him gave way and he fell in the river. We screamed for Pa as John was struggling in the swift current, trying to keep his head above water. As the river carried him farther down stream, Pa dove in and tried to save him. We all stood on the rivers edge, helpless as John was carried out of sight by the rushing waters. Louisa ran home to get the Negro men to come help. Later as we stood on the bank waiting in anticipation, Sam, our worker walked up to where everyone was waiting with little John's lifeless body in his big strong arms. He had been taken down in an undertow and came back up and his little body had snagged on a piece of driftwood on the river's edge. I will never forget that sorrowful day that my sweet little brother went to be with the angels. Ma blamed Pa and Louisa for the loss of her precious son. She was never the same after that day. The love went out of her heart like snuffing out a candle and being left in the dark, never seeing that beautiful light of love again. Pa and Louisa would come to know what a person without love can become. I would learn this first hand myself.

The year is 1911 and I am nine years old. I have one sister and a brother older than me, Maud, thirteen and Earl, ten. Ma comes from a fine old Southern family, McKinstry; my grandfather came from South Carolina and was Scotch Irish, while Grandma, Laura was born in Mississippi in 1859. Sarah Daisy is my Ma's name, she was born in 1879 and she married John Keeton in 1896 when she was only seventeen years old. My Pa was born in 1868 and was ten years older than my Ma, Daisy. It was his family that owned our home in Angie, Louisiana since before the Civil War.

When my Ma was sixteen, she met and fell in love with a local boy. When her parents found out they forbid her from seeing him, she had already been promised to my Pa Keeton. She was broken hearted and never forgave them for making her marry another. She became a bitter person and her sweet demeanor changed into a scorned woman. My grandma told me how sweet she used to be. I have never seen the gentle, sweet person she once was. I think she takes the heartbreak of this, plus the death of little John out on my poor Pa, because I cannot ever remember him having been treated kindly by her. In fact, she was cruel to all of us. The burden of children was not something she was interested in, if it did not benefit her in some way.

I was seven years old when my Ma gave birth to a baby girl. She named her Eloise. She is a sweet little thing, but I could tell Ma was not happy about having another baby. She thought birthing babies was over. She has turned her over to Louisa, our maid, to nurse. We have a cow so Ma does not even feed her. She is totally unconcerned about her existence. I tried to help Louisa with her as much as I can. Maud is twelve years old, but seems preoccupied with her own little world and could care less about helping in the care or attention of Eloise. Louisa is a wonderful loving person and enjoyed taking care of the baby; she almost acted as if she belongs to her.

Louisa is a light-skinned mulatto and she is very good to us. She is half-French and half Negro, which makes for a very pretty young woman. She has coal black hair that is wavy and long, beautiful large black eyes and a pretty mouth. When she is upset with Ma she speaks broken French, that makes Ma extremely angry so angry that she will strike her across the face. Poor Louisa will just stand there and take it. I can imagine what she would like to do to my Ma. Sometimes in the evening when the moon is full, I would sneak out to her little shanty and watch her thru the window, she had candles lit everywhere and she was in a kneeling position on the floor, putting different liquids in a bowl mixing it and then drinking the mixture. I noticed she had a little doll that was dressed in pieces of fabric from one of my Ma's dresses and its hair looked like Ma's, which was the same color as mine, but straight. She stuck a hatpin in the stomach of the doll and as she did this, she spoke some strange words I did not recognize. I heard loud screams from inside our house in the direction of Ma and Pa's bedroom. I ran up onto the porch and looked into the French doors of her room. Ma was not in bed, she was bent double in pain and screaming out, then as suddenly as the pains came, they stopped. She got back in bed and blew out the light. I stood there on the porch for a considerable time thinking about what all of this meant. I had heard the Negros talking in whispers when they didn't know I was listening about something called Voodoo. Strangely, as I thought about the connection of the doll and Ma's pain, I didn't care. She probably deserves it. My mind wandered as I looked up at the beautiful full moon and out across the lawn. The dancing shadows of the moss swaying back and forth on the branches of the old trees gave an eerie scene of dancing creatures of the night playing their little mystic games, that can only be seen by certain individuals like myself or people who believe in fairies and such. Watching this lovely festival of the night fairies made me very sleepy, maybe because they sprinkled sleep dust in my eyes. Anyway, I went into my room, crawled into my soft cozy bed, and fell into a deep sleep only to dream of very strange things.

Our life in this peaceful setting is anything but peaceful. Ma continues to make our lives almost unbearable. She is evil and mean, poor Pa seems to get the worst of it. He is such a kind and gentle man. Everyday I see him looking sadder and sadder. It breaks my heart, because he has so much love to give. He seems to love for me to come into his study where he spends most of his time now. He shows me his prized book collection and points out the ones he thinks I should read as soon as I am old enough. Before I leave him to his solitude, I give him a kiss on his cheek and tell him how much I love him. He gets a big smile on his face and says he loves me very much too.

Now, Pa has given up his mercantile store and has withdrawn completely from life. He stays in his study with the door closed and only lets me in when he wants me to spend time with him. Sometimes I hear Ma in there with him, screaming about how worthless he is.

My Ma and Pa are taking a trip to New Orleans. He has some kind of business he needs to attend to. We have been left in the care of Louisa while they are gone. They depart from the train depot in Angie, very near where we live. They are going to be gone a few days. I would not know at the time, but when I kissed my Pa goodbye early that Monday morning; I would never see him again. We were told my Pa was killed in a freak accident falling from the train while in full motion. He was thrown beneath the train and run over. His body was so mangled they had to have a closed casket funeral. I have often wondered if it was really an accident. Did he fall or did something else happen? I will never know for sure, He had told me before he had left that when he was gone I would need to be strong and trust in God in the years to come, because he probably wouldn't be back here to protect me.

Our life changed forever. Ma's cruelty took on a completely new form. She seemed possessed, she screamed at all of us, we couldn't do anything right. I think she has lost her mind. Word of Ma's insanity has slowly gotten around in our little village; so much that we don't get visitors anymore. Even family members have begun to stay away. Some are saying she is grieving for the loss of her husband and little John. Some say it is a spell that has been cast upon her, while others just say she was always evil and it has just come out in her. We are almost outcast in our little village. My Ma has always been a beautiful woman, with black hair and brown eyes, but now her face has a different look. She looks crazy out of her eyes.

One day Louisa was polishing the silver when Ma came in the room. When I came down the hall, I heard loud arguing in the kitchen it was Ma and Louisa.

Ma suddenly screamed at her and said, "You sorry gal, you think you are a Voodoo Witch! If you believe I am afraid of your spells, you are mistaken. I'll teach you a lesson or two!"

Louisa screamed, "Mistress Daisy, you need to beware of what you do to me."

Ma replied, "You little witch, I'll do whatever I want to you, no one cares what happens to a Negro around here, you should know that fact."

As I stood in the doorway watching their fuss-fight, Ma hit Louisa with a heavy cooking spoon, she suddenly fell back and hit her head on the brick fireplace. She collapsed to the floor, limp as a rag doll. I ran to her, blood was flowing from her head puddling on the hearth. Her face had gone pale; she looked as white as me. Her eyes open, I called to her to answer me, I didn't know she was dead!

Ma screamed out, "Oh God, what have I done! Ouida, get your sister Maud." I asked Ma why she had done this to our sweet Louisa. Ma said that she didn't mean to really hurt her, it was an accident.

I said, "I hate you for killing Louisa and I will never forgive you!" I told Ma that I loved Louisa more than I had ever loved her.

Ma sat down at the table with her hands covering her face, crying, "What is going to happen to me next, I can't take anymore. I am losing my mind! First my precious little John, then your Pa and now I have killed Louisa and you hate me for it." Ma told me that I could never tell anyone about what happened here today. Ma said that she would have Sam to come get Louisa and bury her in the cemetery plot for the Negros out in back of the house. They will have a funeral for her tomorrow. She told Sam she fell and hit her head and died. He didn't question her, he knew better.

Every morning I awake, I know not what the day will bring for me. Please God, help me to be strong like my Pa said and keep my faith in the Lord. I am young, but I am strong and **I WILL** get through this somehow, someway!

With Louisa gone the burden of all the household duties have fallen on us. My mother would not dare hire another maid. In fact, I have become a prisoner in my own home. I can only go out with her at my side and that is just to purchase the necessities to sustain us. No visitors are welcome anymore. Our life in the social world was over forever. What is to become of me? Will I live out my life as my mother's prisoner? Will she finally decide to murder me as she did Louisa? Right now, she needs me and maybe as long as I am useful to her as a slave she will keep me alive. She is not as cruel to my sisters and brother, but then they don't know what she did!

Everyday we work so hard to keep this big house clean, but I am still just a child. I pretend I am a princess locked in a castle by a wicked witch. Living in my dream world helps me to escape from my real world. If I do something that doesn't please her she hits me with Pa's ole razor strap. She always locks me in my room after supper, that is if I even get any supper. I have learned how to sneak food without her knowing. I put pieces of meat and bread in my pockets. One day she caught me eating a few bits of food from the stove. She put my hand on the hot stove griddle; the pain was almost unbearable. That night before supper, Ma was still in her room, which was strange at this time of evening. I went to her closed door and listened. I heard her talking as if someone was in the room with her. I looked through the key hole and I saw her standing in front of the mirror. She was all alone, but talked as if someone was there. She was ranting about something to do with her life as a young woman when she was in love with the young man her parents forbid her to see. She became very angry.

She screamed at the mirror, "You ruined my life, you knew how much I loved him, he was a good person, and he could have made me happy, instead of what I have become."

I felt sorry for my Ma; I guess I never realized just how much she loved that young boy. It makes me understand things a lot better now. Why is she so cruel to me? I will never tell her secret. No one would believe me anyway. I am just a child with a big imagination.

My grandma Laura has come to visit. I heard her and Ma talking in the parlor. "Sarah Daisy, you need a change. I am going to deed the house I own in Laurel to you, you remember seeing it. It is a nice house really close to town and not so much to keep up. I have been hearing a lot of gossip around, so I think it is time to move on with your life and start afresh. I also want Maud and Eloise to come and live with me, since your father has died I am very lonely and it will be good for everyone concerned."

Well, I can tell you right now I am not happy about leaving I love this old house. I feel as if it speaks to me. Since Louisa and Pa have left this world, I feel their presence here. The soft whispers in the night, foot steps on the porch and someone looking over me while I sleep. I see her shadow crossing the lawn to her shanty at night. I call out to her, she stops and turns for a moment and then she is gone into the mist. I miss you Louisa and I love you. She was so good to me. She used to comb my long curly hair at night before I went to bed. She helped me dress in the mornings. I felt a kindred spirit to her. She seemed more like a sister to me than Maud ever did. I miss you too, Pa. I will always love you; you will always be in my heart.

The old house is empty; everything has been packed and loaded. As I take my last look around the house, it feels as sad as I do. Dark and lonely it seems to be moaning as the wind whistles thru the halls and rooms. My eyes are filled with tears as I look out toward Louisa's little shanty out back. Somehow, I feel I am leaving behind everything and everyone I ever loved. Even though I know my Pa and Louisa are only spirits that still cling to their last earthly home, it is, after all the only place I will ever sense their presence and when I leave, I leave the ones I truly loved behind, forever. As we drove away I looked back I could see Louisa's apparition standing on the porch, her long hair moving softly in the breeze, her beautiful sad eyes looking at me until I could no longer see the house. I put my head in my arms and cried all the way to our new home.

Photo from True Crime Magazine in 1935.

CHAPTER II

We entered the city limits of Laurel. We drove down the boulevard; it is a pretty street with lovely young trees on either side of the road with flowering bushes in between. Beautiful houses on the left side and the railway tracks on the other. We passed a beautiful building on the left just before we got to town. The trolley cars were coming down the road as we passed on into town. We were on Front Street and the town was bustling with business. Motorcars were pretty new, but I saw several on the streets, wagons pulled by mules, loaded with cotton, were coming into town to sale their goods. People were all up and down the streets. It was extremely exciting to see a place so busy with people after living in our little village of Angie, Louisiana. We crossed under a railroad bridge and at the top of the hill was our new home. It is a beautiful dark red house sitting close to the ground. It has a big wrap around front porch with posts supporting the roof and it sits on a large lot with nice trees and pretty flowering plants. Inside it has a large parlor, dining room, kitchen on one side and three bedrooms on the right side. It also has an indoor water closet with a bathtub and everything. The kitchen has running water to the sink too. I think all of Ma's antiques will be very pretty in this house. There are fireplaces in every room, except the kitchen.

We are getting settled in now. The year is 1913. I am eleven years old. Ma has seen that we are enrolled in school. There are two schools very near our house, Central School and Silas W. Gardiner School. Earl and I started out in Central School. We had very little schooling in Angie, Louisiana, but we caught up pretty quick. I love school, because it gets me away from Ma. The teachers are very stern, but very kind. They make sure you learn your lessons. One day a bully jumped on Earl and called him an ugly name "COONA**" I don't know if he really knew what it meant or not, but Earl did. The fight began, they were tumbling in the dirt, socking each other and shirts were torn. Both got black eyes, before it was stopped by the Principal. They both got a good whipping by the Principal as well. It turns out that the bully became Earl's best friend at school. I loved the lunches that were served. When we brought our money we could eat a hot meal for five cents, otherwise you had to bring a pail with milk and a cold biscuit inside.

I had several young boys that liked me and wanted me to be their sweetheart, but I was not interested in that at all. Many of them told me I was the prettiest girl in school, whether it was true or not they wanted to win me over- it didn't work. One boy stole a kiss from me when he called my name and I turned around with his face near mine. I gave him a good slap on the face. When I got home from school, Ma had plenty of chores for us to do. By bedtime, I was so tired sometimes I fell asleep in my clothes on top of my covers. This was nothing like living in Angie. When I dream, I always dream of our home in Angie and Louisa. I miss the beauty of the country life. The sweet smells of jasmine, sweet olive and honey suckle vines, the big century old trees shading the lawn. Sometimes I would lie beneath one of them and dream of places long ago. I would watch the little squirrels running up and down the tree I was laying under never realizing I was there. Louisa would sometimes come and lay on the cool grass beside me. She would talk of spirits that walked this earth that were once alive who died with unfinished business or died violent deaths, never being able to go to heaven, wandering hopelessly throughout eternity. She said sometimes you could talk to them and they could hear you. She would say they are so sad and lonely. She could feel their sorrow in her soul. Only a few can sense there spirits, she said it was a gift of an open spirit or aura around you that makes them know you can sense their presence.

"Ouida," she said, "You have that gift. When I die you will be able to see me, because I feel very strongly I will die a violent death and the person that causes my death will meet with a violent death as well. You hear me good and remember what I have told you."

Her words came back to me from a memory I had put back in my mind trying to forget the horrible day when I was nine years old. When I wake in the morning, I always remember my dreams. I feel as if Louisa is calling to me, trying to tell me something, but I don't know what. In the recesses of my mind, she is always there. I can see her face as clear as if she was standing here at the side of my bed, watching over me as she did so many times when I was a small child.

CHAPTER III

There is a war in Europe. America is not involved yet, but I think it is only a matter of time. The year is 1915. I am thirteen years old. The news of the war is terrible, so many young men dying. For what? I don't understand wars; maybe I am just not old enough to understand the waste of human lives for some lost cause. Thank God, Earl is not old enough to be drafted, if we get involved in it.

Life on Cross Street is about the same. I like the fact that we are within walking distance to school, town, the railroad and parks. I love school it gives me another escape from what I have to face at home. Ma is no better; she seems to be more dominating with me that usual. She gets angry with me over nothing. I think her life is so lonely and miserable. She has nothing else to do with her life, except to make my life miserable like hers, maybe she is afraid of being alone, or could it be she is haunted by the terrible thing she did to Louisa, maybe she has the same gift of an open spirit as I have. I am beginning to believe this is inherited, or is it just my imagination being carried away again.

One of my escapes is going to the Bijou to see moving pictures. I enjoy going to see this wonderful new form of life on film. It is a way for people to see the world and actors and it only cost a nickel. What a fantastic invention.

Grandma Laura has come to visit. She has news for us; Maud is engaged to marry David McRae, a young man from a prominent family in Laurel. He is twenty-three years old and Maud is seventeen now. Grandma is very excited. I am very happy for Maud; she is a good person and deserves happiness and love. He is a businessman and owns a service station on Ellisville Boulevard.

Eloise is six years old now and is turning into a very attractive young girl, but I can tell you one thing she is a little spitfire. I can only imagine what she will be like as a young lady. Grandma Laura is fifty-six years old now. I hope she can handle Eloise without Maud, but I understand she has a wonderful Nanny for her. Ma acts like a different person when Grandma comes to visit. How can you turn insanity on and off when ever the need arises? I promise she acts like a sweet and caring daughter in front of her mother. Grandma knows she was going through a bad time in Angie, but I think she thought it was just grief and stress, but now she doesn't have a clue. I wish I could move in with her. Of course, Ma would never let that happen for fear of what I might tell. My life as an adolescent is doomed until I am a grown woman.

It is now 1916 and I am fourteen years old. The older I get the more argumentative Ma is with me. She fusses about everything I do. I can't do anything right. I can't polish the furniture and silver to please her. She doesn't like my cooking; she claims I am stealing her money. I have my own inheritance from Pa I don't need her money. She is paranoid about all of the possessions in this house. What does she think I would do with them? I can't take them somewhere else; I have no other place to go. Her madness is driving me mad. I don't know how long I can bear this life with her. I am only fourteen. I am not grown.

I stay away from Ma as much as possible. I try to stay in my room when I have finished my work in the house. I feel so helpless, because no one in my family believes my life is this miserable. Earl knows, but he wants to live here as long as he can. Therefore, he is not going to ruffle any feathers. I asked Maud once if I could live with her and she said I needed to stay and take care of Ma. My God, if they only knew what a HELL I am living in.

I am doing well in school. I love learning new things. I want as good an education as I can get. I want to be completely independent when I am of age to go to work. My fifteenth birthday has come and gone and my existence is just that, existing. There is no happiness in my life, no love from anyone. My Grandma says she loves me when I see her, but that is the extent of it. Just words no actions. We only see her about once a month. Eloise has a wonderful life. She has everything she could possibly want or need. She does as she pleases and doesn't have to lift a finger if she doesn't want to. Maud is happy with David. I guess I am becoming jealous and bitter like my Ma. I have lived around her so long; her ways are rubbing off on me. Heaven forbid!

The older I get the more Ma wants to control my life. She doesn't want me to go anywhere without her. I am forbidden to leave the house without her, unless it is to go to school. She keeps the doors locked when I am home.

CHAPTER IV

The year is 1918 and I am sixteen years old. As time goes on, I have become adjusted to my life. My body is blossoming out. I have the figure of a young woman now. Only thirty-five, Mother's beauty is fading like a rose withering on the vine. She is even more wicked now that her beauty is going and mine has arrived, I can feel her stares on me. She hates my youth and beauty. Yes, I think I am beautiful, but only from comparing myself to pictures in books. My hair is very long, flowing down my back in ringlets of curls of a dark brown color. I have large brown eyes, full lips of a natural rose color. My skin is very fair and I have a very smooth complexion. I have a fairly large bosom, a small waist and nice full hips with shapely limbs. I am wearing Ma's older clothes, which fit me nicely. She lets me try on ready-made dresses in the economy store. She has purchased cheap frocks for me. Between my Pa's estate and Ma's money, we are still well to do financially. We can afford anything we could possibly want or need, but Ma just lets the money collect interest in the bank, because she only spends it on food and other necessities. We don't even have a horse and carriage.

Ma is beginning to become forgetful. She has left the door unlocked several times. One day she left the key in the door and as you know with it being a skeleton key it will unlock the front and back doors. I was afraid to try anything thinking she was testing me. Later on, she did it more and more. One day I got brave, unlocked the back door, and stepped out on the porch. It was wonderful to be outside in the fresh air all alone.

As time went on, I began to go out when I knew she was napping. One day I dressed in Ma's prettiest dress when she was young and fixed my hair as I saw in a book of Pa's. I walked out the front door as bold as brass with gloves on, a dainty purse and a parasol. I also had a pin watch on to keep up with the time. I will never forget that day. It was summer, a beautiful cloudless day, I was seventeen and I felt as though I was the most beautiful belle of the town. I strolled down the street feeling like a bird out of a cage.

I passed some nice folks as I walked, the gentlemen tipped their straw hats and the ladies said, "Hello, How are you today?"

I just nodded. As I began to feel more comfortable, I began to speak back when I passed some people. I decided I should turn around and head back home, when suddenly as I turned my parasol was in front of my face and I ran into someone. When I moved it out of my eyesight, there stood a tall handsome young man in front of me. He was beautiful!

As I stood there in front of him, we were both speechless, what seemed like an eternity passed, and then finally he said, "Hello, Who are you? And where have you been all of my life?"

I was so set back with his remarks that I didn't know what to say.

He asked me if I was a mute, I knew what that meant from the books I had read.

I replied, "NO!"

"Good", he said, "because I wanted to hear a voice from that beautiful mouth that goes with the most beautiful face I have ever seen in my life, please tell me what your name is, where you live and will you marry me?"

Again, I was stunned by all of his words that I could hardly reply. I finally said my name is Ouida and I live, uh---, out of town. I politely said I had to go and it was nice meeting him.

He quickly said, "You can't just walk out of my life, now that I have found the prettiest girl in town." "What is your last name and who are you visiting and where do they live?"

I said, I am not at liberty to give you that information, but if you happen to be at the park tomorrow at 3:00, I will probably be able to see you there. I said I had to go because I was already late. Therefore, I said goodbye and went on my way back home. As I walked home, I felt as though I was floating. It was shear heaven! Is this what the life in Laurel is like? Natures beauty unfolding before my eyes, wonderful people living in a perfect world, handsome young men just waiting for a pretty young girl to pluck from her obscure life and take her to his castle and be his princess. Can this be really happening to me? I snuck back into the house at the back door, knowing my ma was still in her room. I quickly ran to my room changed my clothes and mussed up my hair. I just hope the joy does not show on my face, that I feel in my heart. I guess I put on a good disguise because she never noticed anything different about me. That night as I lay in my bed I thought about the day's events that I couldn't sleep a wink all night long. I was so excited about my meeting the handsome man in the park; I could hardly contain my feeling in front of Ma. The next morning I watched the old clock in the front hall all day, nervously anticipating the afternoon to come. When Ma went to take her afternoon nap, I scurried to my room to get changed into another pretty dress of Ma's. My life was suddenly filled with promise. I never thought about what the outcome could be. I was only living for the moment. Who cares about tomorrow, when I have today? My heart was overflowing with joy, I tiptoed down the hall in my sock feet; I went out the back door this time. I sat on the porch bench to put on my shoes and I walked around the front of the yard and started on my way to the park.

As I started walking down the sidewalk an old neighbor recognized me, "Lordy, Miss Ouida, how you have grown-up! How is your Ma and why is it I never see either of you anymore? I thought you had dropped off the globe. You are more beautiful than your mother ever thought to be, I bet she is real proud of you, if only your Pa could have seen you grow-up into such a lovely young lady, that is a mighty pretty frock you have on, but it is a little ole fashioned isn't it?"

I said, it was very nice to see you, but I am in a bit of a hurry, please excuse my haste. Oh Lord, what it she decides to pay us a visit and Ma opens the door and she tells her about seeing me. What will I do? Will Ma kill me or just beat me and lock me in a closet for the rest of my life? As I thought about the consequences, I turned and ran back to the neighbor and told her NOT to go to our house for a visit, because my Ma was very ill and couldn't have visitors at all.

She said that she was sorry to hear it and if there was anything, she could do. I said we had everything we needed, but thank you very much for offering. I also added, please don't mention it to anyone about seeing me, it would hurt my Ma knowing I had left the house and left her alone. She said it would be our secret. I thanked her again and hurried on my way.

I arrived at the park and as I approached the stone bridge that goes over the little creek that runs through the park. I saw him standing there as handsome as I remembered. He turned and saw me and smiled. As we came together, he took my hand and kissed it, ever so sweetly.

"Hello Ouida, my mystery lady." Why do you call me that? I asked.

He said he enquired about me and no one in the whole community knew who you were.

I told him I had not been in town for many years and the people probably wouldn't know me for I have grown-up since they saw me last. He accepted this answer and we began to talk about him and about his family. He said his name was John, he was nineteen years old and his family is one of the prominent families of our town. His father is a lawyer and one of his uncles is a doctor. They live on one of the avenues in the nicest area in town. I wanted so bad to tell him who I really was, but I didn't dare. How could he understand about my insane mother? He would run from me as fast as he could. I wanted so bad to be able to be truthful to him, but that was not possible.

He has graduated from high school and has begun his formal education at the University of Mississippi to become a lawyer like his Pa. We talked about many things. The time went by so fast; it was time for me to leave him before I knew it. He asked if he could pick me up and take me to a dance at the Tallahoma Club. They had balls there on weekends. I said I would have to think about that and tell him later. Could we just go on meeting like this for now? He said ok, we parted with a kiss on my hand, and I walked away with my heart so full I almost started crying. I felt emotions in my heart that I did not quite understand. I have read stories of young lovers, but was the feelings I felt love? I don't know because other than my Pa, I have never known what love feels like! As I walked home, my mind became confused and frightened. I knew if we did fall in love, it would involve meeting his family and his meeting my Ma. As we know, that could not be possible. So, what can this relationship lead to, if not a broken heart? I don't know if I can bear a disappointment of this kind. I have lived with pain so many years now, but this kind of pain already hurts me more than the physical pain I have endured for so long. He is so sweet and caring I think I will die if I cannot be with him.

When I got home, I went to my room as I began to undress I looked into the full-length mirror on the armoire. There was the image of a young woman that had bloomed to her fullest potential. I looked at my body in my corset and petticoat and my thoughts were of loving John and he returning that love in a passionate way that was meant for lovers who have spoken their wedding vows. I felt emotions in my body that stirred my soul. I desired John's embrace, his tender touch on my body, and his kisses on my lips. Oh, how I longed for his love. I lay on my bed, my mind filled with thoughts of our lovemaking. Can the love that I feel ever be? Maybe, if he does really love me we could run away together to a place where no one can find us. Am I just dreaming or is it possible I could finally be free from this prison and find love and be happy for the rest of my life? I began to cry, because I didn't really believe it could be possible, I have lived in a dream world for so long, to escape my pain and loneliness that I am imagining things that will never be. Now that I know what I am missing, I don't know if I can bear living this life of seclusion, to go to a life in all of its beauty and love, and actually living like a normal person. Oh God, help me now in my time of need. Help me to be strong.

When we have dinner in the evening, Ma likes candles lit. Our home has gas lighting in all the light fixtures. The room was lit with candles on the table and the buffet as Ma, Earl and I sat down to eat supper. We sat there in silence. Ma gives me stares that feel like daggers piercing my heart. The soft glow of the room and the flickering of the candles give her face a look of shear evil. Her eyes were filled with hate and the wild expression coming from them seems to be glassed over, as if she is in a trance. I fear her madness had taken on a different form. She almost seems to be oblivious to the world around her. She moves from room to room aimlessly, as if she has no purpose in her actions. She gives me her commands by the pointing of her finger and from the look in her eyes, I know she means for me to do it now.

As I go to my room to go to bed, I could feel Ma watching me as I went. I wonder what she is thinking. Maybe, she is remembering her youth and the happy days she once knew as a young girl. My heart aches for her even though she is so cruel to me. I know she was beautiful from portraits hanging in the parlor and everyone said she was a real beauty. How sad it is that she knew so little happiness in her young adult life. A beautiful life wasted and lost from all hope of any peace in this world. I think it would be a blessing for her life to end instead of living with her mind trapped in the evil bondage of the devil. I pray that because I am of her blood that her own daughter does not inherit this insanity. My mother was a normal person until she was nineteen years old, when her life was suddenly shattered into pieces, like a delicate crystal vase thrown on the floor, impossible to mend.

I can't think these thoughts, it worries me too much. I must think of John and figure out some way for me to have a life with him. There must be a way, their must! I didn't sleep much last night. I kept having crazy thoughts and when I did sleep, I dreamed awful dreams of my mother dying a terrible death. I so hope when she does die she can make her peace with God and die knowing she will go to heaven. She is my mother and I can't help having feelings for her soul.

When I arose, I felt very tired. I washed my face from the basin to freshen up. I did my toilette and went to the kitchen to get the stove started. The morning sun shinning in the kitchen windows and a fresh breeze coming in the room renewed my spirits. The sound of the morning doves cooing in the distance sounded so sweet. I almost forgot my life as it is. I got the coffee started. Then I began making the biscuits. The old dough bowl I use is over a hundred years old. A slave, that was a master carpenter, owned by my mother's grandparents, who carved it from wood.

My mind wanders as I finish preparing breakfast. I have sliced the bacon and put it in the iron skillet to fry. The biscuits are in the oven. I have cooked a small pot of grits and I am frying the eggs over easy in the bacon fat. I learned how to cook by watching Louisa as a young girl. Cooking seems to come natural to me and I have a wonderful old Mobile cookbook with everyday recipes in it, with complete directions on preparing a meal. This part of my labors is actually a joy to me. I hate the other chores.

In our home we have many beautiful objects d' art, beautiful Angelica Hoffman vases on the mantle with a lovely bronze clock with porcelain inlays, little cupids on the sides, a pair of candelabras', one on each side of matching bronze. Ma's China cabinet is a marvelous piece of ornately carved Rococo style. It is filled with Meissen China, Bohemian glass of a beautiful ruby color with gold etching all over each piece. So much beauty around her, she obviously had wonderful taste in picking excellent pieces of art, including the artwork hanging on the walls. There were wonderful paintings of pastoral scenes that seem to go for miles into the depths of the painting. Lovely ladies in beautiful satin and lace dresses with faces so elegant and graceful they seem to be so real they could speak. My favorite painting of all on a grand scale is of Old Rome, consisting of scenes of the city in the distance with St. Peter's Cathedral rising above the other buildings. The ole' remains of the Roman aqueducts in the foreground, peasants coming home from market in their ox drawn wagons, ladies carrying vessels on their heads filled with water just drawn from the ancient fountain, all of which are painted in the picture. Finally, but not least, the picturesque, magnificence of the setting sun over the Campagna. This gorgeous masterpiece is framed in a highly carved gilt frame; it hangs in the parlor over a lovely Victorian marble-topped side table. The parlor furniture is early Victorian settees, sofas, ladies and gentlemen's chairs, marble topped small lamp tables, a beautiful square grand piano of rosewood. I try to play it, but my lessons stopped when Pa died, so my repertoire was unfinished and I only know the basic. As I polish everything in this room, I go to a place in time of long ago and I am a Southern Belle in the days of the antebellum South.

I imagine our home is a large plantation and I am waiting for my true love to ride up on his beautiful black stallion. He comes into the room and embraces me, he smothers me with kisses and our hearts beat as one. His kiss on my lips last an eternity, I almost swoon in his arms. This handsome gentleman of course, is John. My daydreams help me to get through each day of my lonely existence. When I meet John, it is as if heaven opens up to me. It is like a world of happiness that words cannot truly express.

The afternoon hour has come again for me to escape these prison walls. I sneak out again as usual and go to our special place to meet the man that makes my life worth living. Now that I have found John, I don't know if I could bear to go back to the life, I once knew without him. As we sit on a park bench under the shade of an ole oak tree, we talk of what we want out of life. I tell John I would just be happy to be the wife of the man I love and go through the rest of my life giving that man all the love I have to give until the day I draw my last breathe. I would like to have a large family with children to cherish and show them love like the one I have never known. John asks me what I mean by that, I quickly answered by saying that my Pa had died and my Ma has never gotten over his death, so she doesn't show me a lot of attention or love.

He said, "Oh I understand and I am very sorry for her and you." John took both my hands in his and said he wanted to tell me something. I nodded my head and said, ok.   "Ouida, you know I have to finish my schooling, which will take three more years before I can get a position to support a family."

"Yes, John, I understand that."

"When I have secured a position as an attorney and have made enough money to build a home, I can then have something to offer a wife."

I paused and waited for him to finish.

"My love, I would ask for your hand in marriage at that time, if you can wait for me and if you love me. You must know I love you dearly and I have since the day you lifted your parasol and I saw your lovely face and looked into those beautiful eyes. I never believed in love at first sight, but now I do. You are on my mind every waking minute of everyday. I want to spend the rest of my life with you. It makes no difference if your family has money or not. I want you as you are. So, please make me the happiest man in the world by saying you love me too and want to be my wife."

I told John that I fell in love with him that first day also and I loved him more than life itself and yes I would wait for him as long as it took just as long as I could see him as often as possible and YES, John I would love to be your wife.

As we parted, my heart was bursting with joy. I wanted so bad to be able to tell someone about my happiness, but of course, I have no one that I can tell. I have a long time to plan for my future and decide how I will work this out. Maybe, I can eventually tell John about my Ma and we can get married without her knowing. I'm not going to ruin how wonderful I feel right now by worrying about the future. I will think about that later.

CHAPTER V

The summer has gone by so quickly that before I knew it John had to return to school in North Mississippi. I won't be able to see him but once a month. This will be a new kind of torture for me. Thirty days without my love, I feel I will go mad. We have arranged for my mail to come to the post office, so we can write almost every day. Our letters are filled with sentiments of love and plans for the future. I am slowly trying to prepare John for what my Mother is really like without saying too much. I'm afraid too much knowledge will drive him away from me. I don't know if anyone could understand me living with an insane Mother all these years. Louisa's death may have been an accident, but she killed her just the same. Even though I was a prisoner in my own home until we moved here. I have tried to forget it ever happened. Maybe, it was a bad dream. When I think back of that day seven years ago the details have become fuzzy to the point I can't remember for sure if it really did happen at all! I have developed such a vivid imagination I may have made it all up in my mind, because after all, who could do such a horrible thing to a human being?

I began working for W.M. Carter at seventeen years of age, as soon as I graduated from high school. He is a very nice man to work for. It didn't take long for him to give me more and more responsibilities. I am clerk in sales and I work as his personal secretary. He is like a father in his attention and kindness to me. The only thing is that he constantly touches me. It started out as a fatherly hug, then more and more, it became obvious that the caresses were anything but fatherly. He rubs against me when passing by and more than once a day, he will touch me in other places and then act as though it was an accident and apologize. I never say anything for fear of losing my job that I love. One day he said he needed me to go to Mobile with him on a business trip. I agreed to go, because there was a bonus in it for me, plus getting away from Mother would be nice. Ma gave me her permission, probably because of the extra money.

We arrived at the St. Andrew's Hotel and checked in. He got adjoining rooms, being that I was so young I needed a chaperon. We went to lunch and stopped by a few business locations for him to sell lumber; I wrote up the receipts for him, but I soon realized he didn't need me on this business trip. It really didn't matter to me, because I was happy to be getting away. That evening we ate at the hotel and had a nice dinner. We then went upstairs to our rooms. I was dressing for bed when there was a knock on the door, it was Mr. Carter. "I just wanted to see if you needed anything?"

I answered, "No, I have everything I need." I noticed how he was looking me over in my pretty satin gown that clung to my body and showed the form of every curve of my figure. I could see in his eyes his desires for me. He came close and put his arms around me and kissed me on my lips.

I said, "Mr. Carter, what are you doing?"

He answered, "Ouida, you are so beautiful, I can't hide my feelings for you any longer. I am a very lonely man since my wife has been sick and I haven't had anyone to make love to in years. Won't you please give a lonely man a little affection?"

I looked in his eyes and I could see his need, I felt sorry for him and I thought if I could give him the love he needs it would not be such a bad thing to do for this man that needed love so desperately. I let him kiss me again; chills went all over my body as I responded to his passion. His hands softly caressed me. As he moved me back towards the bed. He laid me down very gently on the soft bed. My head was spinning as I felt emotions stirring in me that I have never known before. I let him have me completely and it was wonderful.

After he left my room I lay on the bed wondering if what we had done was really a sin and if it was could God forgive me for giving my most cherished gift to a older married man, instead of saving myself for the man I will marry someday. I didn't sleep well that night, as our lovemaking kept going through my mind. I am not quite eighteen yet and I have lost my purity already. Thoughts of all of this filled my mind with guilt, but yet I didn't completely regret what I had done.

I have become a familiar face on the streets of town, at the stores, in the Bistro's and soda fountains. I have even purchased a few dresses and personal items of my own. As I learned, the fashions have changed considerably from those dresses I had been wearing of Ma's. I can't believe John did not say something about how I dressed.

When John comes home on monthly trips on the train and I meet him at the depot. We are being seen together more and more. He has not asked me to meet his parents yet, because I begged him to wait on that until later and he knows from what little I have told him that my mother will not receive him yet.

At home as long as I cook, clean, and stay out of Ma's eyesight, she does not beat me as often as she used to. I think she is weakening with her madness. It has taken a toll on her body and mind. As time goes on, I see her slowly losing her sense of time, she sleeps twice as long as she used to. When she goes to her room for naps, she sleeps four hours instead of two. She gets up late in the mornings. Sometimes she thinks it is breakfast instead of lunch. Her ranting has increased to the point of talking to herself all the time and answering back as if someone else is talking aloud to her, but in another voice. I guess this means she has taken on two personalities now. I have studied one of Pa's books on mental behavior. It had made me more knowledgeable of my Ma's condition. She should have been put in an asylum years ago. Earl is too busy to worry what goes on at home. I won't let myself think for a minute that she is so weak she can't defend herself. She still has the demonic mind she always had and when the need arises she is able to come up with an inter strength to throw pieces of furniture about the room. Therefore, I don't dare cross her or let my guard down. When I am sneaking out of the house, I am afraid one day I will come home, she will be waiting for me (instead of napping), and I will get her full wrath! If she ever finds out what I have been doing it might just be the end of me. I know she is capable of anything.

I have become a mature woman now. I don't live in a dream world anymore. I deal with the reality of my life as it really is. As a rational, intelligent person, I know my limitations as long as I have to live in this house with my mother. One day I will be free of her bonds on me and I will be able to live my life as I see fit.

I have taken control of some of my life. I have been to an attorney and I have found that my father left money for me in his Estate after his death, when I turned eighteen. I am now nineteen, it is 1921 and I have learned that I am worth a fair amount of money, so I have opened an account at the bank and I spend my own money when I need things. I decided to purchase a new motor car, a 1921 Ford. John has taught me how to drive. I park it at a nearby gasoline station, because I don't dare take it home. John does not own a motorcar yet. He is going into his last year of law school. He is very frugal with money. When we are out together, we have a wonderful time. We drive everywhere in the county. We have learned all the country roads. The only problem is none of the roads or streets are in very good condition if it has rained. We have been stuck several times. On beautiful sunny days, we go to the lakeside and have a picnic, then rent a boat and row out on the lake for hours. This is a very pleasant pass time for many. Sometimes the lake is crowded while other times it is not.

I have become one of the most fashionable ladies in town. Wearing the latest fashions from the best shops in town. In addition, I wear lovely plumed hats from the nicest millinery shop in town.

I have finally decided to tell John why he can't meet my mother. I have told him she is very ill and has a condition called epilepsy, which causes convulsions' and have added that it can cause ranting, all of which are uncontrollable. He has accepted this and has explained this to his mother and father. They are very nice and seem to understand. He said that it is time for me to meet his family, so I will be going over for tea this Sunday. The time is perfect, because Ma will be asleep. They said everyone in town is buzzing about me and it is time they met the mystery lady everyone else already seems to know.

It was a lovely afternoon. I was dressed in my white organza dress, being of fine translucent muslin, it was lined with a lacey silk under-liner. The dress flowing softly to the ankles, tight lace sleeves with tiny pearl buttons at the wrist and the same pearl buttons down the back. My white straw hat had a full pink plume with ribbons of pink satin, a pink satin sash around my tiny waist, white gloves, white beaded purse and a white lace parasol and finally white strapped shoes. My dark brown hair in ringlets down my back tied up in a pink ribbon.

The tea was in the rose garden, so when we arrived we were ushered through their lovely home to the open French doors to the patio and garden. There were about fifteen people there in all to meet us and as we walked onto the brick floored patio everyone's mouth dropped open. All the gentlemen stood and the ladies looked from under their large hats at me. I looked at John and he smiled with delight as they were all looking at ME in astonishment. I knew I looked good, but I think I looked more than good to them by their stares. John's mother walked over to me and said how very pleased she was to finally meet me and she wanted to introduce me to her other guests. John's father was very nice and polite and he told John he knew now why he had kept me a secret, because I was so beautiful, I would surely be stolen away if he had let his gentlemen friends and family meet me before now.

The afternoon passed delightfully. I really like his Ma and Pa. It must be nice to have parents that are normal and loving. I could only imagine what a wonderful life John had growing up in such a home as this. They all seemed to like me. John's father remembered my grandpa and said he was a fine gentleman. They said they had heard of my Ma's illness and were very sorry to hear it. When I got home, I rushed to my room to undress as I ran to the door of my room I noticed Ma's door was open! Oh, God! I walked into my room. The whole room was strewn with pieces of my beautiful clothes. Some torn, some cut by the knife she was holding in her hand!

Her eyes were vivid with rage, she came at me with the knife, "Where have you been, what have you been doing? You will never leave this house again, as long as I live." She grabbed me, I pulled away and my dress tore off my body. She began grabbing and tearing my clothes, with one hand she was scratching my flesh with her fingernails and stabbing me with the other. She kept missing me with the knife as I fought to get away from her; she then cut my hand and arm with one slash of the blade. I threw a small stool in front of her and she stumbled and fell. She was stabbed as she fell on top of the knife. She struggled to get up, as she rose to her feet I screamed when I saw the knife imbedded in her side. My brother heard my screams and ran in my room. I told him to get out and go to his room I told him that Ma had fallen while holding the letter opener and it had stuck in her. I said that I would take care of Ma and he could see her later. When I got back to Ma, blood was streaming down her side and as she managed to go down the hall to her room, she left a bloody trail. I slammed my door and locked it, I ran to the pitcher and basin, I cleaned my cuts and put iodine on them. Luckily, they were not deep because the knife she had used was actually a knife she used for a letter opener and it was quite dull. I wrapped my cuts as best I could with a piece of my torn nightgown and tied it up. Thoughts of her lying in her room bleeding to death went through my mind. I wished her dead and then I prayed she wouldn't die. I was so angry at what she had done to my beautiful things and me, that my heart was full of hate. I had never felt these emotions before. Am I becoming evil like her, or is this a normal reaction from the traumatic experience I just had?

After about an hour, I couldn't bear not knowing if she was all right or was she dead. I unlocked my door quietly for fear she maybe lurking outside in the hall, she wasn't. I walked down the hall to her room, the door was ajar and I pushed it open. She was lying across the bed moaning. The covers were red with blood. I walked over to her to see her face. The loss of blood made her pale.

"Mother," I called out, "Can I help you?"

She opened her eyes and said weakly "Yes". When I rolled her over, the knife had been pulled out. I saw it on the floor. I cleaned her wound, which was not very deep, it mostly went in the fatty part of her side and I don't think it cut any vital organs. I wrapped her with a sheet that I tore into strips after applying iodine. She was so weak she could barely move. I arranged her in a clean bed, pulling all the bloody covers off and covered her up. I turned her lamp down to a dim glow and locked her in her room. Just in case she started feeling better and decided to stab me in my sleep. I locked my door too. Moreover, I had all the keys. I was so exhausted I fell asleep almost immediately. I awoke early to see the reminder of last evening's events. My room was destroyed; almost everything I owned was in pieces, including all of my perfumes and toilette articles. My mirror at my dressing table was shattered. I began to cry as I surveyed the damages. I just sat on the floor in the middle of what was left of my lovely wardrobe. After having a good cry, I got up, composed myself and cleaned up all the mess. I went to Ma's room she was still sleeping. She was breathing normal so I didn't wake her. The bleeding had stopped. I went to the kitchen to prepare some breakfast. I made her a bowl of grits and poured a cold glass of milk from our icebox. The iceman had already delivered the ice and put in the box. The milkman had made his delivery the day before. I sliced her a piece of bread and put it all on a tray and took it up to her room. I woke her up, arranged her head on some pillows, and put the tray on her lap. She was still very weak as she looked up at me. I saw an expression on her face that I had never seen before, she seemed almost normal, her eyes showed gratefulness. I fed her the grits and bread, she drink a little milk.

As I wiped her mouth, she said, "No more." As I picked up the tray she grabbed my hand, I was afraid at first, but it was a gentle touch I felt. As she looked into my eyes she said, "Ouida" that was all she said. Nevertheless, in my heart I heard words of regret. I guess with the state her mind is in that is all I can expect from her, but at least I know she is still capable of compassion. I didn't know what tomorrow would bring for me, because when Ma gets well I'm sure she will live up to her word. She will try to stop me from leaving the house without her.

I took care of Ma until she gained her strength back. Each day she reminded me of my disobedience to her and that, I would have to pay for it with punishment. She slapped my face hard and then she said for me to sit down and listen to what she had to say, because there would be new rules in her house. I had to continue all the household duties, but she wanted me to start going out with her more and do our shopping together. That way she could keep an eye on what I did and where I went, because she would always be with me. I decided to tell her about my motorcar I had purchased with my money Pa had left me. She was angry at first, but when I took her for her first ride she loved it, but she wanted to know what this horseless carriage cost. When I told her $1500.00 dollars, she was shocked. She soon got over the expense when she saw what a wonderful machine it was and how it made life easier.

I didn't dare tell her about John. I don't know what to do about our relationship. John and I didn't see each other for months. I tried to think of how I could introduce him into our lives without her knowing we were in love and engaged. I finally slipped a note to him, for him to meet us at the general store and for John to make a big to do over her, telling her how beautiful she is and could he come to visit us. So as I had asked John to do, that day at the store he approached us and began to boast on how beautiful my Ma was. Ma had not had a man make over her in years; she was completely taken away by his actions. She said he could visit Sunday afternoon. This was in the summer months and John had just graduated from law school. All he had to do now was pass the bar and he would be a lawyer. Ma was very impressed with John. It didn't even occur to her that he would be interested in me.

I have turned twenty, John is twenty-two, and the year is 1922. Ma made me clean the house from top to bottom. She had a black lady to come and take out all the carpets and beat them on the clothesline. She also had a man come and manicure the yard. Ma decided to have the house painted on the outside and in the main rooms on the inside. She has had a telephone installed, also she has had them come and put in electric lights in a few rooms like the kitchen, the halls and the water closet. It is a marvel, invented by Thomas Edison, who has been to our hometown to do business with one of the wealthy businessmen. Our town started out a sawmill town, because of the vast acres of virgin pine timber located in this area. Our part of the state is called the Piney Woods Region.

Ma has come alive since going out into the world again and having attention paid to her. After years of seclusion, I am seeing a side of her I never thought existed. The only problem is the attention is coming from my beau. She is buying new clothes and dressing in the latest fashions, of course, I had to buy all new clothes as well.

John comes over several days a week. We have wonderful dinners together, all three of us. Earl never joins us he eats in the kitchen and leaves. I have asked Ma if we can invite some other guests to our house.

She says, "ABSOLUTELY NOT! I am not ready for social life again."

She is probably right about that. Even though she is quiet the talker and flirt with my John, she must think she is still a young woman. She is thirty-nine years old now. There is still some beauty left in her face and her hair is still dark. Her piercing brown eyes are almost hypnotic to her victim. I catch John starring into her eyes as though she has truly mesmerized him with her stare. I bring him out of it by getting his attention with some small talk. As the weeks go by, I am actually beginning to hate his visits. She completely manipulates the whole evening. She shows him all of her beautiful things in the parlor and goes into detail on every piece, of course, she does have a way of making it sound very interesting. Her elegant Southern voice almost captivates me. She did get a formal education and went to a French Finishing School in New York when she was young. I do envy her. At dinner, she loves to use her French, in a way it makes me nauseous. I'm afraid her captivating manners and her sensual maturity is stealing my love away from me. John seems to be infatuated with her. I don't know what I am going to do.

I can't find a moment alone with him. Finally, one evening Mother had to excuse herself to go to the powder room. I asked him if he still cared for me, he said he did, he just hasn't been able to have anytime alone with me. I was not convinced of his feelings. There was something missing in his voice. I tried to tell him that my mother was not everything she portrayed. I didn't want to drive him away, but I also wanted to try to make him know what an evil person she really is without just coming out and telling him. I said, "John, don't be fooled by her soft Southern manners, she can be a cruel person when she wants to. I know you are captivated by her charms, but please believe me she is not what she seems."

John said, "Oh, Ouida don't be childish, your mother is a lovely lady and you are acting so immature." These words broke my heart, because he never said he loved me. When John left, I went to my room and cried all night. I have given him all my love and my evil mother has stolen him from me.

CHAPTER VI

The next morning as I was polishing Mother's beautiful silver coffee service, which had belonged to her Mother, there was a knock on the front door. I went to see who it was. There stood a man, probably about 35 to 40 years old, with a small bag in his hand. We don't get many salesmen where we live. I asked him what he wanted, because he was a stranger to me. He said he wanted to see my Mother, please. Ma was drinking coffee in the kitchen. As I turned to go get her, she was standing behind me. The look on her face was astonishment.

I asked her what was wrong, she quickly said, "nothing, go back to your polishing, I will take care of this."

The man was handsome in a rugged sort of way. His hair was a tossled mass of dark red curls; his build was muscular, tall, and lean and tanned from being outdoors a lot. His suit wrinkled to the point of looking like a hobo (a homeless person who travels the country in boxcars).

I tried to hear Ma as she talked to him on the front porch. I heard her say, "Where have you been all these years?" I couldn't hear his reply, but she obviously knew this unkempt man. The next events completely took me back. As she brought him in the house and took him straight to the kitchen, I walked in the room and saw that she was giving him some of the left over breakfast. She gave him a couple of biscuits, some bacon and grits that were still warm on the stove. She poured him a cup of coffee and sat down at the kitchen table with him.

When she saw I had walked in the room, she said, "I told you to get back to your work, get out of her, now!" They stayed in there for over an hour. When she came out, she said I want you to go up to the attic and get out some of Pa's old clothes from his trunk. We need summer clothes, shirts, pants, socks and so on, plus Pa's shaving things. Ma sent him to the water closet to bathe. I gave him a suit of clothes after I shook them out real good. I did everything Ma told me to with apprehension, I was not about to disobey her, plus I figured she knew what she was doing. This stranger must be someone she knew well. I am so anxious to find out who he could be. He seems to be Ma's age, maybe he is a long lost cousin I never heard of. His life seems to have been a hard one from his appearance. Well, well miracles never cease. Coming down the hall is a very handsome man that could only be mistaken for a real gentleman. I am amazed at the transformation. Ma seems pleased at what she sees.

Finally, she has decided to tell me who he is. She said to me, "He is a very dear old friend of her family that has come on hard times; we will make him at home here with us as long as he needs." His name is Luke; there is something about him that is so familiar to me. He looks more like kin that just a friend. Ma has really taken him under her wing. They talked for hours alone. She does not want me around him for some reason. I do not understand. I hear whispers of days long ago. He seemed to know about Ma before she married Pa.

How would he know about that? I thought it was the family secret. Only Ma, her parents and the man she married, my Pa knew. Well, actually someone else did know, the young man she loved and had been forced to stop seeing. This was the tragedy that started a spiral of events that broke my Mother's heart and caused her madness. Oh, my Lord, can it be? Oh, no, I am getting crazy ideas; this couldn't be conceivable I am letting my imagination go wild again. How could that be possible after all these years that he would just show up at our door out of nowhere? My Ma is being very secretive about him, but then we are dealing with an unbalanced person.

As I found out Luke was Ma's lost love, in 1901, when Earl, my brother was a baby. Luke came back into Ma's life at a time when she was most unhappy and on seeing him again, after almost five years, the feelings for him that my Ma had had never changed. She still loved him desperately. They had to sneak around to see each other. There was an old shack way back on the property where no one ever went. They would secretly meet there at night and make love. Luke had been on hard times, with his family dead and gone. Ma gave him money. He had become a vagabond going from town to town working enough to get a meal and a place to sleep. He was a handsome young man, tall, thin, thick curly dark red hair and beautiful green eyes. Ma loved him so. She would have gladly left with him, but he wouldn't let her. He had nothing to offer her. He said one day I will come back and we can be together always, just please wait for me. She said she would, but with tears flowing down her face she said please come back to me, Luke, I will love you forever.

There might be one good thing to come out of all of this. John, my sweet love, maybe we can begin our life together again. Perhaps Ma will be so distracted with Luke, she will not be interested in John anymore and possibly, she will allows us time together, alone. I pray to God she will have a change of heart.

Luke has been here with us for two weeks. I have had a few opportunities to talk to him. He is really a nice person. He told me after high school both his Ma and Pa died in a flu epidemic, his little sisters were taken away to an orphanage, and he never saw them again. He was old enough to make it on his own, so the authorities didn't take him, but times were hard and trying to make a living was harder than he thought. He did odd jobs for people, usually just for a meal and a barn to sleep in. He went from town to town. He did work some, in the sawmills, but times were so hard that they got to where they gave out tokens instead of money. These were used in the general stores owned by the sawmill owners. They were not much use to a homeless young man except for some cooking utensils, canned goods and such. He said, "I got by okay until I met up with the wrong bunch of men. I had been "hopping trains" which meant jumping in boxcars mostly while they were in motion to keep from being caught, because it was unlawful and a prison sentence if caught. On one occasion while camping on the side of the tracks, a farmer, with a gun, walked up and told them to get off his land. One of the hobo's was a mean man, he shoved the old farmer down, and when he got up, he raised his shotgun at the man. The hobo grabbed the end of the gun and it went off, blowing a hole in his stomach so big you could see his intestines; it was a gruesome sight as he lay on the ground dying. Instinctively I hit the old farmer, not knowing my strength, he fell back and hit the ground, his head struck a large stone. It killed him instantly. It didn't take long for the law to catch up with me. I was tried and sentenced to prison for 2nd degree murder. The other men in our group told the sheriff what happened and I guess that is why I didn't get life. I was sent to Angola Penitentiary in Louisiana. My sentence was fifteen years hard labor. I worked on a chain gang. They beat us on a regular basis. We were forced to cut cypress trees in the swamps. Many died from snakebites and alligators took many limbs and sometimes took whole men away. The site was horrible. We were in fear of death every day. We worked from sun up to sun down in the hot sun with only a few breaks. Some men died of heat stroke. After ten years of good behavior, I was released and here I am."

"Ouida, I know I have led a hard life and I am not proud of everything I have done. I am not a bad person; I just had some truly bad breaks in my life. I once had a lot of hopes and dreams, but I guess it just wasn't to be. I want to try to live the rest of my life making something out of the time I have left. Can you understand that Ouida? I hope we can become really good friends, it would mean the world to me. That is one reason why I wanted to tell you about my life, so we can start with a clean slate. Your Mother and I were very close many years ago. We want to try to rekindle the relationship we once had when we were young. I hope you are ok with that, because how you feel is very important to me in away you can never know."

I said, "ARE YOU MY FATHER?"

Luke stood there speechless. He looked down at the floor, he was wringing his hands, he looked up, and I could see how nervous he was.

"Why do you ask me that?"

"Because it is obvious, you are in love with my Mother and you seem to care a lot about what I think about you. You have been building me up to break the news to me, worrying about what I will think and will I respect you with the history you have. Only a man that cared like a Father would be concerned that much if I accepted you or not. So answer my question. Are you my real Father?"

"Yes, Ouida, I am your real Father! I have wanted for almost twenty years to be able to say those words to you." As he spoke, tears flowed down his cheeks and he grabbed me and held me in his arms. I began to cry too. There we stood in the middle of the parlor holding each other and crying. "I promise you I will love you and protect you for the rest of my life, but you haven't told me if you can love and accept me as your Father."

"Yes, I can and I do. This is the only the second time in my life I have been truly happy. First, was falling in love with John, now finding my real Father, and knowing in my heart that I have always loved you, but didn't know who you were until now."

Luke smiled and said, "Thank you, my sweet daughter for making my life worth living."

Ma, walked into the parlor I could tell she had heard most of what we had said to each other. In her own way, she seemed pleased, but she didn't say anything. She walked up to Luke and put her arm around him, in a way of approval. I know her gestures so well; she doesn't have to say anything. I said I would go and start dinner, but I stopped and asked Ma if I could ring John up and invite him and give him the good news. Ma had a funny look on her face.

Luke said, "That would be wonderful Daisy, wouldn't it?"

She paused and looked at Luke, and then she said, "Yes, that would be nice." Therefore, I got the operator to ring the home of John's parents, I got him on the line, and I asked him to dinner. He said that would be great. I decided to cook something special so I got in my motorcar and drove to the butcher shop and picked out a nice roast, I stopped and picked up ice cream for dessert.

I was very excited, it has been a wonderful day so far, and I hope it can be the rest of the evening. I asked Ma if I could use some of her fine China and crystal and Grandma's silverware. She said, okay. I set the table with all of her finery and I picked fresh flowers for the table arrangement it all looked gorgeous. My roast was in the oven with potatoes and carrots, fresh green beans on the stove, with creamed corn I fried in the skillet. I baked dinner rolls they came out perfect. The seafood man had come by this morning and I bought some fresh shrimp, caught in the Gulf of Mexico, brought in on Mississippi shrimp boats, we get fresh seafood every week when in season. I made a beautiful shrimp cocktail for an appetizer with a cocktail sauce. Our dessert will be pound cake, fresh strawberries and ice cream, served with coffee. I put candles on the table, as Ma likes it. I fed Earl in the kitchen when he came in from work and he went out afterward. He is twenty-one and has been working at Masonite since he got out of school.

John arrived at eight thirty. We had a little wine before dinner. I told John we had some news for him. He has only been over a couple of times since Luke arrived, because he has been very busy lately. I told John that Luke was my real Father and when he and Ma were young, something happened and they couldn't marry, so she had to marry someone else. I told him how happy I was to find my real Father. In addition, Ma and he are going to marry! Ma and John both looked shocked the room went silent.

Then Luke broke the ice by saying, "Thank you Ouida for those words of acceptance and thank you for wishing us to marry, I have not asked you Ma yet, but you have certainly prepared the way."

John, spoke next, he raised his wine glass and said, "This is wishing all of you happiness and thank you for making me apart of your life."

I looked at Ma; I couldn't read her expression, as I always have been able to do. We sat at the beautifully appointed table and enjoyed a delicious meal, if I do say so. The candles lit on the table made for a romantic scene, two couples sitting there together with at least two of the people very much in love, maybe all four, but with whom are they in love?

The evening ended without much conversation. I walked John to the door. All he said was, "Thank you Ouida for a beautiful meal." Then he said in a whisper, "We need to meet and talk tomorrow in the park at the usual time." He kissed my hand and left. I went to bed not knowing what to think of the evening and John's words and reactions. He still seems distant. I had hoped that with Luke on the scene, John would act more attentive to me, but he almost acted jealous of Luke and Ma. Has my plan of John showing Ma attention so he could be near me backfired? Has he fallen in love with her? What have I done? I will hate them both if this has happened. I will hate myself! Oh God, make it NOT so! I guess I will find out tomorrow. I fell asleep with my heart aching. I had so hoped tonight would have been the finish to a wonderful day.

I dressed in a violet colored dress, the sun was hot, and so I wore a wide brimmed white hat with purple plums. This color looks good on me. My dark curls are very long now, hanging over my shoulders, I hardly ever wear my hair up. I walked to the park with Ma's permission; she thinks I am going alone. I saw John waiting he looked handsome as always. As I approached, he met me and we sat on a bench.

I began the conversation by saying; "Well what do you want to tell me?"

He started his prepared speech, as an attorney would do. "Ouida, I have done everything you asked me to do for us to be able to see each other, but I was not prepared for Daisy, excuse me, your Mother! I will just have to tell you, I am confused about my feelings for you right now. I think until everything is clear to me, we need to put our plans on hold. I do plan to continue visiting your home and I hope we can be friends. You are still young and have led a sheltered life, so as you mature you will see I am right in making this decision for you."

I immediately jumped up and said, YOU FOOL! Just go ahead and love my Mother and one day you will be very sorry you ever met her. I am not going to tell you what she is really like. I will just let you find out for yourself. I was the best thing that ever happened to you and you threw it away like a piece of trash. You will be sorry, one day, very sorry! I walked away from him acting tough as nails, with my heart crushed completely. I wanted to throw myself in front of the train as it passed on its usual route on its way to New Orleans. I walked and walked, I couldn't go home yet. I walked until my feet were aching. Finally, I went home. I went up the porch steps and lay on the wicker sofa on the porch. I began crying uncontrollably. I felt the tender touch of a hand on my shoulder, I hoped it would be John and he was sorry and wrong and he loved me after all, but it was Luke, he picked me up as if I was a rag doll and sat me in his lap and hugged me.

He said, "Baby, don't cry your Papa is here and I know what is wrong. I know you have been hurt very bad. I saw it coming when I first arrived. You deserve better. I said I would protect you and I will just wait and see."

I felt secure for the first time since I was a little girl. He gave me an inner peace with his words of comfort. My tears stopped. Someone I loved has left me alone and broken my heart, but someone new has come and made my heart whole again and given me a love that never changes or stops, just unconditional love, A Father's Love! I asked Luke how he and Ma were getting on. He said he had always loved her, but she had changed thru the years. He said he still loved her.

"That is it! This situation with John is a problem that will have to be fixed. I saw that John was infatuated with her from the start, which sometimes happens with young men and an older more mature beautiful woman. It never works. It is just a passing fancy, but one that has hurt someone very dear to me. I will NOT tolerate him in this home any longer!"

Luke stood strong to his word. I heard him and Ma arguing about John the next day.

She screamed at him, "You don't tell me who can visit in my home. I'll have him here anytime I want!"

Luke said, "You do that and you'll be sorry. Do you want me to leave? And another thing you should be thinking about your daughter, don't you know she was in love with him?"

Ma said, "What are you talking about, he loves me." "You foolish woman, he is half your age, Ouida and he were in love until you got your claws in him." Ma said, "I'll kill her if she tries to have a lover."

Luke said, "What did you say? Have you ever hurt her before? If you ever lay a hand on her it will be the last thing you do in this life!"

Luke came to talk to me. "Ouida I want you to tell me the truth. Is your Mother mean to you?"

"No," I said.

"Tell me the truth, I won't let her do anything to you, I promise."

I said, "But what if you leave one day, Luke?"

"I promised to protect you and I meant every word of it."

I began to tell Luke about the cruelty since I was nine years old. The beatings, the burns, her stabbing me, keeping me locked in my room. What I didn't tell him was about Louisa. I didn't think he would believe me, because he does love her. He asked why she would do such things to her own daughter. I told him that I thought she would go crazy sometimes, maybe because she was so lonely.

"Please don't tell her I told you."

He said he wouldn't.

A few days later, I was in the kitchen preparing supper when I heard voices on the front porch, I went to the front door and Ma met me there, she heard the noise too. I opened the door, it was Luke and John, they were arguing. Luke told him he wasn't welcome here anymore.

John said, "Daisy would have to tell him that it was her home."

Ma said, "John, do as he says." John looked at me and then looked at Ma. He said he didn't believe Daisy wanted him to go and left. I couldn't believe Ma did as Luke wanted her to do. I was so glad he was here with us now. The rest of the day and evening passed quietly.

CHAPTER VII

The next day I went shopping, I really needed to get out of the house. Ma has not said anything to me about leaving the house since Luke arrived. He has been a knight in shining armor.

After I did some shopping, I stopped in at the Mississippi drug store; they have a wonderful soda fountain bar. I sat down at a small table and ordered an ice cream soda. It was a hot humid day and I thought a soda would cool me off. Our weather here in South Mississippi is very much like the tropics.

As I was enjoying my ice cream, I heard a nice voice say, "Hello, how are you on this beautiful summer day?"

I looked up and there was a young man standing at my table. He was strikingly handsome, tall, and thin with very dark hair, almost black, piercing blue eyes and a beautiful smile. I answered him by saying, "I am fine and how are you?"

He said, "I am doing wonderful, would you mind if I joined you, if you are alone?"

"I guess it would be all right."

He sat down and ordered a Coca-Cola. He said, "My name is Thomas and who do I have the pleasure of meeting?"

I told him, "Ouida Keeton."

He asked me all kinds of questions. Was I from here, where did I go to school, where did I live, did I have a beau? I answered as best I could. He said he was from here too. He said he lived in town. We had a nice talk, and then I said I should be leaving. He asked where I went to church. I told him we had not been in church for some time now, because of my Mother's illness. He asked if I would like to go to church with him. I said that would be nice. He said he would pick me up Sunday morning at 9:45 a.m. I said all right and left. I felt very up lifted after meeting him, but I was going to be very cautious about getting involved again. I told Ma I was going to church Sunday with a nice young man I met in town. She very indifferently said what ever you want to do. I am amazed at her change of attitude since a man was introduced into her life, first John, and then Luke. She acts as if I don't exist, except for ordering me around as her servant. She doesn't have to say much about household duties, because I have done it for so long, it is a part of my daily life.

Sunday morning came and I got up early to cook breakfast and cook dinner ahead of time, since I would be late. I made biscuits, fried thick slices of ham and cooked eggs. I fried a fresh chicken, made mashed potatoes and gravy, blacked eyed peas and cornbread for our lunch. I kept it warm on the stove. I went to my room and dressed for church. I wore a lovely blue linen dress trimmed in eyelet lace at the neckline and sleeves, a pretty, wide brim navy colored hat with silk flowers and ribbons. I put a large silk flower on my sash. Thomas came to the door. Luke answered the bell and asked him to come in. He introduced himself as my Father, which pleased me. I heard him as I was coming down the hall. Ma stayed in the kitchen. This was fine with me. We went to the Methodist Church on Fifth Avenue. He is a member there it was a nice service. It has been so long since Ma and Pa took me as a child, I barely remember going. Thomas brought me straight home and walked me to the door. He is a real gentleman, not like John at all. He owns a motorcar. His Pa gave it to him when he turned twenty-one it is a 1920 Chevrolet. He is in school at Mississippi State University to be a Doctor of Veterinarian Medicine. He is twenty-two years old. I do not want to get serious in this relationship; I would like to be friends. I have never had a friend, someone I can talk to and tell my dreams to. Someone I can confide in when I am sad or hurt. Thomas seems to be a very caring and compassionate person. He is a good Christian and his family is too. He has talked to me about their love of God and trusting in him for everything. I have prayed many times to God, but only when I needed him. I have never read the Bible and I never thanked God for the good things in my life. I guess I need to become closer to God. I think my friendship with Thomas can help me to become a Christian. Thomas comes to visit, we sit in the parlor, I serve teacakes and coffee and we talk about many different things. I so enjoy his company. He fills a void in my life that makes me complete again, I can't fully describe how good and spiritual he makes me feel, but it is a special sensation of fulfillment.

As the months pass we have become great friends. We go for long walks in the park, we walk all over downtown. Laurel is a busy little town. We have a Bijou (moving picture show); plays are preformed there and it is also a theater. Dress shops, banks, hardware stores, general stores, mercantile stores, several soda fountains and drug stores. We have barbershops, service stations, shoe shops and of course doctors, lawyers and dentist offices. There are more, but this is giving you a general idea of the nice growing town we live in. I can walk to town; we live across the railroad tracks down from the depot. There are other homes near us. Our house is on a hill at a fork in the road. Some of the roads are still dirt, which does make for a mess downtown for motorcars and wagons loaded with goods. Many times people get stuck. Thomas has taken me to the silent movies and to some plays at the theater. We just saw the newest moving picture out, "The Birth of a Nation," directed by D.W. Griffith. We have also seen the picture, "Carmen" starring the opera star Geraldine Farrar, directed by Cecil B. Demille. I loved watching Mary Pickford and Douglas Fairbanks. Theda Bara plays roles of a vamp, which is shocking, especially in the company of a man. Before meeting Thomas, I saw a moving picture by myself. It was wonderful it stared Sarah Bernhardt, the great French actress of stage in the film, "Queen Elizabeth." I was in awe after seeing it.

After doing all of my housework, Thomas came over. We sat on the front porch swing. As we were in the middle of a conversation about Thomas' practice with animals and building a clinic on the edge of town, we heard loud arguing within the house.

It was Ma and Luke I heard her shouting, "I am not going to allow this relationship to go on any longer."

Then she said, "I'm not going to let her have a beau, EVER!" Luke loudly told her she would not interfere with my love life or she would be sorry. I was so embarrassed I didn't know what to say to Thomas. I asked him to excuse me and I would talk to him later. He left, but before he did he said, "I'm sorry your Mother is treating you this way, you know I care very much for you, Ouida, more than you know. If there is anything I can do for you please let me know."

I went in the house, in the front hall stood Luke and Ma. I told her she was not going to destroy my life again, I let her do it once before, but I am not going to this time. I am not afraid of you anymore and if you try to stop me, I will tell your secret to everyone. Luke looked shocked; I don't know if it was because of me standing up for myself, or the words "secret" that I said.

Luke spoke, "Ouida, what secrets are you talking about?"

I said; ask your love Daisy to tell you. He turned to Ma and asked her.

She said, "Nothing important enough to talk about after all these years, it happened a long time ago."

I went to my room. The thoughts of the incident that just happened kept going through my mind. First, Ma wanting to start to dominate my life again, then what Thomas said about how he cared for me. Is he falling in love with me? I know I feel very strong feelings for him and I can't think of my life without him in it. I would be living in a very lonely world without his presence.

There was a knock at my door. It was Luke, he wanted to talk to me, I was afraid of what he was going to ask me.

He said, "We need to talk about your Mother. I'm afraid she is mentally unstable and I worry about what she is capable of doing. Sometimes she is sweet and loving and then she changes into a person I don't know, she seems almost evil. Has she always been this way?" I told Luke, that she has been this way most of my life and I added that I think it all started when she was forced to stay away from him and marry another.

Next, he asked the question I was afraid he would. "What secret were you talking about?"

I said, "Luke I can't tell you anything other than the events happened when I was a child and that I no longer know if they are true or imagined and I just can't talk about it. I should have never said what I did in front of you, so please, don't ask me to say anything else about it."

He said, "Well, I'll leave it alone for now, but there may come a time when you have to tell it all." He left my room and I was relieved that he accepted my answer for now.

I called Thomas on the telephone and asked him to meet me at the park. I have decided to walk, because it was a lovely fall day and the weather was breezy and slightly cool. I saw him waiting for me as I walked on the little brick path to the benches. We sat and began to talk.

He started the conversation. "Ouida, I think it is time I confessed something to you. I know you wanted us to be friends, but I can't hold what I feel in my heart any longer. I am desperately in love with you. When I look into your beautiful eyes, my heart melts, when I touch your hand I want to embrace you in my arms and tell you how much I love you. Your heart is so pure and innocent it makes me feel a spiritual oneness with your spirit. I can no longer hold back expressing my eternal love for you. Please, don't break my poor heart by saying you don't love me too."

"Thomas," I said, "I do love you too, very much. I tried to think it was a love of a friend, but I realize I can't think of life in this world without your love. I need you so very much, please promise your love is true and will last for the rest of our lives."

"Yes, yes I love you as much as I love God and my love is true and everlasting. I will cherish you, protect you and keep you as long as I draw breath and then I will you in heaven forever." We drew near and he softly kissed my lips. We embraced and kissed. It was the most wonderful kiss I have ever known.

He suddenly jumped up with his arms in the air and shouted, "Thank you Lord!" Then he said we must go right now to tell his parents.

"Oh, Thomas, right now?"

"I can't wait any longer I am bursting with happiness. They love you too, and will be so excited to hear the news."

We drove in his motorcar to his home, his parents are very happy, but they want to know when we will become engaged. I was a bit embarrassed, because he has not asked me to marry him. He told them not to ruin his surprise. After we left, he said he wanted us to go to dinner tonight. We have never been anywhere together at night. He is taking me to our towns' finest dining restaurant and hotel, the Pinehurst Hotel; it was finished one year earlier. He took me home to get ready. I am very excited, because I feel certain he is going to propose marriage to me tonight.

I saw Luke when I went into the house. I told him what was going on with Thomas and me and if he could please distract Mother this evening. I prepared a cold dinner of chicken salad and went to dress. I took a fresh bath and washed my long hair. It takes about an hour for my hair to dry. I sat at my dressing table brushing my long dark curls. As I looked in the mirror, I saw a young woman whose happiness shined on her face.

I said a prayer, "Oh Lord, please let this blissful feeling I have last, is it not finally my time to be happy. Please grant me this prayer Oh Lord, and I will be your faithful servant, giving you the praise." I put powder on my cheeks. I dressed in my most beautiful evening dress that I had purchased in our most fashionable dress shop in town. It is deep purple silk and completely covered in

44

heavy lace, the newest style of 1924 with a matching cape. I am wearing a very delicate, intricately designed necklace and earrings of metal with tiny diamonds and amethysts stones. My hair is up with curls cascading down. I think he will approve.

As I quickly slipped down the hall I saw Luke, he stopped me and said, "Let me have a look at you. You are positively the most beautiful young lady I have ever seen. I hope you have a wonderful evening."

Thomas came to the door and I opened it before he could knock. When I opened the door the sun was setting across the autumn sky, and shining was on my face.

Thomas saw me and stepped back, "Oh my God, you are more beautiful than Venus with the sun glistening off your beautiful eyes and your hair is like the dark autumn leaves shining in the sun. You are making the God's jealous of me right now. You are gorgeous, Ouida. How it frightens me to think of it, your beauty within illuminates outward to a divine beauty that I see before me." He made me feel glorious. It was only a short drive to the restaurant. We went to the door and the Maître D' seated us. Thomas had made reservations. He sat us at a quite corner table, the room was softly lit and the feeling of romance filled the room with violins playing, accompanied by a piano. We had a divine meal of prime rib, au jus, roasted new potatoes and snow peas with fresh tomato slices. We also had a nice Italian wine with dinner. When we finished with our coffee, we walked to the outside courtyard. The full harvest moon hung low in the sky I felt the soft October coolness on my skin, it was a beautiful evening.

Thomas got down on one knee and as the violin players played Paganini's Rhapsody, he said, "Ouida, you are the moon and the stars shining in my soul. I love you with every beat of my heart and I give it to you my love. My heart and my soul is yours forever, will you be my soul mate in this world and heaven and be my wife?"

I began to cry as I said the words, "Yes my love; I will be your wife forever." Not realizing it, but everyone in the restaurant was standing at the open French doors watching us. They all applauded. Thomas took me in his arms and kissed me so passionately I thought I would faint. I almost lost my breath. He presented me with a gorgeous diamond ring set in platinum. It was a marquis shaped diamond set tightly in small prongs. We went back inside and we danced for hours. He is a marvelous dancer. (Luckily, I taught myself to dance by buying a victrola and dancing instructions several years ago) It was the most romantic night I have ever known. When we left the restaurant he drove to my house and we sat in the motorcar for a while talking about our future. He held me in his arms and kissed me. He said, "You know I have desires for you that can only be expressed when we are married and we become one. I am a passionate man, but I will wait until we are married. Kissing you makes these feelings rise up into my very soul. We need to say goodnight before I lose control of my passions." He walked me to the door and kissed me goodnight I went into the house and to my room. Wonderful sensations filled my whole body. Every minute of the night went thru my mind repeatedly. I was so intoxicated from the memories of the night's events I felt like I was floating on a cloud. Thomas is a warm and loving man; he is also a real gentleman. I don't really know if I could have resisted his passions, but he controlled his and I am grateful for that. We have decided to marry next spring. I want a big wedding, but I don't know if my Mother is going to be receptive to any of it. She is giving me a hard time by just having Thomas as a friend. What will she say if I tell her I am in love with him and we want to marry? This is a job for Luke; I need his help to convince her to have a change of heart. I don't know why she cares if I marry and leave. She seems to hate me. What is in her mind that makes her want to dominate my life? I wish I could understand her thoughts.

Cold weather is here. This is one of the coldest winters I remember. Thomas had opened his clinic practicing Veterinarian Medicine. He gives medical care for horses, cows and any farm animal and domestic animals such as dogs and cats. He is doing quite well. I go over to his clinic to see him and take him lunch. Our relationship is going well, but I still have not worked everything out with my Mother.

I talked to Thomas this morning about bringing lunch, but he has an emergency out in the country on a mare that is in trouble with giving birth to her foal. The weather is awful it is sleeting and very cold and the roads are treacherous, I wished he didn't have to go out in such weather, but it is part of his job. I phoned back to his clinic three hours later and he still wasn't back. I am getting worried that he is stuck in the mud and freezing out there all alone. I called again before dark and still no answer. I called his Ma and Pa to ask if they had heard from him. They had not heard a word and were worried too. We don't even know what farm had called him to come out. I called the operator to see if they could help me trace the call. They remember the Doc getting a call from the Smith farm out near Wayne County. The operator connected me with the county Sheriff. The Sheriff said there was nothing he could do tonight. He said he probably got stuck, then went to the nearest place to stay overnight; out there, no one has a phone. They have to go to the nearest country store to call anyone. He said don't worry I'm sure that he's okay. I went to the house of Thomas' parents, because they were going to call the Smith farm to see if they had seen the Doc or if he had even made it to the farm. They called the Smiths and Thomas had left their place around 2:30 p.m. this afternoon. I called home and told Luke I was staying here with his parents tonight. We didn't sleep a wink all night. We all prayed together. The whole town knew by now and everyone prayed and held their breath. The next morning we got in their motorcar after calling the Sheriff and started out that way to look for him. We stopped at every house on the way asking if they had seen the Doc. No one had. Finally, we saw motorcars stopped in the road ahead of us.

Thomas' Mom and I grabbed each other's hands and started praying,

"Please God let him be all right." As we got closer, a tow truck was on the scene, we thought, good he got stuck after all. As we neared, the area there was a bridge ahead. We both screamed, **"OH GOD!"** We stopped the car, got out, and ran as fast as we could in the icy slush. When we came on the scene, the tow truck was pulling Thomas' motorcar out of the creek. As the motorcar was coming up to the bridge the door on the driver's side flung open and Thomas' frozen body fell half way out. **I SCREAMED!** I woke up in the back seat of a stranger's car; a lady from church was holding my head I was covered in a blanket.

She said, "There now honey, you'll be ok God will see you through this." They took me to Thomas' house and put me in his bed in his room. The Doctor was there and gave his Ma and me something to sleep. When I woke, I didn't know where I was and what had happened at first. As I lay in Thomas' bed I looked around at his things, I remembered everything.

I began to cry and I cursed God. **"Why GOD Why!** Can I ever have happiness in my life? Why do you keep punishing me? What have I done to deserve this? My beloved is dead! Now I am left behind in this hateful world to suffer unbearable sorrows alone. Why, Why? Lord please take me too, I can't live without his sweet love that made my life complete." I freshened my face and went downstairs. The house was filled with people. I saw the Sheriff and I heard him say the roads were icy and his motorcar slide off the bridge and into the freezing water. His head hit the stirring wheel and knocked him unconscious and he drowned before reviving. It probably happened about 3:30 yesterday. No one saw it happen, because of the weather and the isolated stretch of road close to that bridge. I am truly sorry, we all loved Thomas, and he was a fine Doc and a good Christian man. He will be missed. The coroner has already given his report. The bruising on his forehead confirmed his diagnosis and the water in his lungs finalized his report.

It seemed as though the whole town came thru Thomas' home today. It never occurred to me how much he was known and loved. Everyone was so very nice to me, because they knew we were engaged. I have never known of what it is like for a whole community to care so much about what happens to one person. It was an uplifting experience. Everyone brought food as well. This ordeal has taught me a lot about people as a whole. How compassionate they can be at a time of real need. I am so ignorant about so many things. I thought I was extremely smart, but theirs is a kind of intelligence that doesn't come from books it comes from experiencing LIFE!

It is 1925; he was only twenty-three. Thomas opened this entire world to me. His life was a blessing to many, including me. Even though it was short, he has left something very special behind. A part of his spirit will live on in many people's hearts. He has left a lasting epitaph of Godliness. I was very fortunate to have known his love. Forgive me Lord for blaming you. I was given a precious gift from you for such a short while and now you have taken him home to be with you. He was too good for this world.

The funeral was beautiful. When I looked upon Thomas' face for the last time he was like an angel. I kissed his lips tenderly and said, "I will see you in paradise." With that thought, I saw a sweet smile appear upon his face, and then I knew it was time to go home.

CHAPTER VIII

Now, I have to start my life over. Nothing seems real to me. I feel as though I am just going thru the motions. I think I may be losing my mind. Luke tries to help by talking about doing things and maybe going on a trip when spring comes. I have no interest in anything. I stay in my room a lot. Thomas' parents still call and ask me to go to church with them, but I have withdrawn completely from life. Months go by, as I see the seasons changing outside my window, but I don't care I just want to be left alone with my memories. Luke has been good to me, he brings food to my room, and he tries so hard to help me. I never see Ma; I guess she is glad I don't have anyone it was what she wanted. I hate her, I hate her soul, I wish she would die and go to hell. The devil needs a good disciple down there.

I have decided to take some courses on business. I need to get out into the working world again and start my life over. I have entered the Soule Business College. I am taking typing, bookkeeping and general business. It is a beautiful school. The course was six months long. I passed with excellent grades. The president wanted to hire me as his personal secretary. He offered me $150.00 a month; Mr. Carter said if I was worth that to Mr. Soule, I was worth $175.00 to him.

I decided to stay at home where I was most needed. Luke is looking bad, his color is gray and even though he is thin, he has lost weight. When I cook a meal, he can't eat very much. I am very worried he has something seriously wrong with him. I have called Dr. McLaurin to get Luke an appointment. He said he could come in this afternoon.

I took Luke to Laurel General Hospital where Dr. McLaurin is. He has run some tests on Luke and we will know something next week. Until then Doc said for him not eat any rich foods, mostly chicken soup for now. The next week, Dr. McLaurin called for Luke to come into his office. I drove Luke to the hospital and went in with him. Dr. McLaurin's news was bad. Luke has cancer in his lower extremities it is advanced. The Doctor said he didn't have very long to live. He told Luke he would give him the strongest pain medication he had, but it wouldn't help a lot, especially at the end. He said he was sorry for such bad news. Luke looked so pitiful when the Doctor gave him the results, but he never said a word until the end and he told the Doctor thank you and he got up and we walked out. My heart was breaking for my Pa, he has had many hard breaks in his life and it seems as though fate has dealt him another bad hand. He is still a young man; he is only forty-four years old. As the weeks go by Luke gets weaker and weaker. Ma is not handling this well at all. She is no help; she is mostly a hindrance, because she can't bear to see Luke deteriorate before her eyes. I have to do everything for him, feed him, bathe him, clean him up, but I don't mind. I love him and he is my Pa. I just don't know what I am going to do without him. He got me through some really bad years with my Ma. He protected me and stood up for me. He was my **ROCK!**

Well, Luke is going fast now. I have been up with him for two days and nights. He can barely talk. He asked for a preacher last week. He prayed with him and he told me that Luke had made his peace with God. I have been reading the Bible to him. Reverend Jones gave me some passages of comfort to read to Luke. I think it has helped, I know it has helped me. At the last, he told me he loved me very much and his time here with us was the only happiness he ever knew.

I began to cry and he said, "don't cry baby," that was his last words. He closed his eyes and he was gone. My heart is shattered. Ma is devastated too. At the funeral, she couldn't stop crying. I know, regardless of how crazy she is she loved Luke very much. He was her first and only love. She doesn't have much to say to me, but somehow I know she appreciated my tender care for the man she loved.

My schooling is finished. I made good grades, jobs are hard to find. Jobs for women are teachers, secretaries and clerks. My home town of Laurel has grown by leaps and bounds since the sawmills first moved here. There are many wealthy people with lovely homes. We have the large industry of Masonite Hardboard Manufactory. Mr. William Mason invented it in 1925 by the pressing of sawdust together in a steam machine to form a hard board. It is sold all over the country. This has brought many new jobs in for the common workers, which were needed, but despite all of this, the economy is bad all over. Many people have lost their homes. We are still doing ok, we still have money in the bank and some invested, but not like the good ole days. I don't know if we are going to be able to keep this big old house. It is costly to heat and gas lighting is expensive.

Mr. W.M. Carter has given me my job back as secretary for his lumber business. I started out at $50.00 a month. I was very proud of that. It was a lot of money at that time. Now, of course, I am making $175.00. Ma is falling back into her old ways. With Luke gone, she is becoming unbearable to live with. She argues with me about everything. She is lucky she has me here with her. Maude and Eloise have been gone for years and Earl has his own life even though he lives here. He is not much help to either of us. His drinking is getting bad.

1929! The country has gone crazy. The stock market has crashed!

People are trying to get their money out of the banks, but the doors are locked. The banks are broke. People of all classes have lost everything. The papers say in New York people are jumping out of windows and committing suicide. They are putting guns to their heads and shooting themselves. Even in Laurel, some of the wealthy businessmen have ended their lives like this. What will we all do? This means we have lost some of our money as well.

W.M. Carter has been quite good to us. Earl has a job and he contributes to our sustenance as much as he can. He works at Masonite. He still lives with us, but he is hardly ever here, except to eat supper and sleep. I guess

50

we are lucky, because Laurel has not been hit quite as hard as the large cities and other places. At least we have jobs right now.

After work today, I went by the grocery store and purchased a few things for dinner. I bought a chicken, some bread, butter, lard, cabbage and a personal item. When I got home, I went straight to the kitchen to start supper. I washed the chicken and put it on the worktable to cut-up; I started the lard in the skillet to fry the chicken. We have a gas stove now, so all you have to do is strike a match to light the top burners and oven. I used some of the melted lard to make biscuits in our old dough bowl. I put the biscuits in the oven, and then I put the chicken pieces in the left over flour, coated and seasoned each piece and put it in the skillet to fry. I washed the cabbage, broke it up and put it in a pot on the stove, seasoned with salt and pepper and dipped a little lard from the skillet to pour it in the cabbage. I heard Ma walk in the room behind me.

She screamed, "Where in blazes do you think this money will come from?" I turned to see her looking at the grocery ticket on the table.

I said, "I charged it as usual, but I'm going to pay the whole bill on Friday when I am paid."

She said, "You know what I'm talking about." she pointed at the personal pads I had purchased. She said, "You can use rags like I always have." She then slapped my face really hard.

I said, Ma please let me finish supper or it will burn and we won't have anything to eat. As I walked to the stove, turned the chicken, and got the biscuits out, she grabbed my long hair and pulled it, so hard I dropped the pan of biscuits on the floor.

Then she hollered, "You look at me girl when I'm talking to you, you little B****, you have dropped the biscuits!" She shoved me down on the floor and told me to clean it up. I managed to save a few biscuits and I wiped the floor clean. As I started to get up, she kicked me in the side.

I said, "Stop Ma or else.

She said, "Or else what?"

I said, "I'm not going to let you abuse me anymore. I am a grown woman and even though you are my Mother, I swear you will be sorry if you hurt me again."

She looked shocked that I stood up for myself without Luke around. She shut up and walked out of the kitchen.

Earl came in the back door, "Are you and Ma at it again?"

"Yeh, Earl, but I'm not gonna take her abuse anymore, you hear me Earl."

"Sure Ouida, I've heard that before. Is supper ready?"

I said, "Let me make some gravy and we can eat." We ate in the kitchen, Earl and I. Ma took her plate to the dining room. This is beginning to be a normal occurrence in our house.

We are going through what they are calling, "The Great Depression", they said the "Panic of 1893," was bad, but this is worse and it is lasting a lot longer. There are food kitchens set up for the many folks that can't find work. The schools are serving free lunches. Teachers have been told to take notice of children that are too thin and prone to fainting spells, this is a sure sign of a family in dire straits and possibly too proud to ask for help. Banks are keeping the grocers in supplies, while they carry people until times get better. So far, I have been able to keep a job, so has Earl.

CHAPTER IX

Mr. Carter is a very nice man, his wife is very sick; I think she may be dying. I think he is very lonely, because he comes to our house quite often. I always give him a cup of coffee and he stays and visits for at least an hour. He keeps telling me how beautiful I am and offers to help us out with anything we may need. I feel so sorry for him; he acts like a lost puppy. We have been having an affair since 1920. Ma still doesn't know or she would probably kill both of us. He is nice looking for an older man and he smells so good. I think he wears Old Spice after-shave and he dresses in nice suits. Every visit now, he brings us something good to eat, one-day ice cream, and another candy. I told him one day that my automobile needed work and I asked him if he knew someone good to repair it. He told me he knew a good mechanic and he could follow me to his garage to see about fixing it, so we went to a garage on Front Street, just a few blocks away, at Mr. Ducksworth's garage. He looked it over and said it needed a new engine it was burning oil bad. I haven't driven it much lately, because I couldn't afford the oil and gas. He said leave it for now and I will see what I can do. I left my telephone number for him to call me. I then got into the car with Mr. Carter for him to take me home.

He asked, "Would you like to go for a ride?" This was one of many excuses we used to be alone together.

I said, "That would be nice, because it was a lovely day for a drive." He drove out Highway 11 North towards Meridian. He asked me if I had ever been to Stafford Springs before and tried the water. I said I had heard of it, but I had never been there and tried it. We drove out of Laurel and passed Sandersville and on until we got to the springs. It was a beautiful place; it had a very large plantation style hotel and a gazebo where you got the spring water. He purchased a gallon jug for his wife. It is said to have healing powers. The Choctaw Indians in this area discovered it many years ago. They called it Boga Hama, "Water of Life." He got us a cup each and we drank it. It was very cool and refreshing.

webpages.charter.net/hondapotamus/staffs.....Stafford Springs, Mississippi.

Mr. Carter asked, "Would you like to come back and bath in the springs sometimes?"

I said, "I would love to." The springs were once a busy holiday spot, but since the depression, not many people came out here anymore. We walked around the lovely grounds. The huge pine trees and lovely flowers were in abundance everywhere. I told him this place was a haven hidden away from all the worries of the world just thirty minutes away. There were very few people there and we got a guided tour of the once beautiful hotel. It was beginning to fall in disrepair. The paint had not been freshened in years; everything was looking old and faded. The beautiful Victorian furnishings needed recovering and the gorgeous silk and damask draperies were tattered and faded. How sad to see something that was once grand, the glorious old days being forgotten by the passing of time. As I looked around tears filled my eyes, oh, how I wished I could have lived here in the days long ago, when all of this was fresh and beautiful, with vivid colors of crimson, gold and purple. The lazy carefree days that was alive with banquets and balls. Carriage rides, lovers and eloquent people from all over the world were coming and going, ladies and gents in all of their finery strolling along the shaded paths with fragrant flowers blooming in every direction.

As the day was ending, we had to leave. I didn't want to go back home, to a place of misery and unhappiness, I would love to stay here and just fade into the wallpaper and become part of the past. As we drove away, the sun was setting against the facade of the beautiful old hotel. As the shadows crept up the walls, they seemed to be the ghosts of guests who never left. I knew I wanted to come back here again.

I told, "Will (Mr. Carter) please bring me back." Will decided to get us a room in a little cottage. We sat on the sofa and watched the sun set from the large window that faced the lake. We talked about being together as a married couple, without the shame of this sinful affair. I so want to be able to tell people I love him and be proud to be his wife. Speaking of wife, Will's wife died a few months ago from a long illness. He says he wants to marry me, but will not commit to a date. I'm sure he loves me, he tells me all the time. These brief moments of pleasure is all we have. Mother, I'm afraid will never accept this or any relationship I will ever have. We have talked about her and what we can do about this problem. Will knows my reluctance to leave her alone. So we are at an impasse. We left after an hour or so. The ride home was quite.

The next morning Ma asked why I was so long getting home. I told her Mr. Carter took me to get something to eat. She seemed to accept that answer, because she didn't say anything else to me. Will came by after I got off work. He brought us some ice cream. He asked if I liked my job and I answered by saying I was happy to just have a job. Then he said he was happy I was his secretary. I was really happy, because I would rather work as a secretary than anything else. I told him I loved the job and thanked him. He said he wished he could give me a raise, but his business has really suffered.

The year is 1933 I have been working for Will since 1920, part time, now I am fulltime and I am making $150.00 a month now. I have a 1930 Willis Knight car that Will helped me get. I have been having an affair with Will for ten years; we are still keeping it a secret. Ma doesn't know, but if she ever finds out it will be bad. We still fight like cats and dogs. She is relentless and meaner than ever. I hate her!

Now at thirty-one years old I have never been married. My older sister Maud has been married for years to a good man. She is very happy. Even my baby sister Eloise, five years younger than me, has been married twice, not counting her elopement when she was very young. I have never known any real happiness in my life, not for long anyway. My Mother has dominated my life and taken my youth from me. I have been forced to find love with a married man, live in sin, instead of the holy union of marriage, and have a life of my own away from her. I hate her so, she has a hold on me I can't seem to escape I can't explain this bond that binds me to her. I am the only one who knows of her murderous past. The evil that has devoured her soul has made a mental prisoner of me. When I sleep at night Louisa's spirit comes to me and reminds me of the revenge her soul seeks for her violent death, her youth taken from her in her prime by my wicked Mother. Why is my life haunted by the living and the dead? What have I done to deserve such a malady of life? I have begun having terrible headaches that sends pains down into my neck and shoulders. I have been to Doctors, but they can't explain the reason for my pain. I have also been to the hot springs several times. Will has taken me several times, it gives me temporary relief. My time with Will is the only joy I have. We have talked of how I can be free of Mother. She will never let me leave her. Only her death can set me free. She is just in her fifties and very healthy, she will probably live to be a very old lady.

I think Will really loves me. He says he would do anything in the world to make me happy. I do love him terribly. I would do anything he wanted me to do to keep us together. He is a lot older than I am, but he doesn't look his age, he is a very handsome man and a wonderful lover. He makes me feel so good about myself; he gives me confidence in my own ability as a smart and caring person, not to say how beautiful he says I am. He truly makes my life worth living. I would go thru hell for him if need be. I don't think I am a strong person mentally, but I think I could endure anything for him. I will NOT let anyone take him from me, not family or foe.

Mother is complaining about my relationship with him. Says she is noticing that it seems to be more than employee and boss friendship. She has also reminded me of how much older than me he is. She says, "He is older than your Father if he were still alive." In addition, she tells me I cannot ever leave her. She makes me feel as though I am the one that is keeping a terrible secret about myself, instead of the other way around. Ma is afraid of me taking all of her money and property. She is so greedy and stingy; I think she plans to take it all to the grave with her. What Ma can't seem to grasp is I would gladly give it all to her just to get away from her grip on me. I dream of moving to New Orleans where Eloise is, but only if Will would go with me. I would love to own a small hotel in the Quarter. Will has said he would support my decision in any business venture I wanted, but of course, he can't leave Laurel and his family obligations anytime soon, but maybe later we can move away together. We sometimes meet in New Orleans at the Jung Hotel, we each take the train, but I take the first one from Laurel to New Orleans, then Will takes the second. We spend the weekend together. We talk of me being free of my Mother one day. We have many plans for a life together. He has made many promises to me I hope they are sincere. I have heard rumor that he has had other affairs besides me. I know he loves me, I am sure of it. If he did have other girl friends before me, they weren't like me. He says he loves me and only me.

The year is 1934, my Aunt Paula, Ma's sister, has come to visit today. She is a very dear person, but she is the noisiest woman besides Ma I have ever seen. I caught her looking in my dresser drawers in my room. She found my love letters from Will. I'm sure she will tell Ma, because she likes to get things started. She also found my special drawer that I have baby clothes in, she thinks I am crazy. I buy baby clothes on sale and when I see something sweet for a little baby. I do plan to have children one day, besides it is none of her business how I spend my money. I asked her politely not to go into my room again. If she had seen my underwear drawer, she would have been shocked. I have some very feminine things in there in black lace and silk. I'm sure she would think me a loose woman, for certain.

CHAPTER X

I have heard about a unique school in Washington, D.C. It is the "Lewis Hotel Training School." I really want to go to this school. I told Will about it and he asked what they offered. I told him they had a master course that included chief clerk and staff, housekeeper and staff, chef and staff of food, cook, butcher, garde manager and carver, chef, baker and pastry chef, Management and Executive staff in bookkeeping, accounting... He asked what the master course cost and how long it took. I told him the price and that it starts in September and ends in January. The price included room and board. I am very excited about this school. I can learn everything I need to know to run my own hotel, including the kitchen. I decided to take the course. Before I left for Washington, Will and I discussed some plans for the future. He told me to think about it while I was away.

I have arrived in Washington, D.C. I came by train, the trip was long, but it gave me a lot of time to think about my future. Washington is a beautiful city. The hotel school is very nice. I am going to enjoy my schooling here everyone is so nice. There are students here from every lifestyle and people from every country you could imagine, especially France. I am having a wonderful time. I think this will be an exciting way to make a living, even if I can't find the hotel I want to buy right away. I can work in management until I can. I have written Will about my excitement and how much I love the school. I am making very good grades in every department of the course. Washington is absolutely beautiful in the fall. I have seen the Capitol and all the wonderful memorials here. I never dreamed it was such a marvel to see. It makes you proud to be an American when you see all the statues and tributes to our countries great men from the past. Everyone who is an American should see this city at least once in his or her life. I have met a very nice man here. We have become quite close.

I have gone through the first round of courses and I have passed with an, "A". The second course is Chef and staff. I have to learn all aspects of the kitchen. Handling food, cooking and I have to learn how to butcher a pig, lamb and a steer. This process is very important for the proper cut of suitable parts; the butcher must know all the desired cuts when the Chef gives an order. A sharp knife is used in many cuts of the animal. The value of good, clean, sharp equipment is the pride of a good butcher. Knives, cleavers, choppers, saws and such are his trademark. His equipment often judges him. Next, all aspects of service equipment; dishes, glasses, silver, steward, pantry girl, salad girl, bartender, ect, and last of the second course; maître d' hotel, head waiter, banquet manager, superintendent of room service and captain. I passed this course with an, "A", also. The last course is management and executive staff training. My final test was for every course I took and I made another "A". I am quite proud of how well I did. It was a joy to learn this hotel training course. I think I am ready for a new life as a hotel manager and owner. I can't wait till I get home and talk to Will about the future with my newly acquired education. Of course, Ma can't be told that I am planning to leave Laurel; I think she thinks I want a job at the Pinehurst Hotel here in town. I think the gentleman I met here is in love with me. I am torn between him and Will. I have not yet given myself to him.

No one met me at the train depot. It was cold and raining, I called my brother in law, David, to pick me up and take me home. He was only just down the street at his filling station. When I got home, Ma was waiting for me.

She said, "Well, it is about time you came home did you make a vacation out of your trip as well?"

I told her, "No, I was in school from September to January and I didn't have money for a vacation, and it was in the wintertime for goodness sakes." I told her in a sarcastic way, I missed her too. She just grunted and walked to the fireplace to get warm. She sat in her favorite chair and sipped on a cup of coffee she had sat on the table next to the chair. I asked if there was any more coffee made. I was chilled to the bone and a hot cup of coffee would be nice.

She said, "Make your own; I'm not your maid."

I went to the kitchen and made more coffee, as it was making I started a fire in my room. The room was freezing; it would take it awhile to warm-up, so I drank my coffee in the living room with Ma. She didn't say much, as we sat there staring at the fire watching the flames burn into what looked like molten lava as it slowly burned into black ash. I added more coals to the fire, Ma, fussed, and said that I didn't need anymore in here, because we would be going to our rooms soon. She has always complained about everything I do, so I didn't pay her any mind. I did go to my room after getting a second cup of coffee and a piece of pound cake I saw in the pie safe. I took it to my room and curled up in my bed with just the fire burning in the fireplace. The sun had gone down and my room was almost dark, as my eyes adjusted to the soft glow of the burning embers, I pulled covers up to my waist, slowly sipped the hot coffee, and nibbled on the cake. I was very tired from the long train ride. I didn't get a sleeper car, so I didn't sleep well at all on the hard seats coming home. I started nodding off, so I got up and dressed for bed. I put on my flannel pajamas, because it was still very cold in my room. Before getting in bed, I put extra coals on the fire. I crawled under about four quilts to stay warm; my head had barely touched my pillow before I fell into a deep sleep.

The morning sun was rising halfway in the sky when I woke; I don't think I moved a muscle all night I slept so hard. I hated to get out of bed, because my room was frigid. My fire was out except for a few smothering coals, I added more coals to the fire to see if it would start up again and it did. I stood next to the fireplace and warmed myself; I put on my warmest robe and slippers and went to the kitchen to cook some breakfast. Ma was up and drinking her coffee. She screamed at me for sleeping so late. I tried to tell her how tired I was from the trip, but it didn't matter to her.

I had almost forgotten how mean she is. I lost my temper with her and said, "I wish you were dead!" She looked shocked, but didn't say a word. I was glad it ended there, because I think it could have gotten ugly. I hate to argue with her and have screaming matches. I know it is not respectful to talk to your Mother like that, but after all these years of mental abuse I have just about taken enough from her. I want to be released from the evil bond that ties us together. Where can our lives lead if not to a disastrous end? I am afraid of my own thoughts. I am still haunted by Louisa's revengeful spirit; I dream of her often. As time passes, I sense her spirit is trying to control my thoughts and actions. If I don't get away from Mother, I fear something terrible is going to happen. I've given up my job at the lumber store I am not well, me headaches are bad lately; nothing I take seems to help! I also feel very anxious and nervous. At night, I try to sleep, but I am so restless and apprehensive. I am fearful of what is happening to me I can't concentrate on anything for very long. My mind seems to be in a far away place, but when I try to think of what I have been thinking, I don't know or remember. This makes me distressed and agitated. I am staying in my room most of the time. I even bring my meals in here. I can't seem to eat with anyone around me without feeling very nervous. I get a strange feeling in my stomach, then it comes up into my throat and I can't swallow my food. Sometimes I get into my car and just drive around in the country to help me relax and forget my fears; it seems to help a lot. I don't know what is happening to me, but it scares me to death. Sometimes hours will pass and I can't remember anything about what I have been doing. Ma is leaving me alone and she is not fussing as she normally does. I think she is seeing familiar signs in my behavior and it scares her. She seems to know something about myself that I don't know. What does she think is going to happen, surely I am not becoming like her. Oh Lord, help me to fight this dementia I don't want to be evil like her, is this our family curse?

When Will and I talk of our life together, we both agree that my Mother is our main obstacle. Even if he cannot go to New Orleans now, he could always join me later when I have established a business there. I just have to be able to get away from her. We have planned to talk to Ma together and break the news about New Orleans. He thinks if he is present it will go over better, him being a businessmen and knowledgeable of such things, but I'm afraid of what might happen, because he has never seen the evil side of her character. I don't know how this meeting will end. We have planned for him to come over this evening. I am very nervous, so much that it has made me throw up. I was working at David's station and I had to go home, I felt so sick. When I got home, she was working in the yard.

I went inside and she called out to me, "Ouida, take me to the grocery store."

I said, "I will later I am sick right now."

She came inside and asked, "What's wrong with you now, it seems as though you are always sick here lately?"

I said, "Ma please lets not argue now I don't feel like it." She went back outside. I took her to the store about an hour later and when we got home, I took a long hot bath, it made me feel a lot better. I dressed and waited for Will to come. He came by early and brought some ice cream and said he would return later.

About eight-thirty he came back. He told Ma he wanted to talk to her about some things. She asked us to come to her room it was warmer in there. She had already dressed for bed, but she had on her pretty kimono on over her pajamas. We sat by the fireplace and Will began telling her of my plans to move.

She jumped up and screamed at us both, "Over my dead body!"

The events of what happened next are public record.

Sometimes I remember things, and then other times I think I dreamed all of it. I guess there is one thing I know for sure, Louisa got her revenge! Some say I am insane, while others say I am just evil! I hear whispering about the illicit affair Will and I had, the dirty secret we kept all those years. It wasn't dirty, I loved him deeply and I still do. I know I said things about Will killing my mother, even if it is true, I should not have told our secret. I betrayed the man I loved, but I will make it up to him someday, somehow.

THE STATE OF MISSISSIPPI

VS.   #577

OUIDA KEETON

Tried in the Circuit Court of the Second District of

Jones County, Mississippi, before the Honorable W.J. Pack, Judge

of the Twelfth Circuit Court Judicial District of Mississippi.

Circuit Court Indictment- Single Count

STATE OF MISSISSIPPI
Circuit Court, February term, 1935.

SECOND DISTRICT

JONES COUNTY

The Grand Jurors of the State of Mississippi, elected, summoned, empanelled, sworn and charged to inquire in and for the Second Judicial District of Jones County, State of Mississippi, at the term aforesaid, of the Court aforesaid, in the name and by the authority of the State of Mississippi, upon their oaths, present that OUIDA KEETON and W.M. CARTER on the 18 day of February, 1935, in the County and District aforesaid did willfully, unlawfully and feloniously, of their malice aforethought, kill and murder Mrs. Daisy Keeton, a human being, against the peace and dignity of the State of Mississippi.

ALEXANDER   CURRIE,   DISTRICT
ATTN.

Copy of article from the Laurel Leader Call; January 28, 1935

Copy of article from the Laurel Leader Call; January 30, 1935

Copy of article from the Laurel Leader Call; January 1935

Copy of article from Laurel Leader Call; January 1935

THE STATE

VS.

OUIDA KEETON & W.M. CARTER

                                    Murder

Witnesses:
Jim Brown
Van Valentine
W.P. Duckworth
Will Saul

A TRUE BILL

H. B. Welborn, foreman of the Grand Jury

Filed this the 18th day of Feb., 1935

T.L. Sumrall, Circuit Clerk

By: Esther Carter, D.C.

Jones County Courthouse in Laurel, Ms.

Inside the Courtroom at the Jones County Courthouse, Laurel, Ms.

CAPIAS- Circuit Court

STATE OF MISSISSIPPI

TO THE SHERIFF OF JONES COUNTY   ---   GREETINGS:

You are commanded to take OUIDA KEETON if to be found in your county, and her safely keep, so that you have her body before the Circuit Court of the Second District of Jones County, in said State, to be hold at the courthouse thereof, in the Town of Laurel, Miss., on the instanter day of Feb., A.D., 1935, then and there to answer unto the State of Mississippi on an indictment found against her on the 18 Day of Feb., A.D., 1935 for murder.

And have then and there this writ.

Given under my hand and seal of said court, and issued this the 18 day of

Feb., A.D., 1935.

T.L. Sumrall, Clerk
By: Mrs. L.M. Martin,
D.C.

(SEAL)   I have this day executed this writ by arresting the within named Ouida Keeton and in default of bond, holding her in jail.
This the 18 day of Feb., 1935
L.C. Jordan, Sheriff
By: T.V., D.C.

THE STATE

VS.   #577

OUIDA KEETON

     This day came the District Attorney, who prosecutes for the State, and the defendant, Ouida Keeton, who being arraigned and required to plead to a Charge of murder, preferred by bill of indictment, and the indictment having been read in the presence of the defendant, Ouida Keeton, and the said defendant, Ouida Keeton, having failed to plead to said indictment, but stood mute, where- Upon the court ordered that a plea of not guilty to said charge be entered in this behalf and that the defendant await trial at a later day of this term of court.

Filed Feb. 21, 1935

T.L. Sumrall, clerk

STATE OF MISSISSIPPI

COUNTY OF JONES

SECOND DISTRICT

VS.

OUIDA KEETON

 Comes now Alexander Currie, District Attorney, and moves the court For a subpoena duces tecum to require Mrs. L.A. Varnado, Manager and Owner of the Laurel General Hospital, to produce in this court at 1:30 P.M., February 22, 1935, all charts and records kept and made in said hospital touching the confinement and treatment therein of Ouida Keeton covering a period of time from February 12, 1935, up to and including today.
ALEXANDER CURRIE
DISTRICT ATTORNEY

Filed Feb. 22, 1935

T.L. Sumrall, Clerk
 Ordered by the court on motion of District Attorney that subpoena duces tecum issue to Mrs. L. A. Varnado to produce in this court at 1:30 P.M., February 22, 1935, records of said hospital as prayed for in said motion.
W.J. Pack, Judge
Filed Feb. 22, 1935
T.L. Sumrall, clerk

IN THE CIRCUIT COURT OF THE SECOND JUDICIAL DISTRICT OF JONES COUNTY, MISSISSIPPI

THE STATE

VS.

OUIDA KEETON, Defendant

   Comes now the defendant, Ouida Keeton, by her attorneys, F.B. Collins and Frank Clark, and moves the court to grant her a severance in the above styles cause, and would show unto the court that in said cause she stands now jointly indicted with W.M. Carter for the murder of Mrs. Daisy Keeton.

She therefore moves the court for a severance of said cause that she may be tried separately and alone

FRANK CLARK & F. B. COLLINS
COUNSEL FOR DEFENDANT

Filed Feb. 22, 1935

T.L. Sumrall, clerk

Mrs. L.M. Martin, D.C.

This cause came on this day to be heard on motion of defendant for a severance of said cause, and it is therefore ordered and adjudged that the said motion be sustained, and that the defendant be granted a severance of said cause from the said W.M. Carter jointly charged with her in said cause.

Filed Feb. 22, 1935
W.L. Sumrall, Clerk
Mrs. L.M. Martin, D.C.

STATE OF MISSISSIPPI

VS.

OUIDA KEETON

This cause this day coming on to be heard upon motion of attorneys for the defendant that she be allowed to remain in the Laurel General Hospital at her own expense, under guard, until Wednesday, February 27, 1935, and until further order of the court, and the court having considered said motion is of the opinion that the same should be granted.

It is, therefore, ordered that the defendant, Ouida Keeton, be and she is hereby ordered placed in the Laurel General Hospital, under guard both day and night; said defendant to bear all expenses of her incarceration in said hospital, together with the expenses of maintaining two guards, one each day and one each night.

It is further ordered that no one be allowed to visit the said defendant except her attorneys, Judge F.B. Collins and Honorable Frank Clark; her physician, Dr. J.B. Jarvis and Dr. Thomas R. Beech, Health Officer of Jones County, provided said physicians may invite other physicians to accompany then.

Ordered, this the 22nd day of February, 1935.

W.J. PACK, JUDGE OF THE
CIRCUIT COURT
Filed Feb. 22, 1935
T.L. Sumrall, clerk
By: Mrs. L.M. Martin, D.C.

STATE

VS.

KEETON

Comes now District Attorney and moves Court to issue a subpoena duces tecum to require First National Bank to produce its records showing all accounts of Ouida Keeton both savings and checking's from 1925 to date.

ALEXANDER CURRIE,
DISTRICT ATTORNEY

Filed March 1, 1935

T. L. Sumrall, Clerk

By: Mrs. L.M. Martin, D.C.

....

On motion of District Attorney, it is ordered that subpoena duces tecum issue requiring First National Bank of Laurel to produce its records showing all accounts of Ouida Keeton from 1925 to date, returnable March 1, 1935 at 1:30 P.M.

This the 1st day of March, A.D., 1935.

W.J. Pack, CIRCUIT JUDGE

Filed March 1, 1935
T.L. Sumrall, clerk
By: Mrs. L.M. Martin, D.C.

STATE

VS.

KEETON

Comes now the District Attorney and moves the court for a subpoena duces tecum to require the Sumrall Funeral Home to produce before this court the certain parts of human body alleged to be that of Mrs. Daisy Keeton and intrusted to their care by the sheriff of Jasper County, Mississippi.

ALEXANDER CURRIE

Filed March 5, 1935

T.L. Sumrall, clerk

By: Mrs. L.M. Martin, D.C.

....

Ordered by the court on motion of the District Attorney that the Sumrall Funeral Home by writ of subpoena duces tecum be required to deliver into this court those certain parts of a human body intrusted to their care by the sheriff of Jasper County, and alleged to be parts of the body of Mrs. Daisy Keeton, deceased.

W.J. PACK, JUDGE

Filed March 5, 1935
T.L. Sumrall, clerk
By: Mrs. L. M. Martin, D.C.

STATE OF MISSISSIPPI

VS.

OUIDA KEETON

        This day came on to be heard before the court, on application or Petition of the defendant for a subpoena duces tecum for Jack Deavours, Alexander Currie and L.C. Jordan, to come into court and produce certain written confessions made by the defendant in this cause, or alleged to have been made by the defendant in this cause, and the court having considered said petition, doth sustain same.

        It is, therefore, ordered and adjudged that a subpoena duces tecum issue for the said Jack Deavours, Alexander Currie and L.C. Jordan, according to law in such cases made and provided, to appear before this court instanter and produce such alleged confessions as they have in their possessions of the said defendant, for the inspection of the attorneys for the defendant for use on the trial of this cause.

                    W.J. PACK, JUDGE OF THE CIRCUIT COURT

Filed March 6, 1935

T.L. Sumrall, Clerk

By: Mrs. L.M. Martin, D.C.

THE FOLLOWING PAGES ARE SOME OF THE TESTIMONIES OF WITNESS FOR THE STATE HAVING BEEN FIRST DULY SWORN:

DIRECT EXAMINATION:

W.E. KENNEDY
BY MR. CURRIE:

Q.   You are Mr. W.E. Kennedy?
A.   Yes, Sir.
Q.   Where is your home, Mr. Kennedy?
A.   My home is up in Choctaw County, my headquarters now is Port Gibson.
Q.   Mr. Kennedy, state whether or not you had occasion to pass through Jones County on the date of January 21st of this year?
A.   Yes, Sir.
Q.   From what place were you traveling when you came into Jones County?
A.   On my way from Quitman to Jackson.
Q.   Approximately what time did you leave Quitman?
A.   Eight o'clock.
Q.   Had you seen her before today here in the court room?
A.   Yes, sir.
Q.   When was the first time you saw her?
A.   The morning I picked her up, on January 21st.
Q.   About what time of morning was it when you picked her up?
A.   I would judge eight forty-five, somewhere along there.
Q.   On which or what public highway were you traveling?
A.   Highway 11.
Q.   Where had that brought you from?
A.   I had come from Quitman here.
Q.   Is that the road leading into Laurel?
A.   Yes, sir.

Q.	The same road that passes through Sandersville?

A.	Yes, sir.

Q.	In what kind of automobile were you traveling?

A.	I was traveling in a dove-colored, 1934 Model Chevrolet Sport Model Coupe.

Q.	What was the condition of the weather on that day?

A.	It was raining and cold at the time I reached Laurel and before I reached here.

Q.	What was the condition of the weather at the point where you picked up Miss Keeton?

A.	It was raining and cold.

Q.	Along what point of the road did you first see her?

A.	When I first saw her, the condition of the road, or lay of the road, you might say, where I picked her up, you come around a curve, and just as I straightened out around the curve, I could see the lady walking.

Q.	About how far were you from her at that time?

A.	I would say twice the distance from here to the back of the courthouse.

Q.	When you observed her and as you approached her, what happened then?

A.	Just before I got to her, well she began to flag me with her left hand, she was walking on the right hand side of the road, and I saw it was a lady and I slowed up, and as I drove by her I opened the door and held the door open and when she got there I asked her what in the World- I said, "Lady, what in the world are you doing out here in this kind of weather?" And she told me her car was stuck and she said, "I want you to carry me to the nearest telephone" and I said, "Lady, I don't know of any telephone any nearer than Sandersville" and she said she would go to Sandersville with me.

Q.	State whether or not she then and there got in your car?

A.	She did.

Q.	In what direction did you then travel?

A.	I came into Sandersville, down Highway 11.

Q.	How was the defendant dressed on that occasion?

A.	At that time she had on a little short fur coat, or imitation fur coat, had that over her head, and she didn't have on any stockings and had on high-heeled shoes, and if I remember correctly, a green striped dress.

Q.	When she had gotten in the car did you have any conversation with her?

A.	Yes, sir, I asked her what she was doing there and she told me she was going down the road- she told me she was on a side road and she started after a lady to stay with her while her mother was in New Orleans and until her Uncle John got back from New York--

BY MR. COLLINS

We object. That is incompetent, irrelevant and immaterial to this Issue.
BY THE COURT:
Overruled.

Q.   All right, what other conversation did you have with her as you proceeded along the road?

A.   Before we reached Sandersville the lady told me her car wasn't stuck very badly, and she felt another car with a chain could pull her out, and she asked me if I knew many people in Laurel and I called over a few people I knew in Laurel, and she said she would come on to Laurel with me, if I didn't mind, that she knew some people here and she would get somebody from Laurel to get her car, and I told her I would be glad to bring her on to Laurel.

Q.   State whether or not you did bring her on to the City of Laurel?

A.   I did.

Q.   After she stated to you she believed she would come in and get someone to get her car, did you talk further with her?

A.   Yes, sir, along on the way down here somewhere, just where I don't know- what place on the road- but I took my handkerchief out of my pocket-when she got in the car I thought probably she was cold, and I rolled the glasses all up, and the windshield got clouded, and I took my handkerchief out of my pocket and wiped the windshield off, and she asked if I wanted her to roll the window down on her side, and I said "No, because you are cold already" and she said no, she wasn't cold, and a little further on she took a deep breath and said "I'm completely broken down", or "a nervous wreak" or something to that effect, "from that walk I took" and when we got in the edge of town her she asked me if I knew where Cross Street was and I told her I didn't, and she said she would show me, and a little further on, just before we got to the place where I put the lady out, or where the lady got out, she asked me how much she owed me, and I told her not a thing in the world, if I had helped her I was glad, and she said she certainly appreciated it, and I pulled over to her house, pulled over to the left side of the road to her house- I say her house, I don't know whether it was her house or not, but I pulled down to the house where she said she wanted to get out, and pulled over on the left hand side and let her out and I worked my way back on the other side of the road and went on toward town- went ahead to Jackson.

Q.   Mr. Kennedy, about what time was it you picked her up- your best judgment?

A.   I would say eight-forty-five, approximately.

Q.   Hove you since that morning been over to the place where you let her out of the car?

A.   Yes, sir.

Q.   State whether or not you have ascertained that that was her home where you let her out?

A.   I have been told--

BY MR. COLLINS:

We object as to what he ascertained.

BY THE COURT:

Sustained.

Q.   Where was the place- describe the place at which she got out of the car?

A.   The place where I put her out of the car is just across the railroad track at the Loreco Service Station, in front of a big brown house just the other side of the street from the Loreco Service Station.

Q.   Have you been back to the place at which she first got in the car?

A.   Yes, sir.

Q.   Have you observed a road, a community or country road that turns to the right north of the place where she got in you car?

A.   Yes, sir.

Q.   What is the distance between the road that turns to the right North of the place that she got in the car and the place at which she did get in?

A.   As I understand you, you mean the distance from the road where she left the car to the place where she got in my car?

Q.   Yes.

A.   A fraction over .4 of a mile.

Q.   a little better than .4 of a mile?

A.   Yes, sir.

Dan Evans, Introduced On Behalf Of The State, Having Been First Duly Sworn, Testified As Follows:

DIRECT EXAMINATION

BY MR. CURRIE:

Q.   Your name is Dan Evans?

A.   Yes, sir, Dan Evans, Jr.

BY THE COURT:

Q.   Dan, it is mighty hard to hear in the court room, you don't mind speaking loud, do you?

A.   No, sir, I don't mind speaking loud.

Q.   Where do you live, Dan?

A.   I live nearer Heidleberg than I do Sandersville, between Heidleberg and Sandersville.

Q. Between Heidleberg and Sandersville?

A. Yes, sir.

Q. How long have you been living up there?

A. I been living there all my days.

Q. How old are you?

A. 37 years old.

Q. Dan do you remember the date of January 21st of this year, anything that happened that makes you remember that date?

A. Yes, sir.

Q. What if anything had you started out to do on the morning of the 21st?

A. On the 21st of January?

Q. Yes.

A. I started out to hunting first thing?

Q. Started out hunting?

A. That day, yes sir.

Q. Do you know the place at which it is said some human limbs and a portion of a body were found?

A. Yes, sir.

Q. How near do you live to the place where they were found?

A. I live a little better than a quarter of a mile from that.

Q. On which side of the road were these limbs and the body found as you travel toward Heidleberg?

A. Well, it's on the right going North and the left coming South.

Q. On the right as you go North?

A. Yes, sir.

Q. State whether or not you are the man that found these limbs?

A. Well, I know I was the only man was there when I went there.

Q. How had you traveled from your home to the place where you found them?

A. How I traveled when I left home?

Q. Yes.

A. Well, when I left home I come down towards the highway and left the pasture from in front of my house and hunted on the West side of the highway plumb on down to just this side of an old house setting side of the road on the west side, and didn't jump anything through there, and I decided I would cross over on some more land, and when I crossed I crossed right in that road and I got my dogs ahead of me.

Q. What road did you cross into?

A. A little blind road that leads East.

Q. Leads where?

A. East, on the east side of the highway.

Q. What did you do then?

A. I was walking along looking along the road, I figured I might see some

80

rabbits sitting in their bed, so my dogs run on ahead of me, they was already ahead of me, I got them ahead of me, and they went on ahead of me, and about twenty steps ahead of me my big black dog begin growling, and I taken notice of the growling and there was some packages laying there, and I thought maybe--

Q.   You can't tell what you thought, just tell what you saw?

A.   Well, there was some bundles laying there and I stopped, and the dogs was growling so I stopped them from growling, and I saw it was flesh in the bundles and I got a stick about 12 inches long off of a plumb bush there, I rolled one of the bundles over, and when it rolled over I begin to see it wasn't hog flesh and it wasn't beef, and I stood there four of five minutes studying what it was, and while I was studying it run across my mind I seed a fellow killed one time at a saw mill, and it put me in the mind of his flesh, and when I discovered it was human flesh I left there, I rolled it back up and left.

Q.   You say you rolled it back up?

A.   Rolled it just like it was.

Q.   Describe to the jury how many packages or bundles you saw there on the ground?

A.   Just them two bundles.

Q.   How many of them did you unroll?

A.   Just the one.

Q.   Tell the jury how you found them- how they were rolled up-What sort of package it was?

A.   It was white- it was in a white cloth that looked to me like sugar sacks, it was just laid in there and rolled right on up, that one I unrolled- that was the one I was taking notice of and doubled up at the end- and when I rolled it over there was a little of it showing, about that much- (indicating)- and I rolled it back after I unrolled it, and I left there.

Q.   State whether or not you notified anyone of the finding of these human limbs?

A.   Well, when I left there I went home--

BY THE COURT:

Answer the question.

Q.   State whether or not you notified anyone of the finding of these human limbs?

A.   Yes, sir.

Q.   Tell anybody about it?

A.   Yes, sir.

Q.   Whom did you tell?

A.   I told my wife and went on--

Q.   All right, did you tell any other person?

A.   Yes, sir, I told my sister, her house is the first house from my house.

Q.   Who else did you notify?

A.　　　I went on down and told four colored fellows, they was killing hogs, and I told them about it, and they told me to go and get Mr. Robert Youngblood and get him to go with us, and I told them out it looked-

BY THE COURT:

Leave off all those details.
Q.　　　Don't tell what you told them- did Mr. Cook finally get word of what you had found?
A.　　　Yes, sir, I got word by Mr. Conliff, he come up- he drove on down the road.
Q.　　　Well, did you go back to the place and show them what you had found?
A.　　　Yes, sir, I did that.
Q.　　　Who if any person did you see there where you found the body?
A.　　　Nobody.
Q.　　　I say when you went back with officers who did you see there?

BY MR. COLLINS:
We don't like to be always objecting, but all these questions are leading.

BY THE COURT:
Don't lead the witness. Refrain from leading the witnesses and we will save a lot of time.
Q.　　　State who you saw there after you had gone back?
A.　　　Well, there was Mr. Griffin Cook, Police Brown, Mr. Kent Huddleston.
Q.　　　Dan, tell the jury about how far the Main Highway, Highway No. 11, this body was when you found it?
A.　　　Well, everybody counted the steps, the same steps-

BY THE COURT:
Q. Tell them about how far it was?
A. All right, I will do that, Judge.
Q. The best you can?
A. I will do it.

BY MR. CURRIE:

Q.　　　In your judgment how far was it?
A.　　　In my judgment about 84 steps from the highway to where it was laying.
Q.　　　About 84 steps?
A.　　　Yes, sir.
Q.　　　How were they situated with reference to each other- how were they

upon the ground?

A.   They was laying right side by side, the two small ends-two ends laying both together, just this way. (indicating)

Q.   Can you identify the cloths in which the limbs were wrapped?

A.   Yes, sir.

Q.   I will ask you to look at that cloth and state whether or not it is the cloths in which one of the limbs were wrapped? (holding up cloth) Mr. Collins continued to question Dan about the clothes that the human limbs were wrapped in.

Mr. Griffin Cook, Introduced On Behalf Of The State, Having Been First Duly Sworn, Testified As Follows:

BY MR. CURRIE:

Q.   You are Mr. Griffin Cook?

A.   Yes, sir.

Q.   Mr. Cook, what if any official position do you hold?

A.   I am constable of Beat 5 in Jasper County.

Q.   State whether or not you received information that a part of a human body had been found on the 21st of January of this year?

A.   I did.

Q.   Do you know who gave you that information?

A.   It seems to me that Kirby Darwin came to the house after me.

Q.   Did you go to the place where it was found?

A.   Yes, sir.

Q.   Did you see Dan Evans there?

A.   Yes, sir.

Q.   This negro who just testified?

A.   Yes, sir, Dan was standing by the side of the road when I got down there. Mr. Collins continued the question as to how Dan got to the location of the human limbs and again about the cloth that the limbs were wrapped in.

BY MR. CURRIE:

Q.   I will ask you to look at this patch on this cloth and state whether or not that is the item of identification that you refer to?

A.   Yes, sir, that is it.

Q.   Now the first cloth that I showed you - the one you said was wrapped around?

A.   The right limb.

Q.   The right limb?

A.   Yes, sir.

Q.   I will ask you if you now observe a discoloration upon that cloth- of green paint?

A.   Yes, sir, there some place on that cloth- I don't see it now- was a spot of paint about as big as my hand, and then it was smeared, and this looks like the place where it was folded back.

Q.   Now when you indicate there you point to this green coloring that is on the cloth?

A.   Yes, sir.

More questions continue about the paint on the cloth and as to how the cloth was wrapped around the limbs. Next comes Mr. Cook as a witness for the State who was duly sworn and some of his testimony is as follows:

Q.   Were there tracks upon the little road that led down to where you found the limbs?

A.   Well, right where we picked up the limbs there had been a car there, but it had rained so much it had almost put out the front wheel track of the car, but where the back wheel stopped you could see where it had backed back to about 50 yards of the road.

Q.   What observation if any did you make with reference to the automobile having struck a pine tree there?

A.   Well, there was a little pine there somewhere about this size I guess. (indicating)

Q.   You indicate by saying this size, how many inches in diameter would you say?

A.   Not over 2 ½ inches-might have been three inches.

Q.   All right, what observation did you make with reference to the pine?

A.   Well, this little pine was skinned where the car backed up against it there, and there was a trench about this deep where the wheel had spun.

Q.   You indicate by saying this deep, how many inches?

A.   About three or four inches where the car wheel had sunk in the dirt.

Mr. Will Saul, Introduced On Behalf Of The State, Having Been First Duly Sworn, Testified As Follows:

DIRECT EXAMINATION

BY MR. CURRIE:

Q.   You are Mr. Will Saul?

A.   Yes, sir.

Q.   Where do you live, Mr. Saul?

A.   Seven miles out North of Laurel, just off of Highway 11.

Q.   Is that between here and Sandersville?

A.   Yes, sir.

Q.   On which side of Highway No. 11 do you live going North?

A.   East side.

Q.   The right hand side?

A.   Yes, sir.

Q.   As you go north?

A.   Yes, sir.

Q.   About what distance is you home from the main highway?

A.   You mean taking the road off or--

Q.   Well, following the road from the main highway to your house, about what distance is it?

A.   Well, it is hardly a quarter of a mile.

Q.   And then from your home, an air line across to the highway, is it a shorter distance?

A.   Yes, sir, it is shorter.

Q.   Mr. Saul, do you remember, or did anything happen on the date of January 21st?

A.   Yes, sir.

Q.   This year?

A.   Yes, sir.

Q.   That called your attention to the date?

A.   Yes, sir.

Q.   What was it that happened that caused you to remember the 21st of January of this year?

A.   Well, I was sitting out on the porch, the front porch, and I looked up the road and saw a car coming and it come on and just before it got- well it got right in front of me and I noticed there was a lady in it, driving the car, and it was raining and the roads was slick and she kind of raised up and looked down the road. It is a narrow road and very, very slick, and she drove on just past, and directly in front of the barn there she jerked the steering wheel, gave it three quick jerks and cut it back into the gate and reversed the car and come back out, shot back out and come on out, and as she turned, I got up and stood up and looked at her, and looked over in the car.

Q.   Now, Mr. Saul, what color car was this lady driving?

A.   It was a maroon body with black top and black fenders.

Q.   What model car?

A.   Well, as near as I could make out, about a 1930 of '31 Model.

Q.   I mean how many doors would you say?

A.   No, I don't know just exactly how many doors, but I think it was a two-door sedan, the way it locked.

Q.   How many seats in it?

A.   It was a two seated car.

Q.   Two seated car?

A.   It is what is called a sedan.

Q.   Yes- Now, Mr. Saul, state who was driving that car?
A.   Well, it was a lady driving it.
Q.   Who was the lady?
A.   Miss Keeton.
Q.   What Miss Keeton?
A.   Miss--
Q.   Miss Ouida Keeton?
A.   Yes, sir, Miss Ouida Keeton.

BY MR. CLARK:
We object to his leading.

BY THE COURT:
Overruled as to that.

Q.   Well, point her out to the court and jury, the lady driving the car.
A.   It is the lady sitting over there.(indicating)
Q.   Mr. Saul, from what direction did the car come as it approached your house?
A.   Well, it came out of the South, you might say the South, you see it was going North.
Q.   Is that from the direction of the main highway?
A.   Yes, sir, she turned there at my barn and went back to the main highway.
Q.   Now is the road that you are on- live upon- graveled- Is it a graveled highway or just--
A.   Just a common dirt road.
Q.   What was the condition of the weather that day with reference to whether it was raining or fair?
A.   It was raining- the roads was very sick.
Q.   You said that she turned around there in front of your barn?
A.   Yes, sir.
Q.   Was there anything unusual in the manner of her turning around?
A.   Yes, sir, the way she jerked the steering wheel in turning around, she seemed nervous and the roads was slick, and after she got on up the road on top of the hill going back to the main highway, there's a hill there, and when she got on top of the hill the car kind of whipped sideways that way (indicating), and she jerked it back right quick.
Q.   Now, Mr. Saul, how is you house built with reference to the road- how near does the road pass from your front porch?
A.   It is 95 feet from where I was sitting to the road.
Q.   Where were you when you first observed her driving the car along there?

A.   I was sitting on the bench against the wall.

Q.   Did you continue to sit there? If not, what did you do?

A.   Well, after she got turned around I got up and walked to the end of the porch and stood on my tiptoes and looked over in the car- the door was down- the right hand door was let down.

Q.   State whether or not you were able, or if you did observe anything in the car?

A.   Yes, sir.

Q.   Where was it and what sort of matter was it that you observed?

A.   Well, there was something in the front with her in there, and it was covered up, and when she got straightened out, she reached and pulled the covering back over it.

Q.   Mr. Saul, what further observation did you make, if any, as to what became of this car and the defendant?

A.   Well, after she went back to the highway, it is less than a quarter of a mile, - it drawed   my attention- I walked to the end of the porch and listened to see if she went back South or went North, and I knew if she went North she would have to change in second gear--

BY MR. COLLINS:
We object to that.

BY THE COURT:
Sustained.

Q.   Just tell what you did, Mr. Saul.

A.   Well, she turned and I went through the hall to the back and I could see up the main highway it was nearer back there and I saw her going down- she went on North.

Q.   State whether or not there is an open view from the back of your house over to Highway 11?

A.   Plain and open, just a plain field.

Q.   And you are able to see automobiles as they pass up and down Highway No.11?

A.   Yes, sir, you can.

Q.   And after she turned around in front of your place and went back to the highway, was she traveling north or south?

A.   She went North.

Q.   State whether or not that is in the direction in which it is said this body was found?

A.   Yes, sir.

BY MR. CLARK:

We object to the direction attorney
Putting the words in the witness' mouth.

BY THE COURT:

Sustained.

Q.   With reference to Sandersville in what direction did she travel?
A.   Well, she went north toward Sandersville.
Q.   State whether or not the car that you saw going toward Sandersville,
and the driver, is the same one that turned around there in front of your place?
A.   Yes, sir.

BY MR. COLLINS:
We object to that as leading.
Questioning continued as to the road and the direction that Miss. Keeton
traveled on the day in question.

Mr. W.P. Duckworth, Introduced On Behalf Of The State, Having Been First
Duly Sworn, Testified As Follows:

DIRECT EXAMINATION

BY MR. CURRIE:

Q.   You are Mr. Duckworth?
A.   Yes, sir.
Q.   W.P. Duckworth?
A.   Yes, sir.
Q.   What business are you engaged in, Mr. Duckworth?
A.   Garage.
Q.   Where is your business located?
A.   Front Street.
Q.   Here in the City of Laurel?
A.   Yes, sir.
Q.   How long have you known her?
A.   Two years.
Q.   Have you in the time past done work for her?
A.   Yes, sir.
Q.   Where was she living, Mr. Duckworth?
A.   On Cross Street.
Q.   Describe the house and its situation on Cross Street?
A.   Well, it is a kind of red looking house- or brown looking house- brown,

I would call it.

Q.   Where is it situated on Cross Street with reference to the New Orleans & Northeastern Railroad and the filling station?

A.   It is setting just opposite the filling station and facing West, at the intersection of Daughdrill-

Q.   Intersection of what street?

A.   Daughdrill and Cross.

Q.   Which side of Highway No.11 is it on as you go North?

A.   Right hand side- East side.

Q.   State whether or not on the date of January 21st of this year, you received a call from Miss Keeton?

A.   I wouldn't say what date it was on, but it was on one Monday, I did receive a call.

Q.   About what time of day?

A.   Between nine and nine-thirty.

Q.   What did Miss Keeton- that was from Miss Ouida Keeton?

A.   Yes, sir.

Q.   What did she say to you when she called you?

A.   She asked me to come and pick her up that she had her car stuck on the Sandersville road.

Q.   What did you do?

A.   I went over there and took my wrecker and picked her up in front of her house.

Q.   What was the condition of the weather at that time with reference to rain or clearness?

A.   It was raining.

Q.   Where did you get Miss Keeton, if you did get her?

A.   Right in front of her house.

Q.   How was she dressed at the time if you know?

A.   She had on a rain coat and didn't have any hose on, and had a parasol, she didn't have on any hat either.

Q.   No hose and no hat?

A.   No, sir.

Q.   What conversation did you have with her when she got into the car or wrecker?

A.   She got in the wrecker and asked me was that all I had to go in and I told her she said she was stuck and I thought probably she wanted to get out, so that was all that was said then.

Q.   As you went along what other conversation if any did you have with her, just tell the jury what you talked about.

A.   She said she was going up to Sandersville to see somebody, I don't remember who she said, but she was on the way to Sandersville and picked up an old lady--

BY MR. CLARK:
We object, he said he didn't know what date it was on.

BY THE COURT:
Overruled.

Q.   With reference to the day that it snowed, what day was it?
A.   It was before it snowed.
Q.   All right- the Monday before it snowed on Tuesday?
A.   Yes, sir.
Q.   All right, what conversation did she have with you when she got into the wrecker, on the way up?
A.   She said she thought she would do this old lady a kind deed and she picked her up and she said the old lady lived the other side of Sandersville and she carried her home and she got stuck.
Q.   Go ahead.
A.   And on further she said something about being afraid somebody might take something off of her car, and then she said something about the wrecker traveling-
Q.   What was it she said about the wrecker traveling?
A.   She said it could travel pretty fast.
Q.   What did you tell her?
A.   I told her yes, it would, that is all I told her.
Q.   Mr. Duckworth, did you pass through Sandersville on the way to get her car?
A.   Yes, sir.
Q.   Tell the jury how you reached the car or located it, after you had passed Sandersville what conversation if any you had with her with reference to locating the car?
A.   Well, we went on up the highway and I asked her how much farther it was and she said a little bit farther up the road, so I kept on going and after a while she said she believed we had done passed it, so she told me to turn around and I did and came on back down there and she said she believed that was where it was, and we went a little bit farther and she said there it was, and I saw the car.
Q.   What kind of car did you see there?
A.   A Willys Knight Sedan- maroon colored.
Q.   Was that the Keeton car?
A.   Yes, sir.
Q.   Did Miss Ouida tell you that was her car which she wanted removed?
A.   Yes, sir.
Q.   Where was it situated with reference to Highway 11, as you go North?

A.	It was on the East side, the right hand side traveling North on a little road, handing off of the highway.

Q.	Did she make any statement to you about how the car got stuck?

A.	No, sir, and just said she was carrying this old lady home and got stuck.

Q.	What directions if any did she give you as to how to remove her car or how to get it out?

A.	She didn't give me any directions to move it. When I got there , no she was afraid I would stick it again.

Q.	I see- now have you been shown the place at which it was said these limbs were found?

A.	Yes, sir.

Q.	Who showed you that place?

A.	The negro boy that found them.

Q.	Dan Evans?

A.	The negro boy that found the legs, I don't know his name.

Q.	Well, have you seen the negro boy here in the room today?

A.	Yes, sir.

Q.	Is that the one?

A.	Yes, sir.

Q.	How much farther down the road was it from where the car was stuck down to where the legs and body were found, in your judgment?

A.	Well, it was a little over half way from where the car was- the car was stuck about half way between the highway and where they showed me the legs were.

Q.	How far, in your judgment was it, from where it was shown you the legs were found back to the highway?

A.	Well, I don't know about how many yards it was, but I guess 75 yards; I reckon.

Q.	And her car was stuck about half way?

A.	Yes, sir, stuck about--

Q.	Between two places?

A.	A little nearer the highway.

Q.	When you were there and getting her car out of that little road, state whether or not you made any casual conversation and if you saw anything out ahead of you on down the road?

A.	I just backed in and lifted it up.

Q.	What was holding it- what fastened it?

A.	A little pine tree.

Q.	A little pine tree- where was that little pine tree located with reference to the road on which you found the car?

More questioning continued about the tree, its location and the condition of the bark on the tree...Also as to how Mr. Duckworth proceeded in getting Miss Keeton's car unstuck.

91

Q.   Mr. Duckworth, you didn't go forward with the car in getting it out?
A.   No, sir, not with her car, I didn't take her car forward.
Q.   You didn't take her car forward?
A.   No, sir.
Q.   You backed it back?
A.   Yes, sir. I saw something white down the road farther.
Q.   That was out in front of you, down the little road?
A.   Yes, sir, up ahead of her car.
Q.   That was the direction in which you would have driven if you had gone down and turned around?
A.   That is what I did, you mean?
Q.   Is that the direction in which you would haven driven if you had gone and turned around--

Objection ensued by Mr. Clark as to the leading of the witness with the court sustaining the objection and Mr. Currie withdrew the question.
Mr. Currie questioned Mr. Duckworth more about the location of where the legs were found in conjunction with where Miss Keeton's car was stuck.
Q.   Did you look inside of her car the morning you pulled it in for her?
A.   Yes, sir.
Q.   What if anything did you see in her car at that time?
A.   Well, there was some paper on the floor board of her car, on the right hand side of the front seat.
Q.   Now the floor board- you mean that is the place where you keep your feet?
A.   Yes, sir.
Q.   Down in front?
A.   Yes, sir.
Q.   On which side of the floor board of the floor were the papers?
A.   Right hand side.
Q.   Right hand side?
A.   Yes, sir.
Q.   On which side of the seat were the papers?
A.   Right hand side.
Q.   Was that on the front or back seat?
A.   Front seat.
Q.   Mr. Duckworth, state whether or not you recall having seen an oil cloth in there?
A.   No-

BY MR. COLLINS:
We object to his leading.

BY THE COURT:
Sustained- but overruled as to that.

Q.   After you had pulled the car back into the highway, you said the defendant drove it on into Laurel?

A.   Yes, sir.

Q.   State whether or not she told you who the old lady was that she was carrying home?

A.   She did not, no sir.

Q.   You say you had been doing her car repair work for about two years?

A.   Yes, sir.

Q.   Did you follow the defendant on into Laurel?

A.   Yes, sir.

Q.   With your car?

A.   Yes, sir.

Q.   State whether or not she drove it on into Laurel?

A.   She did.

Q.   Where did she stop, if you know, when she got here?

A.   She turned in her driveway.

Q.   Where is that driveway with reference to the house?

A.   It is on the North side of the house, turning off of Cross Street.

Q.   Where does it lead to after you leave the street and turn into the driveway, where does it go to back there?

A.   Well, it goes to the garage.

Q.   Where is the garage located with reference to the house?

A.   It is on the back- kind of back end of the house.

Q.   Is that the place that you saw the defendant turn her car into?

A.   I didn't see her drive in the garage, she drove it in the driveway.

Q.   What did you do?

A.   I come on- I didn't even stop.

CROSS EXAMINATION

BY MR. COLLINS:

Q.   Mr. Duckworth, how long did you say you have known Miss Keeton?

A.   Two years.

Q.   When you first knew her she was a much stouter and heavier girl than she is now, wasn't she?

A.   Yes, sir.

Q.   In other words, when you first knew her, she weighed about 150 pounds, didn't she?

A.   She was lots heavier that she is now.

Q.   You see her as she sits there now, Mr. Duckworth, she weighs about 105 or 110 pounds, and won't weigh over that, will she?

93

A.   I wouldn't judge her to.

Q.   Well, when you saw her that day, she wasn't much heavier than what she looks to be right now, was she?

A.   No, sir.

Q.   In other words, within the last two years, Mr. Duckworth, she has greatly emaciated in weight, hasn't she?

A.   Yes, sir.

Q.   She doesn't look much like the same person, does she?

A.   No, sir.

Q.   All during that time she has appeared to be very nervous, hasn't she?

A.   Well, I don't think so, I hadn't-- I couldn't say, I never--

Q.   Well, you do say, Mr. Duckworth, that during the past two years she has fallen off considerably?

A.   Yes, sir.

Q.   And doesn't look like the same girl?

A.   No, sir.

Now comes Mr. Cook to be cross examined as to what was done with the parts of the body that was found.

Q.   You state that you are the one who delivered the portion of the body found to the undertaker?

A.   Yes, sir.

Q.   When you delivered it to them was the portions found attached to each other, or had they been severed?

A.   They were severed.

Q.   I hand you a photograph- I will ask you if- to tell the jury what that is a photograph of?

A.   This here is--

Now the attorney objected to this line of questioning saying that it was irrelevant and that the witness is incompetent to identify the photographs as being photographs of the limbs.

BY MR. CURRIE:

Q.   Mr. Cook, when you took possession of the limbs, I will ask you who you turned them over to?

A.   I carried them to the Sumrall Funeral Parlor, and young Mr. Sumrall and the other gentleman there, Mr. Robert--

Q.   Mr. Allen?

A.   Yes, sir, Mr. Allen, I believe it is.

Q.   Mr. Allen?

A.   Yes sir, I turned them over to them.

Q.   That is here in the City of Laurel, Mississippi?
A.   Yes, sir.

Now comes Mr. E.S. Conliff to testify as follows:

BY MR. CURRIE:
Q.   You are Mr. E.S. Conliff?
A.   Yes, sir.
Q.   Where do you live, Mr. Conliff?
A.   Laurel.
Q.   Mr. Conliff, did you go out to the place at which it is said a portion of a human body was found?
A.   I did.
Q.   On January 21st of this year?
A.   I did.
Q.   Just in your own way describe that place in which the body was found- how did you get to it and so on- tell the jury about the description of the woods and so on?
A.   It is about 75 or 80 yards from the highway. This young fellow, a red headed fellow, flagged me down North of there about 200 yards and told me about it--
Q.   Were you able to see the limbs from the highway?
A.   If you looked real close, I believe you could.
Q.   What did you do?
A.   I had the negro to walk around it so as not to blur up the car tracks and we walked in and I told-- excuse me-- I had the negro to get a stick- a small switch and pick up the cloth so I could look at it and see what it was.
Q.   When you examined the content of the wrapping, what did you find it to be?
A.   The lower part of a body and the upper part of the limbs from the knees on up.
Q.   Up to how high on the body?
A.   The lower part of the body.
Q.   How many portions of the body did you find there?
A.   Two.
Q.   Where were they-- were they united or disunioned?
A.   They were cut in two.
Q.   How were they placed upon the ground- how did you find them lying and being?
A.   They were placed about- I should judge- about five feet from the car tracks- five or six feet; placed with the top part together, and the knees were open a little, the right side open more than the left.
Q.   Then were they lying side by side?

95

A.   Yes, sir, they were lying practically like they were cut off of the body.
Now comes Mr. Neville G. Allen, to testify as follows:

DIRECT EXAMINATION
BY MR. CURRIE:

Q. What is you name, please sir?
A.   Neville G. Allen.
Q.   Mr. Allen, where do you live?
A.   535 Meridian Ave, Laurel, Ms.
Q.   What work do you do?
A.   Funeral director.
Q.   And by whom are you employed?
A.   Sumrall Funeral Home.
Q.   Mr. Allen, I will ask you to state whether or not on the date of January 21st, this year, portions of certain- certain portions of a human body were turned over to the Sumrall Funeral Parlor?
A.   Yes, sir.
Q.   And do you know those limbs when you see them?
A.   Yes, sir.
Q.   By whom were they turned over to you?
A.   The Deputy Sheriff from Jasper County, Mr. Griffin Cook.
Q.   About what time of day did he deliver them to you?
A.   Between four and five o'clock, I would say.
Q.   How many portions did he bring to the undertaking parlor?
A.   Two.

Now the court recalls Mr. Griffin Cook for direct examination as follows:
BY MR. CURRIE:

Q.   Mr. Cook you were formerly on the stand this morning, and asked about the condition of the portions of the body when you found them, I will ask you to look at these photographs that have been introduced as exhibits, and state whether or not they correctly represent the condition of the portions of the human body as you found it there on the ground, and if not what is the difference?
A.   That shows the body after it had been sewed back together.
Q.   What does Exhibit "4" show?
A.   It is the same.
Q.   Exhibit "5"?
A.   It is a back view, one is a front and this is a back view of it- and this is the front.
Q.   Are these pictures of the exact portions of body that you found on the

ground?

A.   Yes, sir, they are.

Mrs. Phil Cook, Introduced By The State, Having Been First Duly Sworn, Testified As Follows:

DIRECT EXAMINATION

BY MR. CURRIE:

Q.   You are Mrs. Phil Cook?

A.   Yes, sir.

Q.   Mrs. Cook, talk so the jurors can hear you, please Ma'am- where do you live, Mrs. Cook?

A.   I live on Cross Street, next door to where Mrs. Keeton lived.

Q.   What distance is there between your residence and hers?

A.   Well, I have heard some of the men say it was about sixty-six feet, there is an alley between us.

Q.   An alley between you?

A.   Yes, sir, but I- my bedrooms are all on the North side of my house and hers were on the South side of her house.

Q.   Your bedrooms are on the side of your house next to Meridian?

A.   Yes, sir.

Q.   And her bedrooms are on the South side of the house?

A.   Yes, sir.

Q.   Mrs. Cook, how long have you lived at your place- at your present place of residence?

A.   Be twenty-five years in May.

Q.   When was the last time that you saw Mrs. Daisy Keeton?

A.   Saturday morning, I will say, the last time was about eleven o'clock, but I know she was there about five o'clock Saturday afternoon, I didn't see her though then, but she gave my little grand-boy some cookies, and he came in and told me Mrs. Keeton-

Mr. Collins objects and states that Mr. Cook can't tell what her grand-boy told her.

Q.   Was that on the date of January 19th?

A.   It was on Saturday, I don't know if it was the 19th or not.

Q.   Was that the Saturday before it snowed?

A.   Yes sir.

Q.   Where did you see Mrs. Keeton on that day?

A.   I saw her going back and forth from her garden to her porch. I was working in my back yard and I could see her across over in her yard, going back and forth from her garden to her porch.

Q.   How did she appear on that occasion with reference to health and activity as compared to other occasions?

A.   She just seemed- she looked like she was all right.

Q.   Who lived there in the house with her?

A.   Ouida.

Q.   Did any other person live in the home with them or at that time besides Mrs. Daisy Keeton and Miss Ouida Keeton?

A.   No, sir, not that I know of.

Q.   Going from the front porch into what part of the house would you enter?

A.   That you went into?

Q.   Yes.

A.   The living room.

Q.   All right, when you got into the living room, what rooms if any were on the right hand side of the house?

A.   Ouida's rooms are to the right and Mrs. Keeton's room is to the right, all the bedrooms are to the right- there are three bedrooms to the right.

Q.   Who occupied the first bedroom?

A.   Ouida.

Q.   Who occupied the second bedroom?

A.   Mrs. Keeton.

Q.   And them there was another bedroom?

A.   Yes, sir.

Q.   Where, if at all, was there a bathroom in the house?

A.   It was between the back bedroom and the kitchen.

Q.   How did you get into that bath room from Mrs. Keeton's room?

A.   You had to go through the back bedroom into- the door that went out of Mrs. Keeton's room, into the back bedroom then right through into the bedroom.

Q.   How do you go out of the bathroom into the kitchen?

A.   Well, the door that opens from the bathroom went into the kitchen, well, yes, it- no, there was a little hall from that bathroom before you got into the kitchen that led from this back bedroom.

Q.   Mrs. Cook, how was that house heated?

A.   Had fireplaces.

The attorney questioned Mrs. Cook more about the fireplaces and as to where the garage was located in proportion to the street. He also questions her as to the time on the day in question did she see Mrs. Daisy Keeton.

Q.   How long, if you know had Mrs. Keeton and Miss Ouida lived in that home?

A.   Well, I can't remember exactly the time that Eloise was there- I don't know exactly when she left, sometime this year she went to New Orleans, the last time, to work.

Q.   Well, some members of the family would come and stay awhile and then go away?

A.   No, sir- well, none only except Eloise- well, Earl and his wife lived there in the home some time, but they moved.

Q.   When did they move away?

A.   Well, I don't know just the time- it was some time last year, I think maybe it was in the summer, I think maybe June or July. Sometime along there, I don't know exactly when they left there.

Q.   How long had Miss Eloise been back- or in New Orleans?

A.   Well, I really don't know when she went there the last time to work, she visited the home Christmas.

Q.   When did you next see Miss Ouida Keeton that you recall definitely?

A.   I saw her Wednesday morning.

Q.   Where and what was the occasion for your seeing her on Wednesday?

A.   I saw her coming from her Aunt's where she spent the night and I saw her coming home from over there Wednesday morning.

Q.   About what time Wednesday morning was it when you saw her?

A.   I think it was about nine o'clock.

Q.   Did you have any conversation with the defendant that Wednesday when you saw her?

A.   No, Sir.

Now Mr. Collins will cross examination of Mrs. Cook. He began by asking her how long she had lived where she lives now and she responded about twenty five years.

Q.   Mrs. Cook, the defendant here- in all of your acquaintance with her, and noticing her, the defendant here has appeared very much devoted to her mother, hasn't she?

A.   Yes, sir.

Q.   Even more than any of the other children, didn't she?

A.   Well, her mother seemed to think she was.

Q.   And from all appearances, Mrs. Cook, the defendant here seemed to be more devoted to her mother than any other child she had?

A.   Well, I couldn't say, Mr. Collins, she was there with her more and they seemed like they were right together.

Q.   And both of them have appeared very much devoted to each other, haven't they?

A.   Yes, sir.

Q.   Well, you knew she went to Hot Springs two or three times in the last two years for treatment?

A.   Yes, sir.

Q.   And you know she has fallen off considerably in the last two years?

99

A.   Yes, I know she is not nearly as large as she was.

Now comes on the witness stand for direct examination by Mr. Collins is Mrs. E.W. Lott.

BY MR. COLLINS:

Q.   You are Mrs. E.W. Lott?
A.   Yes, sir.
Q.   Where do you live, Mrs. Lott?
A.   I live on Cross Street.
Q.   How near to the home in which Mrs. Daisy Keeton lived?
A.   There is one house between- two houses between us- one between me and Mrs. Cook.
Q.   Did you know Mrs. Keeton?
A.   Yes, sir, I knew her.
Q.   Mrs. Lott, give the jury the best description you can of Mrs. Keeton, as to age, size, and weight and so on?
A.   Well, she was a right tall woman-
Q.   Talk a little louder, please Ma'am?
A.   She was tall and pretty large, she weighed about 175 or '80 or '85, somewhere along there, I don't know just what she weighed.
Q.   And about what was her age?
A.   She was fifty something, I don't know just what her age was, but I suppose she and I were about the same age.
Q.   What was the color of her hair?
A.   It was gray streaked, it had a little black in it.
Q.   Mrs. Lott, who lived in the home with Mrs. Daisy Keeton?
A.   Ouida lived there.
Q.   How long had the two of them lived in that home?
A.   Well, ever since I have known them.
Q.   On the 19th of January of this year- on Saturday the 19th, state whether or not you saw Mrs. Keeton?
A.   Yes, sir, she came up to my house.
Q.   What time of day did you see her?
A.   Just before noon.
Q.   You said she came to your house- what for?
A.   She came after buttermilk for Ouida.
Q.   Did she get it?
A.   Yes, sir.

At this time Mr. Earl Keeton is called to the stand to show that Miss Ouida Keeton had given the authorities permission to investigate and search her home.

Q.   Mr. Keeton, were you present- and state whether or not Miss Ouida Keeton- what instructions she gave you and to Chief Brown and other about going to her home and investigating the matter?

A.   The instructions she give me was I could do as I pleased.

Q.   Did she turn the home over to you?

A.   Well, it wasn't turned over to me at the time because it was under charge of the law, they had guards there.

Q.   Were you with Mr. Brown and other persons when they went to the home to investigate this matter?

A.   I was.

Q.   I will ask you if Miss Ouida didn't tell Mr. Brown to go ahead and make the investigations?

A.   If I was with him.

Q.   If you were willing?

A.   She was willing.

Q.   And you were willing?

A.   I said, if I was with him.

Q.   I say you were willing?

A.   She said if I was with him it would be all right.

Q.   If you were with him?

A.   Yes, sir.

Q.   And you were with him?

A.   Yes, sir.

Q.   And you were willing?

A.   Yes, sir.

Q.   And it was with your permission and consent that the investigation was made?

A.   Yes, sir.

Q.   And Miss Ouida was present and said it was all right?

A.   She said if I carried them it would be all right, or if anybody went with me, and whatever I done it would be all right.

BY THE COURT:

Q.   Where was Miss Ouida at the time?

A.   In Mr. Deavours' office.

Q.   Who made the request of her at that time?

A.   I did.

Q.   You made the request to go into the home?

A.   Yes, sir.

Q.   For the purpose of making inquiry and investigation necessary there in the home?

A. Yes, sir.

BY MR. COLLINS:

Q. And they kept Miss Ouida there in that office for twenty hours, didn't they?
A. Well, she was there until something after four o'clock that morning.
Q. Four o'clock the next morning?
A. Yes, sir, but it was about four o'clock that afternoon she gave permission to go to the house.
Q. And one person right after another grilled her, didn't they?
A. Well, she was asked questions.
Q. By first one and then another?
A. Yes, sir.
Q. All night long, that's true, isn't it?
A. Yes, sir.
Q. And nobody in that room warned her that anything she might say would be used against her, and that she didn't have to talk if she didn't want to?
A. Not that I know of.
Q. You didn't hear it, did you?
A. No, sir.
Q. Yet on the other hand they questioned her, one of them right after another, trying to elicit something out of her?
A. Yes, sir.
Q. And first an officer, then a layman, then a lawyer, and just anybody that wanted to ask her questions were asking them, weren't they?
Still more questioning resumed on the questioning of Ouida Keeton and to the investigation of the home.
Q. Have you seen-- when was the last time you saw your mother alive? Approximately- your best recollection?
A. Well, I have seen her--
A. I talked to her on Wednesday.
Q. What Wednesday, Mr. Keeton, with reference to this date?
A. Previous to the day this was supposed to have happened.
Q. Did you talk to her in person?
A. I did.
Q. Where was she when you talked to her?
A. She was at my house- out in front of it at least.
Q. What condition of health was she in at that time?
A. Well, she said she had been sick, but she was able to be up, going.
Q. Who lived in the home with you mother?
A. Miss Ouida.
Q. Who if any other person lived in the home with her.

102

A. There was no one since I left there.

Q. And when did you leave there?

A. I left there this October a year ago, about eighteen months ago.

Q. About eighteen months ago?

A. Yes, sir.

Q. Did you see Miss Ouida on Sunday after it is said this occurred on Saturday the 19th?

A. I did not.

Q. Did you see her on Monday?

A. I did not.

Q. When was the first time that you saw her after this Saturday?

A. In Mr. Deavours' office.

Q. And that was on--

A. Friday.

Q. Friday- and about that time on Friday?

A. About like I told you, between three-thirty and four.

Now comes the Cross Examination of Mr. Keeton by Mr. Collins.

Q. Fact is, Earl, she was- seemed to be more devoted to your mother than any of the other children, didn't she?

A. She was.

Q. That's right- now, Earl, in the last two and a half years, Ouida has been rapidly falling in health, hasn't she?

A. She had. She has been sick off and on.

Q. While you lived there in the house with them, night after night your wife has gone in when Miss Ouida would be complaining with her head and back and bathe her shoulders and her back, hasn't she?

A. She went in at times and worked two and a half or three hours putting hot towels on her back.

Q. And she was complaining with severe pain in the back of her head and her shoulders?

A. She was.

Q. Earl, she has been to Hot Springs three or four times in the last two years for treatment, hasn't she?

A. Been a good many, I don't know just exactly, but she has been over there several times.

Q. And she has been to the doctors here in town for treatment, hasn't she?

A. She has.

Q. Been to New Orleans- Been down there to Dr. Elliot for treatment, hasn't she? And examination?

A. I don't know.

Q. Earl, for the last two years, there has been a definite change in Ouida,

103

physically and from all appearances, hasn't there?

A.   Well, she hasn't been the same girl she has always been, because she has been sick a lot.

Q.   She had in other words a kind of melancholy expression?

A.   Well, she just wasn't the same person she always had been.

Q.   You just knew she wasn't the same person?

A.   (no answer)

Re-direct examination by Mr. Currie.

Q.   And on this- at this time, before the 19th of January, where was Miss Ouida working?

A.   She had been working for David McRae, half the day, for something like a month or so.

Q.   And was working up until the 19th?

A.   I couldn't say whether she was working until the 19th or not. I don't know whether she was working or had quit.

Mr. Bill Hinton, Introduced On Behalf Of The State, Having Been First Duly Sworn, Testified As Follows:

DIRECT EXAMINATION

BY MR. CURRIE:

Q.   You are Mr. Bill Hinton?

A.   Yes, sir.

Q.   Mr. Hinton, do you know where Mrs. Daisy Keeton lived?

A.   Yes, sir.

Q.   Have you been to her home?

A.   Yes, sir, I was over there on Friday night, I think about the 25th, if I'm not mistaken.

Q.   Mr. Hinton, did you while there, take certain objects or parts of facings and other objects from the building- saw them out?

A.   I cut a piece of door facing and a piece of jamb and the stop off of the bathroom door.

There were more questions about where and what parts of the house did Mr. Hinton remove resulting with this answer.

A.   Those came from- there was a base joist under the middle bedroom, right next to the fire place, and it came from there.

Q.   Base joist?

A.   Floor joist, under the middle bedroom, where it connected up with the fireplace, the fireplace is under the corner of the room, and this set in like this.

Q.   State whether or not you removed any of the soil--

A.   No, sir.

Q.   directly under the piece of floor joist that you cut out?

A.   No, sir, I didn't remove any of the soil.

Q.   You didn't participate in the removal of any soil?

A.   No, sir.

Q.   Did you see Mr. Hamilton when he did?

A.   Yes, sir, Mr. Hamilton was under there and filled a little jar with dirt from underneath the fireplace.

Q.   From what place under the house did he get the dirt?

A.   Right under the fireplace of the middle bedroom, right under where I cut the piece out.

Q.   Mr. Hamilton, did you go into that home after the date of January 19th for the purpose of making investigation into the purported death of Mrs. Daisy Keeton?

A. Yes, sir, the following Friday.

Q.   Friday following what day?

A.   The 19th.

Q.   Who if any persons were in the home with you at that time?

A.   Well, Chief Brown and Mr. Deavours and Miss Ouida and Miss Richeimer- Miss Jean Richeimer.

Q.   Miss Ouida Keeton was there when you first went there?

A.   Yes, sir.

Q.   The defendant?

A.   Yes, sir.

Q.   State whether or not on that occasion the defendant gave permission for you to come into the home and examine the home-

This question was objected to by Mr. Collins and sustained as loaded by the court.

Now back to questions as to what other materials were gathered from the house of Ouida Keeton.

Q.   What other matter if any did you obtain at that time?

A.   We got some dirt that was directly under this and some cobwebs off of the floor joist, and it was saturated in oil-

The Court ask the question if Mr. Hamilton was able to say what was saturated into the soil, he stated that it is some kind of grease.

BY MR. CURRIE:

Q.   Give a description of it with reference to odor or other properties.

A.   Well, it turned the color of the wood and looked like grease, and it has the odor of tallow.

Q.   Now, Mr. Hamilton, from just what place did you obtain this soil or dirt that you said you got there?

A.   Right under the edge of the hearth, there is a cement hearth that comes out to the floor, about twelve inches, and there is a little crack between the edge of the hearth and the floor, a kind of chipped this place, and this grease had run through that place on the ground and it wet the floor joist, the one that runs straight across where this angle meets here, and run through there and dripped on to the ground.

Q.   Mr. Hamilton, I show you a jar, there is some substance in it, I will ask you to look at it and state if you know where it came from?

A.   Yes, sir, that came from out from under the house.

Q.   At the place you have just mentioned?

A.   Yes, sir.

Q.   Mr. Hamilton, what was the condition of the hearth in the middle room when you first saw it after January 19th?

A.   It was freshly painted.

Q.   What was the color of the paint?

A.   Green.

Q.   Green?

A.   Yes, sir.

Q.   What was the condition of the floor immediately in front of this fireplace?

A.   Well, when we were there on Friday there was several spots there, and the girl had been scrubbing.

Q.   What girl?

A.   Miss Ouida.

Q.   All right-

A.   She was scrubbing when we went in the house between the rug and the fireplace, and it was a highly varnished floor, but between the rug and the fireplace she had scrubbed the paint all up, and there was two or three little spots there that had showed up, at that time the floor was wet with water, but these spots looked like grease-

Q.   Well just describe--

A.   Well, it appeared to be grease on the floor, and--

A.   Then when the floor got dry several more of these spots showed up and that is the reason I went under the house to look for this.

Q.   Mr. Hamilton state to the Court and jury whether or not you made any other observations and what if anything you found?

A.   Well, on Friday night- Friday night- afternoon or night after we were over there the first time, we looked on the floor and on the wall immediately at the head of the bed in the center bedroom and we found several small specks of blood and it was on the floor and on the wall right at the head of the bed, and then we followed those on in the room, the last bedroom in the back and in the bath room, and then we found them on the door facing entering from the bathroom into the kitchen, there were several of those, they were small specks but they showed to be blood.

Q.   What if any observation did you make as to finding any blood on a bed mattress?

A.   There was some in the center of the bed mattress.

Q.   And in which room?

A.   In the center bedroom.

Q.   Where with reference to the head of the bed, and on which side of the bed did you find the blood?

A.   The blood was on the side next to the door, right at the head of the bed, about where the post come to.

Q.   What if any observation did you make with reference to blood stains or any blood on any chair cushion?

A.   I didn't see that.

Now Mr. Clark will cross examine Mr. Hamilton.

Q.   Mr. Hamilton you stated to the District Attorney that you found blood in the house?

A.   Yes, sir.

Q.   How do you know it was blood?

A.   Well, you can tell blood when you see it.

Q.   How big were those specks?

A.   They were small specks.

Q.   Mr. Hamilton how big specks were they?

A.   Well, from the size of a match head down, they were small; that is, in the bedroom.

Q.   Specks of blood about the size of a match head?

A.   Yes, sir.

Q.   How many specks did you find?

A.   I didn't find but twelve or fifteen in all at that place.

Q.   Twelve or fifteen?

A.   Yes, sir.

Q.   How big a blood spot was it in the bed?

A.   Well, it was about a foot and a half or two feet across- it was a big spot.

Q.   You mean there was a blood stain in the bed a foot and a half or two feet across?

A.   Yes, sir, the mattress was stained in a pretty large space.

Q.   And you found that on what day, Mr. Hamilton?

A.   That was on Friday night, after the 19th, I couldn't tell the exact date, but it was on Friday night after the 19th of January.

Q.   And you don't know what kind of stains is on this wood?

A.   Blood stains is all I know.

Q.   You won't tell the jury that is blood stains?

A.   Sir?

Q.   You won't tell the jury that is blood stains on that piece of wood?

A.   Yes, sir.

Q.   You don't know what kind of blood it is, do you?

A.   No, sir.

Now re-direct examination by Mr. Currie.

Q.   Mr. Hamilton, how large a space under the floor was in the same condition as that exhibit you have in the bottle there?

A.   A place about 24 inches long, about 6 inches broad and about two inches deep in the deepest place.

Q.   And how about the sill out of which this exhibit was cut?

A.   It was wet clear to the top, it was an 8 inch sill and the 8 inch sill was the width of the hearth, it was wet all under the hearth.

Now comes Mr. Valentine to be questioned as follows:

Q.   Did you, yourself, make any observation as to blood stains or other discolorations on the door facing of the bathroom?

A.   I did.

Q.   Mr. Valentine, you said you went into the first bedroom-

A.   Yes, sir.

Q.   On the right?

A.   Yes, sir.

Q.   Did you see any object- or was there any object taken into possession while you were in that room?

A.   Yes, sir.

Q.   I will ask you to look at the object I now hand you - observe them and tell the jury if you know where they came from?

A.   Out of the fireplace in the first bedroom to the right.

Q.   What is it?

A.   A pair of stockings- hose.

Q.   What is the color of these stockings?

A.   Kind of brownish gray.

Q.   Brownish gray- who took possession of these stockings and who got them out of the fireplace?

A.   Chief Brown.

Q.   That is Mr. Brown, Chief of Police of the City of Laurel?

A.   Yes, sir.

Q.   What was the condition- when did he get them?

A.   On Friday evening, the 25th day of January.

Q.   What was the condition of those stockings at that time with reference to odor?

A.   The right stocking had a very strong odor on it.

Q.   Mr. Valentine, did you see body, or portion of the body that was recovered?

A.   I did.

Q.   State whether or not there was any similarity- or what condition if any existed between the odor of the body that was recovered and the odor of the stockings?

A.   Yes, sir, there was.

Q.   Describe it to the jury- tell the jury about it?

A.   Well, the stockings had the same odor that the body did- those legs did.

Q.   You have a normal sense of smell, have you, Mr. Valentine?

A.   Yes, sir.

Q.   And what was done with these stockings?

A.   Turned them over to Mr. Deavours.

Q.   I next show you a pair of shoes and ask you to take them and look at them and examine them and tell the jury if you have seen them before?

A.   Yes, sir.

Q.   Where did you first see those shoes?

A.   In the first bedroom to the right of the Keeton home.

Q.   When did you see them?

A.   On Friday evening the same time the stockings were found.

Q.   State whether or not there was any odor emitting from the shoes when you found them?

A.   There was on the right shoe.

Q.   On the right shoe?

A.   Yes, sir.

Q.   What sort of odor was it?

A.   A very bad, strong odor.

Q.   I will ask you to state how the odor on the shoe compared in its nature to that as you have testified about on the right stocking?

A.   Same thing.

Q.   How did the nature of the odor on the shoe that you found compare with the odor of the body?

A.   They smelled alike- same odor as the body.

Q.   State to the court what observation generally you made in the house in your investigation of this case?

A.   Well, in the second bedroom on the right there was blood stains on the floor and on the facing of the wall, and there was one drop of blood on the head of the bed and some blood on the rug on the floor.

Q.   Where was the rug that you have mentioned finding the blood on?

A.   It was in the second room of the house.

Q.   Go ahead and tell what other observations you made?

A.   In the third bedroom there was some blood on the floor and then there was some blood in the bathroom- on the door facing--

Q.   Mr. Valentine, did you make any observation about the hearth in the middle bedroom?

A.   Yes, sir.

Q.   Tell your observations there?

A.   Well, it had been re-painted- the fireplace had and the walls.

Q.   Just what had been repainted- explain it to the jury?

A.   On each side of the fireplace and the hearth had been repainted up by the wall around the fireplace had been repainted and the floor in front of the fireplace was greasy looking.

Q.   What about there being any evidence if any on the floor in front of the hearth being scrubbed?

A.   Yes, sir, it was wet.

Q.   The rug that you spoke of having blood on it was in that middle room, you say?

A.   Yes, sir.

Q.   Now, Mr. Valentine, did you look into the fireplace there and make a careful examination of it?

A.   I did.

Q.   And of its contents?

A.   Yes, sir.

Q.   Describe to the jury any marks or evidence or anything that you saw in the walls of that fireplace?

A.   To the left of the fireplace, facing the fireplace, the left wall had some blood stains that run down on the inside wall of the fireplace.

Q.   Describe their condition and the general appearance of them?

A.   It just appeared to be blood that had run from the top, cattycornered across down from the fireplace wall.

Q.   You said you were present when an examination into the fireplace was made?

A.   Yes, sir.

Q.   I will show you an object here and ask you to look at it and examine it and tell the jury where that came from.

A.   That came out of the back yard of the Keeton home.

Q.   Whereabouts in the back yard?

A.   Well, as you go out of the back door it was to the right of the door steps out there in a pile of ashes.

Q.   Look at the content of that vial and tell the jury where that came from?

A.   That came out of the fireplace out of some ashes that we swept from the fireplace.

Q.   You tell the jury that the content of this vial came out of the fireplace?

A.   Yes, sir.

Q.   What is that in there?

A.   It is a piece of bone.

Q.   What fireplace did that piece of bone come from?

A.   The fireplace in the middle room of the Keeton home.

Q.   Here are vials containing other small objects, where did they come from?

A.   They came out of the fireplace of the Keeton home.

Q.   There is another container with a number of smaller objects in it, one of which I now hold before you, where did that come from?

A.   Come from the back yard of the Keeton home.

Q.   What immediate place?

A.   To the right of the door as you go out of the back door, out of an ash pile.

Q.   I hold another object before you, what does that appear to be?

A.   Piece of a hat- it appears to be.

Q.   Where was it obtained?

A.   It was in the back yard to the Keeton home, out of a pile of ashes.

Q.   Mr. Valentine, where did you first see this object?

A.   In the second bedroom of the Keeton home.

Q.   What is that object?

A.   A fire poker.

Q.   Describe it into the record.

A.   It is- it's about a half inch iron rod with a brass handle on the end of it.

Q.   How long?

A.   About twenty-six inches long- or twenty-eight inches-

Q.   What did you do with the poker and these other objects when they were recovered there and reclaimed on the premises?

A.   They were brought to the Sheriff's office.

Q.   Delivered to him?

A.   Yes, sir.

Mr. Currie now introduces the contents of two pasteboard boxes, contents being, three vials, the bone and the piece of burnt substance which the witness designated as a piece of hat.

Q.   Now where did you find this object?

A.   In the back yard of the Keeton home.

Q.   What is that?

A.   Fingernail file.

Q.   Of course, Mr. Valentine, this other stuff, you don't know what it is, it was just picked up around the house and you don't know what it is- don't know anything about what it is or anything about it?

A.   It came out of the ashes.

Q.   But I say you just picked it up out of the ashes and you don't know anything about it or what it is?

A.   Well, part of it is bones.

Q.   Bones- and you don't know anything about what kind of bones?

A.   I know it is bones.

Now Mr. Collins recalls Mr. Wayne Valentine for further questioning.

Q.   Now, Mr. Valentine, you were talking about these- you testified about these stockings a few minutes ago? Do you know whose stockings those are?

A.   No, sir, I do not.

Q.   You don't know where those stockings came from when they were placed in the place over there where you found them?

A.   No, sir, the first time I saw them they were in the fireplace.

Mr. Valentine was questioned more about the odor and the shoes that were found. Now Mr. John M. Dannker is called on behalf of the State being direct examined by Mr. Currie.

Q.   What is your name, please sir?

A.   John M. Dannaker.

Q.   Where do you live, Mr. Dannaker?

A.   New Orleans, Louisiana.

Q.   What is your profession or business?

A.   I am City Chemist for the City of New Orleans.

Q.   Are you a graduate chemist of any College?

A.   Tulane University.

Q.   How long have you been employed as City Chemist for the City of New Orleans?

A.   I was assistant city chemist from July 1920 until December, 1920, them I was again employed as assistant City Chemist from May 15th, 1925 until May 1st, 1928, and on May 1st, 1928, I became City Chemist of the City of New Orleans and have held that position since.

Q.   Mr. Dannaker, does the science of chemistry teach and enable one to diagnose blood and other elements- chemically analyze them?

A.   It does.

Q.   Is you training such as to qualify you, and do you do that kind of work?

A.   I have had considerable experience in that type of work.

Q.   Were you called upon to make a chemical analysis of certain materials and matter furnished you by Mr. Jack Deavours?

A.   I was.

Q.   Mr. Dannaker, did you take any substance from that exhibit which you made certain analyses of? If so, indicate to the jury where you got it.

A.   I did. Where the paint has been removed as shown by the white spots, inside those marks, is where I removed the paint to make the examinations such as I made.

Q.   What sort of process did you go through with in making that examination- describe it to the jury.

A.   These chips of paint were treated with distilled water and what is known as a normal salt solution. By this process, any blood which may have been present on those chips would be dissolved in these two solvents-...If we get no positive reaction for blood stains it is an indication that blood is positively absent, however, if we get a positive test for blood stains by these chemical reactions, it is not an indication that blood is present. Following my chemical tests, I placed some of this material on a slide and examined it in the microscope, non-nucleated red blood corpuscles were distinctly visible. That is one of the positive tests. These specimens were then tested with this anti-human serum, and we obtained from these pieces of framing and from the solutions pressed from the chips taken from the pieces of frame, positive reactions for the presence of human blood.

A.   The result of my examination is that the stains which are found on this piece of wood are human blood.

Q.   Describe this object so that it may be marked as Exhibit to your testimony?

A.   This is a piece of molding and I have the exact dimensions of it, if I may refer to my original notes. It is a piece of wood molding, 1 ½ inches by ½ inch by 20 ½ inches.

Again test were made on the scrapings - these spots where you see the paint has been removed had a positive reaction for the presence of human blood by chemical, microscopically and biological tests.

Q.   Mr. Dannaker, I next hand you a fire poker and ask you to take it and examine it and tell the jury who if anyone delivered that fire poker to you?

A.   Mr. Jack Deavours delivered this fire poker to me.

Q.   Did you perform any chemical analysis to discover whether or not there was any foreign substance upon it, if so, tell the jury about it.

A.   I did....and then again we obtained positive reactions for the presence of human blood by chemical, microscopically and biological examination.

Q.   Now, Mr. Dannaker, from the examination you made of the object about which you have testified, state whether or not you found the positive elements of blood upon all of them?

A.   I did.

Q.   State whether or not that was human or animal blood?

A.   That was human blood.

Q.   Mr. Dannaker, state whether there was any soil substance furnished you?

A.   There was.

Q.   Did you make a chemical analysis to determine the content of that matter in that jar?

A.   I made certain chemical examinations on this soil.

Q.   Tell how you did it and the result it had.

A.   When I received this soil and I noticed that it had a distinctly fatty or greasy odor- from 25 grams I obtained 3.169 grams of an oily or fatty looking material.

Q.   Did you also make an analysis of the wrappings or cloth that were delivered to you?

A.   I also made examination of some cloths that were delivered to me.

Q.   Did you remove any part of this cloth?

A.   I cut two pieces from that cloth.-- I cut this semi-circular piece from the cloth and cut this six inch square piece from the cloth.- The semi-circular piece of cloth had stains which were suspicious of being blood stains- these stains- this cloth was treated in identically the same matter as described in connection with the stains on the wood framing.-The square piece of cloth that was cut from the cloth just exhibited was six inches square, because of the fact that the soil and the cloth had the same greasy or fatty odor, I made the same tests with the cloth as I did with the soil, with the six inches square of the cloth, and again I obtained an oily or fatty substance amounting to 1.985 grams.

Q.   Mr. Dannaker, how did the odor that you found upon the cloth compare in its character and nature to the odor of the soil that was delivered to you?

A.   The odor of the sack and the odor of the soil that was delivered were both distinctly fatty or greasy.

Q.   Did you perform any test to determine the content of that with reference to grease or oily matter?

A.   There are stains on both sides, both of the two inch sides of that block that appear to be oily in character, I cut sections four inches long completely across the two inch sides of that block, and--again I obtained an oily or fatty looking material, amounting to 3.5922 grams.

Q.   Mr. Dannaker, would a human body heated to a high temperature give off oily tissues or a greasy matter such as you have indicated and testified you found in the soil and in the wood?

A.   It would give off- the heating of a human body would necessitate some fatty material being given off when the tissues were burned.

Q.   Mr. Dannaker, were you delivered a pair of stockings at this same time?

A.   I was. Those are the same stockings that were delivered to me by Mr. Jack Deavours.

Q.   Did you make any chemical tests of the content of those stockings- of the stockings?

A.   I examined one stocking, namely the stocking that had the brand mark stamped at the top.

Q.   Look at the stockings and tell the jury which one you made the chemical test of?

A.   Well, there was nothing foreign on this stocking. On the other stocking, which has no brand name in the top, I found a distinct stain down the back of the stocking from the knee to the foot of the stocking.

Q.   What if anything did you do to make that test?

A.   There were certain fragments of material adhering to this stocking throughout the stain, I removed some of the pieces- some of the fragments of this material that was adhering to the stocking and placed it on a microscopic

114

slide and examined it microscopically and found that the fragments adhering to that stocking were particles of vegetable matter, apparently undigested.

Q.   Mr. Dannaker, have you any other slides of exhibits there that you have obtained in your tests?

A.   I have another slide made from a shoe.

Q.   What is that on that slide?

A.   That is vegetable matter, apparently undigested and similar in character to that removed from the stocking.

Q.   Who furnished the shoe, or from whom did you get the shoe from which you got the matter you have testified about?

A.   I received a pair of brown suede, low quartered shoes, from Mr. Jack Deavours at the same time I received the other articles.

Mrs. O.H. Gibson, Introduced By The State, Having Been First Duly Sworn, Testified As Follows:

DIRECT EXAMINATION

BY MR. CURRIE:

Q.   You are Mrs. O.H. Gibson?

A.   Yes, sir.

Q.   Where do you live, Mrs. Gibson?

A.   302 Daughdrill.

Q.   302 Daughdrill Street?

A.   Yes, sir.

Q.   How near is that to the Keeton home?

A.   Well, I don't know, it is across the street.

Q.   Mrs. Gibson, I will ask you to state to the court and jury whether or not at that time, about the dates mentioned, your attention was attracted to anything- to any unusual smell or odor in that community?

A.   It was on Sunday night about-between ten-thirty and eleven and twelve o'clock, and it smelled like burning wool and rubber.

Next Mr. J. W. Smith is questioned by Mr. Currie about the smell.

Q.   Mr. Smith, I will ask you to state if in sometime past- recent past- you attention was called to something burning, or a smell or scent there in your community?

Q.   When was it, Mr. Smith, you say you smelled this odor?

A.   On the 20th day of January.

Q.   This last January?

A.   Yes, sir.

Q.   What time of day or night was it that you smelled this odor?

A.   Between nine-thirty and ten o'clock, best of my recollection.

Q.   Where were you at the time you detected the odor?

A.   In my back yard.

Q.   Describe to the jury the best you can the kind of odor it was that you smelled?

A.   Well, it smelt like hair burning and also wool- kind of like a horn burning....Well, it smelt very strong- the odor was very strong.

Now Mr. Clark asked Mr. Smith about the odor.

Q.   Mr. Smith, don't tell me what you think now- will you tell the jury on your oath whether you smelled hair or not?

A.   Yes, sir, it was hair burning.

Q.   It was hair, and you are willing to tell the jury that?

A.   Yes, sir, hair was mixed in it.

Q.   What was that?

A.   Hair was mixed in the scent.

Q.   Can you tell the jury on your oath whether or not you smelled wool burning?

A.   I couldn't say whether it was or not, but I know hair was burning.

Q.   Now are you willing to swear you smelled wool?

A.   I don't know what it was Mister, but it was a different odor just to hair alone.

Q.   You told the jury you smelled hair, wool and horn?

A.   Well, it was all three.

Q.   Do hair and wool smell alike?

A.   No, sir.

Mr. Virgil Sumrall, Introduced By The State, Having Been First Duly Sworn, Testified As Follows:

DIRECT EXAMINATION

BY MR. CURRIE:

Q.   You are Mr. Virgil Sumrall?

A.   Yes, sir.

Q.   Mr. Sumrall, where do you live?

A.   I did live- I live with my father now- I lived at 648 Cross Street- I did live there.

Q.   State whether or not at any time your attention was attracted to any peculiar odor or scent?

A.   About eight o'clock I --on Monday night, I think, I wouldn't be for sure, it was about the 21st, somewhere thereabout, it was the night it rained so before the snow and freeze.

Q.   Give the jury the exact character of the odor that you smelled, or as near as you can?

A.   Well, it was- it smelled like wool and grease, or something like that, is the nearest I could tell you.

Q.   Have you- state whether or not you had ever smelled anything that had the exact odor that you smelled on that night?

A.   Well, yes, sir, I have.

Q.   Where was it that you experienced such a smell?

A.   It was in the Canal Zone, at the crematory, where they burn bodies.

Q.   Burned what kind of bodies?

A.   Human bodies.

Q.   Have you smelled human bodies that were being cremated- burned?

A.   Yes, sir.

Q.   How did the odor of this that you smelled on this night, compare to the odor that you smelled at the crematory where you say you have smelled human bodies burned?

A.   Well, it smelled nearer like that than anything I have smelled.

More questioning resumed about the odor and now comes Mr. Brown to be questioned. He was questioned about the body parts and how they were positioned on the ground.

Q.   How was the- how were the portions of the body themselves situated?

A.   Well, the large part was facing South and where they was cut off at the knees was facing North and they was both lying right side by side.

Q.   Mr. Brown, describe the condition of these portions of the body, with reference to blood stains or other evidences that you observed there?

A.   Well, the parts from where they was cut up to here was perfectly clean, but on the ends, why they looked to me that they had black looking mud on them.

Q.   Mr. Brown, when you reached the home and the defendant had answered the door, what did you say to her?

A.   She asked me in the house, asked me to have a seat and I sat down and she sat down and I told her my business over there that morning was to see her mother-

Q.   What was her answer?

A.   She said, " Mother is not here." I asked her where her mother was and she said that she had gone to New Orleans on a visit and I asked her when she left and she said she left on Tuesday morning-

Q.   Then what followed, Mr. Brown?

A.   She said that she had a letter from her that morning, and I asked her if I could see the letter and she said right at that time she didn't know where it was, so I asked her who taken her mother to the train and she said she did, that early morning train going South. Then I asked her if she would have any objection to me looking at her automobile and she said she did not and invited me back through the house, through the dining room and kitchen and to the back door and when we got there ,there was a big police dog out there that seemed to be very vicious and I wouldn't go out on him, and she undertaken to tie the dog but

117

never did tie him and I told her to just leave the dog alone that I would walk around and come around the other way, and I come around another way and looked at the automobile and come back around and she dressed and we went from there to Mr. Jack Deavours' office.

BY THE COURT:
Q. Mr. Brown, did the young lady know you   were a policeman at the time? Did she know you?
A. Yes, sir. I told her my purpose over here was to see her mother.
Q. You tell the court she invited you into the house?
A. Invited me in the house and invited me to have a seat and she taken a seat herself.
Q. When you made known to her that you desired to make further investigation of the premises, what if anything did she say or do?
A. She said, "You are perfectly welcome, come right back this way."
Q. Directed you where to go?
A. I was in the front of the house and she directed me and went with me from the front of the house through the dining room and kitchen and to the back porch.
Q. Now then, when you had seen what she pointed out to you- or did she point out anything to you or give you the privilege of observing your self?
A. She pointed the car out to me and told me I was perfectly welcome to look at the car.
Q. When you were through with your investigations   there on the premises, did you then put her under arrest?
A. I brought her on up for investigation.
Q. What if anything did you tell her when you went to carry her?
A. I asked her to come go with us up town.
Q. Sir?
A. I asked her to come go with us up to Mr. Deavours' office.
Q. Who was with you at that time'?
A. Mr. Deavours, and Mr. Hamilton.

BY MR. CURRIE:
Q.   Mr. Brown, after the defendant had been carried by you down to the County Attorney's office for inquiry and investigation into the matter, I will ask you to state whether or not she gave her consent for you and others to search the residence?
A.   Yes, sir, she did.
Q.   From the time that you arrested her on this first visit and you went back on your next trip, state if the defendant gave her full consent and permission for you and other to go into the house and search the house for evidence in this matter?

A.   She did.

Q.   State whether or not on that occasion her brother, Earl Keeton, was there?

A.   Yes, sir.

Q.   And if she also gave her permission and consent that anything he might do in that regard would be agreeable with her?

A.   Yes, sir.

Q.   Mr. Brown, you were being asked about your going to the home on Friday about ten o'clock.

A.   Yes, sir.

Q.   I will ask you who answered the door when you got there?

A.   Miss Ouida Keeton came to the door.

Q.   What if anything did you say to her at that time?

A.   I just spoke to her and she spoke to me and she invited me in and asked me to have a seat and I told her my purpose and business was to see her mother-

Q.   What, if anything, did she say?

A.   She told me- she says "Mother isn't her and I told her it was important that I see her or get in touch with her and told me she was visiting in New Orleans, had left there on Thursday morning-

Q.   Go ahead, Mr. Brown?

A.   And I asked her then if I might have permission to go out and look at her automobile and she said yes, so we went from the first room through the dining room and kitchen to the back door and when we got back there, there was a vicious police dog...

Q.   Did you go out to the garage?

A.   Yes, sir.

Q.   What kind of automobile if any did you find in the garage?

A.   It was a Willys-Knight.

Q.   What color? Give a description of it to the jury?

A.   Well, it is a sedan car, Willys-Knight, and maroon colored with black fenders.

Q.   Now, Mr. Brown, did you make any examination of that car with reference to whether or not there were blood spots or stains upon it?

A.   Yes, sir, I looked at the right hand side of the car first-

Q.   Tell the jury what if anything you observed with reference to the right hand side of the car?

A.   Well, the right hand fender, right up on the top of the fender, looking down over it like that, you couldn't see anything, but you could get back and look at it, and it looked as though something had been drug across it, some sticky object I made the remark- I said--

Q.   You can't tell what you remarked.

Q.   Was she present?

A.   Yes, sir, she was right there.

119

Q.   All right, tell what you remarked.

A.   I said "Wonder what that is on that fender?"

Q.   What was it you remarked to her Mr. Brown?

A.   I just asked her- I says "I wonder what that is on the fender" and she taken her hand like that, and begin trying to rub it off.

Q.   And that was the right front fender?

A.   Right front fender.

Q.   The limbs were on the right hand side of the car tracks?

A.   Yes, sir.

Q.   And you say this sign was on the right fender?

A.   Yes, sir.

Q.   After you had seen the car what did you them do, Mr. Brown, on this Friday?

A.   Come on back around and she went in the house and dressed, and we told her we were going to take her up town to Mr. Deavours' office.

Q.   For the purpose if investigation--

A.   Investigation, yes, sir.

Q.   -- the cause of Mrs. Keeton's death?

A.   Yes, sir.

Q.   Mr. Brown, I will ask you to state whether or not the defendant gave permission for you and other to enter the home there and conduct a search of the premises and the home in making an investigation of this matter?

A.   She did.

Q.   State whether or not Mr. Earl Keeton, the defendant's brother was present at that time?

A.   He was.

Q.   State whether or not thereafter Mr. Earl Keeton went with you on occasions into the home to conduct investigation?

A.   Yes, sir.

Q.   Mr. Brown, state to the court and jury what Miss Ouida Keeton said to Mr. Earl Keeton, if anything, about permitting an investigation of the home?

A.   She told him to take charge of the house and let any of the officers- all of them, make any investigation they wanted to. Earl Keeton and myself went over to the house. It was on Friday afternoon, on the 25th of January.

Q.   Do you know what room was occupied by Miss Ouida Keeton as her bedroom?

A.   No more that what she told me.

Q.   What room did she tell you was her bedroom?

A.   The first room on the front on the right hand side going in.

Q.   Mr. Brown, did you remove any article of wearing apparel from that room?

A.   Yes, sir.

Q.   What did you take from that room?

A.   I taken a pair of gray stockings or hose out of the fireplace of that room and laid them upon a little bench that was setting to the right of the fireplace.

Q.   Mr. Brown, what was the condition of the hose that you took from the fireplace of the defendant's room with reference to odor at that time?

A.   Well, they had a very offensive odor. It was a kind of sour, stinking smell, is all I know.

Q.   You said you saw the portion of the body that was found-

A.   Yes, sir.

Q.   And examined it- state whether or not there were some of the intestines attached to the portion of the body that you found?

A.   Yes, sir.

Q.   How did the odor of the stockings compare in quality and character to the body?

A.   I never got any odor from the body.

Q.   You didn't?

A.   No, sir, I couldn't smell any odor to the body or the part that I seen.

Q.   Mr. Brown, I will show you a pair of shoes, brown suede shoes, have you seen these shoes before?

A.   Yes, sir. Them shoes had the same kind of odor on them that was on the pair of stockings.

Q.   Tell the jury what you saw in the second bedroom- just describe it in your own way?

A.   Well, in the second bedroom it had been scrubbed in front of the fireplace- it had been scrubbed until all the varnish was scrubbed off of the floor pretty near the length of the fireplace on the floor, and the hearth and the sides that run up to the mantel had been freshly painted and there was some- I don't know just how many, but a few little specks of blood around the fireplace, and I turned the rugs back and the rug come up in about four or five inches of the concrete on the fireplace, and I turned that back and there was a lot of white powder under there.

Q.   What was that white powder?

A.   Well, it was some kind of scrubbing powder.

Q.   Mr. Brown, what color had this hearth in the middle room been painted?

A.   Green.

Q.   Mr. Brown on the Friday morning that you first went to the home, state to the court and jury whether or not- What was the condition with reference to any water faucets, or whether there was running water in the house?

A.   The water in the bath tub was running full force.

Q.   Was the defendant full dressed at that time?

A.   Yes, sir.

Q.   Was Miss Jean Reicheimer fully dressed at that time?

A.   I didn't see her but one time, she was dressed when I seen her.

121

Q.   You said the water in the bath room was running full force?

A.   Full force- and the cork was out and it was going down- the water was running out of the faucet and going out as fast as it come in.

Q.   It wasn't being accumulated in the tub?

A.   No, sir.

Q.   Now, Mr. Brown, I will ask you whether or not you found any gun in that house?

A.   Yes, sir, I found one.

Q.   Where did you find that gun? Describe its position to the jury?

A.   I found it in Miss Ouida's wardrobe, there was a wardrobe there with two doors-

Q.   This gun was in the left hand side of this wardrobe about half way between the top and bottom, sticking up between some clothes or cloths, I never examined that part of it?

Q.   Between some-

A.   Cloth.

Q.   Mr. Brown, you said that you saw the limbs as they lay on the ground up there where they were first found?

A.   Yes, sir.

Q.   And that the nubs or ends of them were filled with dirt? Have you been in the Keeton back yard?

A.   Yes, sir.

Q.   State whether or not you have made observation as to the character of the soil and dirt at that place?

A.   Yes, sir, it is kind of blue looking soil, black looking.

Q.   How did the color of the dirt or soil that you saw on the ends of the limbs compare to the soil that was in the back yard of the Keeton home?

A.   They was about the same color. Same kind of dirt.

Q.   Sir?

A.   About the same kind of dirt- same color.

Q.   Mr. Brown, state whether or not there is a toilet or commode in the Keeton bathroom?

A.   Yes, sir, there is.

At This Time The Jury Is Excused From The Court Room And The Following Testimony Is Taken In The Jury's Absence:

Q.   Mr. Brown, I will ask you if on Sunday, January 27th, of this year, if you visited or saw the defendant, Miss Ouida Keeton, here in the Jones County jail?

A.   I did.

BY MR. COLLINS:

If the Court please, we want the record to show now if they propose to introduce any statement or confession of this defendant, that we object to the evidence for the reason, first: That the corpus delicti has not been established, and second: Because the confession is not free and voluntary and it is therefore inadmissible and incompetent.

BY THE COURT:

The Court holds that there has been sufficient evidence introduced into the record to make it competent, so far as the corpus delicti is concerned. Any testimony the State has to offer touching a confession- the Court will hear further testimony with reference to the competency of a confession.

BY MR. CURRIE:

Q.   Were you present when the defendant made a confession or statement concerning this matter Mr. Brown?

A.   Yes, sir.

Q.   Where was it that you heard such a statement?

A.   It was upstairs in a cell in the county jail.

Q.   Who was present at that time, Mr. Brown?

A.   Yourself, Mr. Van Valentine and myself.

Q.   Mr. Brown, state to the Court under what circumstances the defendant made a statement?

A.   She made a voluntary statement.

Q.   Detail to the Court what condition, if any was given her about her making a statement or whether or not she had to- just state the circumstances of it?

A.   She was told that if she made a statement that it would be of her own free will and it might or might not be used against her.

Q.   State whether or not there was any threat made against the defendant?

A.   No, sir.

Q.   State whether or not there was any promise, or hope of reward held out to her?

A.   No, sir.

Q.   What if anything did the defendant herself say as to her desire to make a statement about the matter?

A.   She said she wanted to make a statement.

Q.   State whether or not it was after the advice that she wanted to make a statement that she did make one?

A.   It was.

Q.   You were present when she was admonished that she did not have to make any statement whatever?

A.   Yes, sir.

123

Q. State whether or not I gave her that admonition?

A. You did.

Q. And state whether or not I offered her any inducement whatever to make any statement?

A. You did not.

Q. Was any promise or any encouragement held out to her to make one?

A. None whatever.

Q. After being admonished that any statement she would make could be used and probably would be used against her--

A. Yes, sir.

Q. in a subsequent prosecution, what did she say then about her desire to make a statement?

A. Said she wanted to make a statement.

Q. Was it after all this procedure that she did make the statement?

A. Yes, sir, it was.

Now Mr. Brown is cross examined by Mr. Currie.

Q. Now, Mr. Brown, when was it you stated that you arrested the defendant?

A. It was on Friday morning about ten o'clock.

Q. About ten o'clock?

A. Nine or ten, something like that.

Q. You immediately carried her to Mr. Jack Deavours' office, didn't you, Mr. Brown?

A. Yes, sir.

Q. And she stayed in Mr. Jack Deavours' office from Friday morning about ten o'clock until four o'clock Saturday morning, didn't she?

A. Well, so far as I know now she stayed in there from the time we brought her in there that morning between nine and ten o'clock until about six o'clock, I left her there.

Q. But you stayed in Jack Deavours' office from ten o'clock in the morning until six o'clock that afternoon?

A. No, sir, I was just in and out there.

Now Mr. Brown is being questioned by Mr. Collins.

Q. Mr. Brown, of course all of you present while you were there, took your turns in questioning the defendant?

A. Well, as far as myself, I asked her very few questions.

Q. You didn't ask her many questions yourself?

A. No, sir.

Q. But others did take their turns examining her?

A.   The only ones I heard ask her any questions was Mr. Deavours, while I was present.

Q.   And of course he was asking her one question right after another during the whole time you were there?

A.   Yes, he questioned her while I was there.

Q.   And Mr. Brown, up until the time you left there at six o'clock, she hadn't been permitted to go out of there for eating or drinking?

A.   Well, I don't know about that.

Q.   Now, Mr. Brown, she made a statement there in the office, didn't she, and was questioned considerably there- that is, she was questioned at considerable length and answered those questions?

A.   Yes, she was questioned.

Q.   Nobody told her in there that any statement she would make might be used against her did they?

A.   I never heard anybody tell her there.

Q.   And nobody informed her that she didn't have to make a statement, did they?

A.   If they did I didn't hear it.

Q.   Mr. Brown, on the following Saturday morning there was a considerable crowd gathered all around the court house and on the lawn and out on the street, and they milled about here all day Saturday, didn't they?

A.   Yes, there was a bunch scattered out there.

Q.   Then on Saturday it was virtually the same way, the street down there and all on the lawn and the court house around there, people was standing all around- there was a considerable crowd of people milling around?

A.   Yes, sir.

Q.   And that was true at the time you went up into the jail to get this purported statement?

A.   As well as I remember there was quite a few people scattered around out there in different places.

Q.   Now, Mr. Brown, when you went up to the cell who was there with her?

A.   She was by herself.

Q.   By herself- and you went up with Mr. Currie and--

A.   Mr. Valentine.

Q.   Mr. Valentine- and it is my understanding and information that she was kept in Mr. Jack Deavours' office until four o'clock next morning?

A.   I don't know how long she was kept there.

Q.   Now, Mr. Brown, the statement you got up there in the jail was practically a reproduction of the statement made down in Mr. Jack Deavours' office, wasn't it?

A.   I don't know what statement she made down there.

Q.   You don't know what the statement was?

125

A.   No, sir.

Q.   You had information she made a statement down there, didn't you, Mr. Brown?

A.   Yes, I had information she had made a statement.

Q.   Now, Mr. Brown, during all this time, from the time you arrested her until you got the statement Sunday afternoon, did anyone in your presence feed this defendant or give her anything to eat?

A.   I didn't see her eat.

Q.   Now at the time they had her down in Mr. Deavours' office during all that time, Mr. Brown, did they permit the defendant to rest, or retire to a rest room in your presence?

A.   Not in my presence.

Q.   Did Miss Eloise Keeton come while you were there?

A.   I brought her there.

Q.   You carried her there?

A.   At Mr. Deavours' request.

Q.   Were you present when Miss Ouida used the telephone?

A.   I was present when she called Eloise.

Q.   From whose office did she call Miss Eloise?

A.   Mr. Deavours'.

Q.   Where did she call for her?

A.   At New Orleans.

Mr. Collins will now cross examine Mr. Earl Keeton.

Q.   Mr. Keeton, while you were in there did anybody warn Miss Keeton that any statement she made might be used against her?

A.   No, sir.

Q.   What they did was just one right after another popped questions to her all the time you were there?

A.   Well, one would ask questions and he would get through and another one would ask her questions.

Q.   And they did that as long as you stayed there?

A.   Well, there was practically somebody asking her questions all the time.

Q.   Practically somebody asking her questions all the time?

A.   Yes, sir.

Q.   You didn't see her eat or drink a mouthful while you were there?

A.   Well, she taken one swallow of coffee and drank one coca cola to my knowledge.

Now the questioning resumes with Mr. Hamilton.

Q.   Do you know whether or not the defendant got any sleep at all Friday night?

A.   No, sir.

Q.   Do you know whether she got any sleep at all Saturday night?

A.   No, sir.

Q.   Do you know whether she got any sleep at all Sunday?

A.   No, sir, I wouldn't say.

Q.   You don't know about that- but all the time you saw her around the jail and around Jack Deavours' office, you know she didn't sleep?

A.   Well, I don't know, I wasn't up in there until Sunday some time during the day I went up there one time.

Q.   She wasn't asleep then?

A.   No, sir.

Now Comes Mr. J.E. Brown, Recalled By The Defendant For Further Questioning, Testified As Follow:

CROSS EXAMINATION

BY MR. COLLINS:

Q.   Now, Mr. Brown, with further reference to the circumstances under which this confession was obtained- now, Mr. Brown, you have known the defendant a good long time, haven't you?

A.   Yes, sir, I have been knowing her a long time.

Q.   And, Mr. Brown, at the time you went to arrest this defendant, did you, when you went into that room there that day, notice that starey look out of her face?

A.   Yes, I noticed that.

Q.   Mr. Brown, tell the court you honest opinion- isn't it your honest opinion, Mr. Brown, at the time you went in there and saw this defendant that she was insane?

Q.   Mr. Brown, you have known the defendant here, as I stated, a long time?

A.   I been knowing her I imagine for about twenty years.

Q.   And Mr. Brown, up until the last two or three years, she was a healthy looking girl, and weighed 160 pounds, didn't she?

A.   Well, she used to be heavier than she is now.

Q.   Considerably heavier- and she used to be considerably heavier that she was at the time you saw her over there the day you arrested her, didn't she?

A.   Yes, sir.

Q.   And Mr. Brown, you have had occasion around town to make observation of her and see her in her everyday walk of life, and her demeanor, haven't you?

A.   Well, I would just see her occasionally.

Q.   And didn't you see a definite change that had been made in this girl from the time you had last seen her and the time you saw her over there?

A. Well, she had an unusual expression on her face.

Q. Well, what was that unusual expression, Mr. Brown?

A. Well, just that stare she had.

Q. A blank, starey look, wasn't it?

A. (no answer)

Q. And you have seen insane people, haven't you, Mr. Brown?

A. Yes, I have seen them.

Q. Now, Mr. Brown, from what you have observed about the girl, and what you saw there that day, isn't it your opinion that at that time this girl was insane?

A. No, sir, I won't say that.

Q. Mr. Brown, regardless of what brought it on, isn't it your opinion that at that time she was insane?

A. No, sir.

Q. It isn't? Now, Mr. Brown, you have talked to me about this, haven't you?

A. Yes, I have talked to you about it.

Q. And you have expressed an opinion to me that this girl was insane, haven't you?

A. I expressed my opinion that it looked to me like the whole job was an insane act. That is the way I expressed it.

Q. And didn't you, Mr. Brown- refresh your memory now- I'm not trying to cross you up- but didn't you tell me you noticed that blank, starey look in her eyes?

A. Yes, I noticed that.

Q. And that in your honest opinion she was insane?

A. (no answer)

Q. That in your honest opinion she was insane?

A. I don't remember telling you that.

Q. You don't?

A. No, sir.

Q. Then do you state, Mr. Brown, that it was or was not your opinion at the time she was insane?

A. Not at that time.

Q. Mr. Brown, I will ask you one more question- you say you don't remember stating that to me. You don't say you did not state that to me, do you?

A. No, sir. I can just state I don't see how any person could do that kind of crime.

The court brings back the jury into the courtroom and Mr. Currie continues to question Mr. Brown.

Q. Mr. Brown, when the jury was retired in order to test the competency of certain testimony, I was asking you if you were in the jail here in Laurel on

January 27th of this year, on Sunday afternoon, in my presence and that of Mr. Van Valentine, the jailer?

A. Yes, sir.

Q. Did the defendant, Miss Ouida Keeton, make a statement there as to the death of her mother, Mrs. Daisy Keeton?

A. Yes, sir.

Q. Mr. Brown, state to the Court and jury as near as you can, what that statement was?

A. Well, she- I asked her if it was a premeditated murder and she said "Yes", that it started being talked about last September, and said last Saturday, or Saturday of the 19th, Mr. Carter come to the filling station on the Boulevard, McRae's Filling Station, where she worked, twice, and it was planned to be done that night, and he told her, says "I have got my alibi" and says "All you have got to do is to do like I tell you to do."

So she says Mr. Carter went to her house where her and her mother lived that Saturday evening about six o'clock and brought some ice cream to the front door and left and was gone until about eight or eight-thirty and when he come back that time he come into the house and the three of them was sitting in her mother's room in front of the fire, her mother was on the right and she was in the center and Mr. Carter to the left, and there was a question and argument come up about how some people raised their children and Mrs. Keeton taken exception to it, which she said didn't amount to much, and at that time Mrs. Keeton walked out of the room and went into the kitchen and come back with a bottle of wine or brandy and was pouring the wine out in a glass on the right hand corner of the mantel and she said that Mr. Carter struck her mother on the right hand side of her head just above her ear with the big end of a fire poker and she fell and she got down over her and caught her by her hand and felt of her pulse and she was dead. Mr. Carter says to her "Pack her clothes" so she got a brown zipper bag as she called it, and packed her mother's clothes and then they taken her out and loaded her up in a big automobile on the north side of the house- she said she didn't know whether it was the Buick or what it was- she said it was a big car and he drove away and was gone just a short time when he come back with these two limbs from the knees up to the hips and brought them in there and told her- says "Here's your part to dispose of, I have disposed of mine" and she says "What in the world did you do with the rest of my mother's body" and he says "I left it down on the Ovett road" and he says "Now I am going to Mobile in my Pontiac" is the way she expressed it.

Q. Mr. Brown, state whether or not the defendant made any statement to you then about her disposing of that portion of the body, and what she did with it? Where she carried it?

A. She said on Monday morning between seven and eight o'clock she got in her car with these two parts and went north on Highway 11 and when she got up about five miles north of here she taken a right hand road and went down and

129

turned around in front of a man's house and come back and hit the highway and went up above Sandersville to a plum orchard and drove down in a little side road on the east side of the highway and drug these parts out- she said she tried to back out and the car- the bumper struck a pine tree or pine bush and the wheels begin to spin and she got out of the car and walked out to the highway and walked down the highway a piece and flagged a man down and got in his car and come back to Laurel to her house.

Q.   Mr. Brown, what if any, statement did she make to you as to sign there on the right fender of her car- what had caused that?

A.   Said that was where she drug the limbs out over the fender.

Q.   What statement if any did she make to you about the painting of the hearth in her mother's room?

Mr. Collins stops the questioning and would like to know if the statement in question was made in writing and signed by the defendant. The court replies to him that he can ask the question on cross examination.

Q.   This statement you are now testifying about to the jury, is the one made Sunday afternoon?

A.   Yes, sir.

Q.   Then state to the Court and jury whether or not the Sunday afternoon statement was written down?

A.   It was.

Q.   Sunday afternoon?

A.   Sunday afternoon- I wouldn't be sure of that.

BY MR. CURRIE:

Q.   Mr. Brown, what if anything did the defendant say as to the painting of the hearth in the middle room, or her mother's room? If so what was it?

A.   She said she painted the hearth to hide some blood stains.

Q.   What statement if any was made by the defendant with reference to the burning of any articles there in the house?

A.   Well, she said she burned her red kimono and a pair of pajamas, as well as I can remember.

Q.   And what was it- I didn't clearly understand you- what was it you said you asked her? If it was a premeditated murder?

A.   Yes, sir.

Q.   What was her answer to that question?

A.   She said it was.

Q.   And what was it you said that she told you about it being planned on that Saturday?

A.   She said it was started to being talked about last September and planned on that Saturday afternoon.

Q.   Now for what reason if any did she assign that the murder was

130

committed?

A.   So that she might have more privileges.

Q.   Now, Mr. Brown, state, if you know, whether or not Mrs. Keeton was a widow?

A.   So far as I know she was.

Q.   You have never seen her husband?

A.   No, sir.

Q.   And she lived there as you have described on Cross Street?

A.   Yes, sir.

Q.   Now, Mr. Brown, refreshing your memory as to the statement about which you have just testified, on the question of whether or not that was a written statement made in the jail on Sunday afternoon just in your presence, Mr. Van Valentine's and myself, the question of whether it was written down or not, you didn't write it down, did you?

A.   No, sir.

Q.   I didn't write it down?

A.   No, sir.

Q.   Mr. Valentine didn't write it down?

A.   No, sir.

Q.   Was there any other person there when she made the statement?

A.   No, sir.

Q.   Then I will ask you whether or not it was written down?

A.   No, sir.

Q.   Then state whether or not it was simply an oral confession made there?

A.   It was. Just as near as I can express it in words, just the way I have told it.

Q.   I see- but name the persons present to the jury?

A.   Well, you was present, Mr. Van Valentine and myself and Miss Ouida Keeton.

Q.   Then I will ask you- Miss Ouida didn't write it down, did she?

A.   No, sir.

Q.   Van Valentine didn't write it down?

A.   No, sir.

Q.   And I didn't write it down?

A.   No, sir.

Q.   And you didn't write it down?

A.   No, sir.

Now Mr. Collins will cross examine Mr. Brown.

Q.   Mr. Brown, what time on Sunday afternoon was that?

A.   It was late in the afternoon.

Q.   Late in the afternoon?

131

A.   Yes, sir.

Q.   About what time, Mr. Brown?

A.   Well, we must have gone in there about- around five o'clock and it was just about dusk dark when we come out.

Q.   And you all went up there for the purpose of getting a statement out of the defendant?

A.   We went up there to talk to her.

Q.   And Mr. Brown, now after you had obtained that statement where she told you that Mr. W.M. Carter was the man that killed her mother, then you asked Mr. Currie if he didn't want you to go and arrest Mr. W.M. Carter, didn't you?

A.   Yes, sir.

Q.   And he told you no, didn't he?

A.   We decided to wait until next morning to see if she stuck to that same statement.

Q.   Then you did that on advice of Mr. Currie, didn't you?

A.   Yes, sir.

Q.   That's right- all right- now that was on Sunday afternoon?

A.   Yes, sir.

Q.   And Mr. Carter wasn't arrested until Monday, was he?

A.   No, sir.

Q.   You remember, Mr. Brown, having driven up this road and stopped on this creek bridge?

A.   Yes, sir.

Q.   And you got out and examined the bridge there, didn't you?

A.   I don't think I got out.

Q.   Well you looked at the side of the bridge, didn't you?

A.   You drove right up by the railing and we stopped and talked about it.

Q.   And a person driving up that road in an automobile that would run up on the side of that bridge, there wouldn't have been a thing in the world to have prevented them rolling those limbs out and off into the creek?

A.   No, sir that would have been and easy job.

Q.   Easily done- all right then, Mr. Brown, you drove with me then on up the road, that highway from there to Sandersville?

A.   Yes, sir.

Q.   And you have investigated lots of crimes, haven't you?

A.   Yes, sir.

Q.   But this thing has baffled you more than anything you have ever gotten into, hasn't it, Mr. Brown?

A.   This is the first thing of its kind I have gotten into.

Q.   That's right- Mr. Brown, you were the man who arrested this defendant the morning she was arrested, didn't you?

A.   Yes, sir.

Q.   And when she invited you into that room there you noticed something peculiar about her, didn't you?

A.   Well, she didn't look like she usually looked.

Q.   You noticed that blank stare out of her eyes, didn't you Mr. Brown?

A.   Yes, sir, she had that stare.

Q.   And, Mr. Brown, you have expressed the opinion that she was insane, haven't you?

Mr. Currie object to the question and Mr. Collins rephrases the question.

Q.   You expressed that opinion to me, didn't you, Mr. Brown?

A.   I expressed that opinion in this way, if I remember right, that I didn't see how any sane person would go through and do just like this was done.

Q.   In other words, Mr. Brown, you never have investigated a crime in your life, or a happening like this where a normal person was acting just like this? Have you, Mr. Brown?

A.   Give me that question again.

Q.   You never have in your life investigated a happening like this where a normal person did a thing like this?

A.   No, sir, as I said while ago, this is the first case of this kind I ever investigated.

Q.   And it is your opinion now, isn't it Mr. Brown, that it is the act of an insane person?

The Court asked Mr. Collins if indeed he was referring to the defendant. Mr. Collins replied that he was referring to the defendant and continued questioning Mr. Brown.

Q.   Isn't that true, Mr. Brown?

A.   Well, I have answered that question.

Q.   Well, that is true, isn't it, Mr. Brown?

A.   It is true that my opinion is just like it was-

Q.   And when you first observed her, that is a year or two ago, why she was a strong, healthy looking girl, wasn't she?

A.   Well, she was heavier than she is now.

Q.   Much heavier, wasn't she?

A.   Yes, sir.

Q.   And had a different expression on her face, didn't she?

A.   Yes, sir.

Q.   And a different look out of her eyes, didn't she?

A.   Yes, sir.

Q.   That's right, there had been a very definite change in her looks, hadn't there?

A.   Well, she looked mighty bad, but for what cause I didn't know.

Q.   Mr. Brown from all of these faces, judging from all of these facts, from you investigation of this affair, and trailing down her actions and from what you have known about her and what you have seen about her, and what you saw over there that day, isn't it your opinion that she is insane?

A.   The only way I could answer that question is that I don't see how any sane person could go through with that thing and carry it out just like it happened.

With this answer the Court stated to Mr. Brown that the question was with reference to being sane or insane--

BY THE COURT:

Q.   Mr. Brown, are you able to answer that question counsel asked you?

A.   Well, I'm not an insanity expert. I give my opinion. My opinion was that I didn't see why or how any sane person could commit that crime in the way it was committed and the general way it was done.

Now the questioning proceeded by Mr. Collins.

Q.   All right, I will put the question this way- if she did it in the way you have learned from your investigation it was done and from what you have seen about her, if she did it, is it your opinion she was sane or insane?

A.   If she did it just like it was done, the way I see it, the part that I have seen, she was undoubtedly insane.

Q.   That is your opinion about it, isn't it, Mr. Brown?

A.   Yes, sir.

Mr. Currie will now direct examine Mr. Brown.

Q.   Mr. Brown, as a matter of fact, you don't know how this crime was committed, do you?

A.   No, sir.

The Court said to exclude the questions and answers of the witness Brown touching the suggestion of sanity or insanity of the defendant, because it is not shown by the proof to be competent- he is not qualified by knowledge and acquaintanceship with the defendant sufficiently and upon which to base that opinion. Also it is stated by Mr. Currie that the State makes it known to the Court that at this juncture it desires to have brought into Court, to be viewed by the jury and all other competent person, that portion of the body found and about which testimony has been given, and asks the Court to direct the Sheriff, with proper assistance to bring them before the jury to be identified. With this evidence being a problem as to whether or not the jury should view the limbs that have been found and with that Mr. Clark adds the if the Court please, he will say for the defense we never anticipated the State would offer to parade the corpse before the jury. Mr. Currie replied that it simply operates to qualify this jury upon the question of identity of that part of the body found; to show that it was a part of the body of Mrs. Daisy Keeton. The issue is who is dead, whether she went to death because of violence- the jury will be able to determine whether or not she came to her death violently. It is relevant to determine the manner of death.

At this time Mr. Currie desires to say to the Court that the limbs have been encased and a glass cover placed on top, there will be nothing unsightly or unbecoming. The State has made the best preparation possible to present them in an acceptable form for the jury. Mr. Clark would state that the defendant further objects to the introduction of this portion of the body for the reason that there is no testimony in this record to show that the exhibit now offered by the State is any part of the body of the person named in the indictment in this case.

Now come Mr. Neville Allan is reintroduced by the State and directly examined by Mr. Currie.

Q. Mr. Allen, there is being brought into the court portions of a human body- have you examined that portion of it today?
A. Yes, sir.
Q. I will ask you to state whether or not that portion of the human body now is in court is the same that was delivered to you by Mr. G.E. Cook?
A. Yes, sir, it was.
Q. And has it been in the custody of the Sumrall Undertaking Parlor since that time?
A. Yes, sir.
Q. And I will ask you to take a look at the contents of this container here now and state whether or not these portions--or if that is a part of the body that was brought to you?
A. Yes, sir.

Dr. C.H. Ramsey, Introduced On Behalf Of The State, Having Been First Duly Sworn, Testified As Follows:
DIRECT EXAMINATION
BY MR. CURRIE:
Q. How long have you been engaged in the practice of medicine?
A. Since July, 1902.
Q. Did you know Mrs. Daisy Keeton in her lifetime?
A. Yes, sir.
Q. Doctor, what in your judgment was her approximate weight?
A. Well, I never did weigh her, but somewhere- judging from her height and size she weighed 170 or 80 pounds, possibly a little more.
Q. What was her height, in you judgment?
A. She was five feet seven or nine inches, something like that.
Q. Doctor, did you examine a portion of a human body down at the Sumrall Undertaking Parlor?

A.   Yes, sir.

Q.   I will ask you to view that- the content of the matter here before the court. Do you want me to open the box? I will ask you to view that part of the remains in the box there, and state first what sex it is. Whether male or female, state whether or not from your examination that you are able to tell whether or not that is a portion of the remains of a male or female person?

A.   Female.

Q.   Doctor, are you able to determine whether or not that is a part of the remains of a female who has borne children?

A.   Yes, sir.

Q.   How are you able to tell that, Doctor?

A.   By this-- if it was turned over you could see the lineal lines broken on the abdomen muscles there, and then also by the vagina.

Q.   Doctor are the limbs of a Caucasian or white person?

A.   Yes, sir.

Q.   State where the limbs are severed- in the lower portions or how?

A.   Well, the lower portion- can you all see that?

Q.   Where are they severed?

A.   At the knee joint.

Q.   How about the top portion?

A.   The top portion right across- right, you might say, just across the umbilicus- the navel.

Q.   How about the back portion?

A.   The back is severed at the left of the spinal column.

Q.   Doctor, what is the length of the bone, if you have measured it, that is, the large bone of the limbs there?

A.   The large bone is 19 ½ inches, that is the femur, extending from knee to hip.

Q.   19 ½ inches?

A.   Is there any rule whereby you can accurately ascertain the height of a person by the length of that limb?

A.   Yes, you can approximant it very close.

Q.   How would you figure the height by the length of that bone?

A.   Multiply the length of the bone by 3.6.

Q.   3.6- Doctor, as you view those limbs and the other portions of the body, what, in your judgment, would be the weight of the person of which they are a part?

A.   Based upon the weight of them which was 32 and 37 pounds, would make about 40% of the weight.

Q.   Did you know Mrs. Daisy Keeton in her lifetime?

A.   Yes, sir.

Q.   Now, Doctor, I will ask you one further question- have you made such a diagnosis as that you can express an opinion- a medical opinion, as to whether or not this person had passed the period of possible childbirth?

A.   Yes, sir.

Q.   What do you base your opinion upon that on doctor?

A.   On the atrophy of the ovary and the womb.

Q.   Then state whether or not, in your medical opinion, this person has passed that age?

A.   It had.

Mr. Currie asked the Court direct for the limbs to be carried back to the funeral parlor. Now Mr. Collins will cross examine Mr. Brown.

Q.   Now, Doctor, what portion of the human body is blood?

A.   What portion of the body is blood?

Q.   Yes, what percentage of the weight of the human body is blood?

A.   About one twelfth.

Q.   And could you judge, Doctor, from the weight of the head about how much a body would weight?

A.   No.

Q.   But you don't know whether this was an average person or not, do you?

A.   No, sir.

Q.   Fact is, you don't know anything about it only just what you saw in looking at it?

A.   From the examination of the parts, yes, sir.

Now Comes Mrs. M.A.Sherrill To Be Direct Examined By Mr. Collins:

Q.   Your name is Mrs. M.A. Sherrill?

A.   That's my name.

Q.   Where do you live, Mrs. Sherrill?

A.   I live about four miles down below here between here and Ellisville.

Q.   On Highway 11?

A.   Yes, sir, Washington Road for about fifteen years.

Q.   I believe you are a sister to Mrs. Daisy Keeton?

A.   I am.

Q.   About how often have you seen the defendant during that time, Mrs. Sherrill?

A.   Oh, I average once a week at least.

Q.   Mrs. Sherrill, state what her physical appearance used to be, up until a year or two ago with reference to whether she was a stout or slender girl?

A.   Well, she was a very stout girl up until two years or a little more ago.

Q.   About how much did she weigh, Mrs. Sherrill?

A.   Well, I guess she would weigh about 150 or more.

Q.   Did you notice any change in her- or have you noticed any change in

137

her physically in the last two years?

A. Yes, a decided change.

Q. What change if any have you noticed?

A. Well, in her physical condition- I notices she had changed lots a couple of years ago, then recently- well, for a year or more ago I noticed some change in her mental condition.

Q. Mrs. Sherrill, as you stated then, she has greatly emaciated or fallen off in the last two years physically?

A. Yes, sir.

Q. Mrs. Sherrill, up until two years ago state whether or not the defendant- what about her mental condition as to whether she was bright, apt and easy to learn?

A. Unusually bright. Up until two years ago.

Q. Well, what do you say with reference to whether she did carry on conversations with you or not?

A. She was very good in a conversation up until a couple of years ago.

Q. Just go on and describe to the jury how she would act in the last two years?

A. Well, she would come in with my sister and we would all three be in the living room and she would pick up one magazine after another and just look through them at the pictures, just like a child, and I would see she was nervous, and I was afraid she would take my sister off-- and I wouldn't want them to go so soon and maybe I would have a dozen more magazines out there and she would say, "Well, I have read them all, let's go, Mama."

Q. State what her condition was there with reference to whether she was nervous or appeared nervous?

A. Yes, sir, very nervous and restless.

Q. State what if anything you noticed with reference to her facial expression?

A. Well, she liked to look in the mirror at herself, and you know, primp, continually, and I noticed her eyes did not look as they should.

Q. In what way had her eyes changed?

A. Well, they just had a wild, starey look.

Q. Mrs. Sherrill, state to the court and jury what if anything you noticed with reference to whether she was devoted to her mother?

A. I always thought she was the most devoted child I ever saw to her. Well, she has been the most devoted child I ever saw from a little child up.

Q. To whom was she devoted?

A. To her mother- she always wanted to stay with her mother.

Q. Was there anything about her actions with reference to that that distinguished her from the other children?

A. Well, yes, the other children would like to get out and go, you know, places, and she preferred staying with her mother.

Q.   What about the condition of Ouida's health for the last two years when you would visit there?

A.   Well, until the last few months Ouida was in bed most every time I would go there. Well, for years back- she would take little spouting- pouting spells and they wouldn't really know what about, and wouldn't come to the table and eat her meals with the rest of them, she would wait and then go eat alone and go back to her work.

Q.   What if anything did you notice with reference to her condition on Tuesday before this thing happened?

A.   Well, I noticed that- she came and my sister and I- I was out in the back yard and I was washing out a few clothes, so my sister told her to go on in the house and she went on just like a child afraid she would take cold, and we went on in the yard, my sister was looking at some of my flowers and we come on around to the car and she got in the car and as soon as she got in the car she went to looking at her face- as I say, she got to where she could look at herself in the glass and went to arranging her hair and fixing her face and she let out a rather peculiar laugh, kind of blood-curdling, I think- I don't know, I can hear it ringing yet.

Mrs. Sherrill is questioned more about her mental and physical condition and then she is asked about what type of work Ouida did and who she worked for.

Q.   Describe to the jury the nature and character of her work while she worked for Mr. Carter?

A   Kept books.

Q.   In fact, she was an expert in that line?

A.   Supposed to be.

Q.   That was the reputation she had, wasn't it- as a most efficient young lady in business? That is the reputation she enjoyed as being a very efficient business woman?

A.   That's what I have heard.

Q.   What you understand- in fact, she was offered a position as secretary to the president of Soule Business College, wasn't she? Offered employment there?

A.   She was.

Q.   And that is a reputable, highly recognized business college or University in New Orleans, isn't it?

A.   Yes, sir.

Q.   Ordinarily they came to visit you Mrs. Sherrill on Sunday afternoon- that was the common custom?

A.   Well, yes, lately.

Q.   Now on Sunday, January 20th, did either of them come to you home that day?

A.   No, sir.

Now Mrs. Earl Keeton, Introduce On Behalf Of Defendant, Having Been First Duly Sworn, Testified As Follows:

DIRECT EXAMINATION

BY MR. COLLINS:

Q.   You are Mrs. Earl Keeton?
A.   Yes, sir.
Q.   How long have you known Miss Ouida Keeton, the defendant?
A.   Almost nine years.
Q.   State whether or not you ever lived in the home with them?
A.   I did.
Q.   When was that, Mrs. Keeton?
A.   We went there in 1930.
Q.   1930, How long did you live there in the house with them?
A.   Almost three years.
Q.   During the time you lived in the house with them, Mrs. Keeton, what was the condition of Miss Ouida Keeton with reference to her health?
A.   Not so good. Well, I know she was in a weak condition- she wasn't strong, like a person should be.
Q.   Did you know her when she was strong and healthy looking?
A.   Yes, sir, I did.
Q.   Did it appear to you- or did she appear to you to be suffering very intensely?
A.   She did. Well, I noticed she didn't notice things like she did- didn't have as bright an expression in her face as she did.
Q.   Didn't notice things like she did?
A.   No, sir.
Q.   Did you have occasion to visit the filling station down here where she worked?
A.   I was there on Friday.
Q.   During those times you visited the filling station down there did you notice anything- any change in her expression and manner and appearance down there?
A.   I did notice a difference yes. Well, I noticed she didn't pay any attention to what we were saying to her.
Q.   How did she do?
A.   She had a far away look in her eyes.
Q.   Mrs. Keeton, did you stay there very long?
A.   I guess we stayed there about twenty or thirty minutes.
Q.   And attempted to talk to her?
A.   Yes, sir, she had a blank look.
Q.   Blank look?
A.   She did.

Mr. Collins will now call for direct examination Dr. J.D. Smith.

Q.   You are Dr. J.D. Smith?
A.   Yes, sir.
Q.   You were reared near Sandersville then in Jones County?
A.   Yes, sir. I attended the medical department of the University of Alabama.
Q.   How long have you been practicing as a physician in Jones County?
A.   31 years.
Q.   Did you attend any other medical schools, Dr. Smith?
A.   Well, I attended this old New Orleans Polytechnic-post graduation.
Q.   In what place, Doctor?
A.   In New Orleans.
Q.   And you have been a practicing physician for thirty years?
A.   Yes, sir.
Q.   General practitioner?
A.   Yes, sir.
Q.   Dr. Smith, did you know the Keeton family?
A.   Yes, sir.
Q.   Did you know her husband, John Keeton?
A.   Yes, sir.
Q.   Did you know the McKinstry family, that is, Mrs. Keeton's people?
A.   Yes, sir.
Q.   How long have you known them, Doctor?
A.   Well, practically all of my life- they are an old family out in that country- both of them lived out there and my people lived there and I have known them all my life.
Q.   Now, Doctor explain to the jury where the families lived, both the Keeton's and McKinstry's.
A.   Well, both families lived in Jasper County- I am not sure whether the Keeton home was above the line or below; the Keeton home was just a half a mile west of Highway 11, at the county line between Jones and Jasper County. John Keeton married and left up there and I never knew much about him after he left.
Q.   That was the father of the defendant?
A.   Yes, sir.
Q.   And the McKinstry's lived over on what was known as the old Paulding and Ellisville road, about a couple of miles west of the Keeton home- they lived a mile on this old road something like a mile north of the county line.
The Judge needs to ask the Doctor a question before he can rule.
Q.   Dr. Smith you claim not to be a psychiatrist, or an alienist?

141

A.   No.

Now back to questioning by Mr. Collins.

Q.   All right, now, Doctor, I believe you have just testified here that you knew the defendant and have known her practically all of her life and that you knew her during her working for Mr. W.M. Carter, that she was an active, bright courteous girl?

A.   Yes, sir.

Q.   And that you saw her twice during the last six months and the first time you saw her in the last six months you didn't know her and had to look at her for some time there had been such a pronounced change in her physical appearance and the expression in her eyes and in her face, and you testified Doctor, that she had a starey look out of her eyes, a faraway look, and you testified, Doctor, that you examined her recently down in the hospital, now from your personal knowledge, Doctor, and from those things you have testified about, is it your opinion, Doctor, that at the time or prior to this when you saw her, that she was sane or insane?

A.   Yes, sir, she was insane. Insane in my opinion.

Dr. Smith will now be crossed examined by Mr. Currie. Mr. Currie questions the Doctor about growing up with the defendants family and different facts that he knew about them.

Q.   Now where is John McKinstry, he is dead, isn't he?

A.   Who? John Keeton- the father of the defendant?

A.   Yes, sir.

Q.   And do you know the mode or manner in which he lost his life?

A.   No, sir, not from any first-hand information I do not- I understand that he fell from a passenger train and was killed.

Q.   Yes- and then Mrs. Keeton thereafter moved to Laurel with her children?

A.   Yes, sir.

Q.   Do you know the sisters of Mrs. Daisy Keeton?

A.   I know this Miss McKinstry that works at Fine Brothers.

Q.   Miss Laura?

A.   Yes, sir.

Q.   All right, now, Doctor- you say you made- about how many times have you seen the defendant since-

A.   Oh, I have seen her twice a day, oftener than that, but I have seen her twice every day since I was called to take charge of her at the hospital about three weeks ago, approximately three week ago, I wouldn't say the exact date.

Q.   Have you made a physical examination of her, Doctor?

A.   Yes.

Q.   And have you made a mental test and mental examination of her,

Doctor?

A. Yes.

Q. Doctor, from what you have seen and what you have observed, from your examination and your tests that you have made, and in the light of your general experience and your training, what is your opinion as to whether she was sane or insane the first time you saw her?

Mr. Currie objects to the question that Mr. Collins has asked Dr. Smith saying that he is does not qualify as an expert. The Court ask the Doctor if he is in a position to give an opinion on that question? The Doctor replied that he was. The Court then asked what he was basing it on. The Doctor said that he based it on the symptoms she has presented and the symptoms that she shows in every examination that he has made and that in his opinion she' quite insane. Well, the Doctor answered, I'm more prepared- the more I saw her- The first time I saw her, of course I took her under observation, and I formed my opinion the second time I attended her. Now the Doctor will be cross examined by Mr. Currie.

Q. What kind of insanity is she suffering from, Doctor, in your opinion?

A. Well, now, Mr. Currie, I will tell you, on the terms of all the different types of insanity, I don't know that I would be very competent- I am very cognizant of that fact- and - well now--Wait a minute-but from the history and the symptoms she presents, I think she is, however, a dementia praecox.

Q. I see-in what form?

A. Well, she has the catatonic type.

Q. And what stage?

A. Pretty far advanced stage.

Q. I see- Doctor, when does that type- the type of dementia praecox you are talking about- when does that set up?

A. That may set up in early life, it is progressive.

Q. You say that type of insanity progresses, or is progressive?

A. Yes, sir.

Q. And you say it is likely to set up in early life?

A. Yes, sir.

Q. And that is you diagnosis of the type from which she is suffering?

A. Yes, sir.

Dr. Smith was questioned more about Ouida's physical and mental condition. Next Dr. Jarvis is being questioned by Mr. Currie about his opinion on Ouida as he had stated before he had given her luminal and is being questioned about that.

Q. How much luminal did you send here?

A. Oh, I had several tablets one and a half grains each.

Q. Doctor, upon whose recommendation did you send the luminal up here?

A. Well, Dr. Beech phoned me the night before, I got the message through him, that Dr. Holbrook had suggested that luminal would be kind to her nervous condition.

Q.   Who is Dr. Holbrook?

A.   Well, he is the nerve man- psychiatrist from New Orleans.

Q.   And he was brought here at whose instance?

A.   I think the State had him summoned here.

Q.   The State had him summoned- so you gave her the luminal then at the instance of the doctor the state had summoned here?

A.   At his suggestion, yes, sir.

Q.   At his suggestion- now when you saw her in the room there, state whether in your opinion that luminal you gave her had any effect on her, towards putting her in the stupor in which you found her?

A.   That is very questionable to me, whether it was or wasn't, I gave her a small dose, that is, small to what we usually give, we usually give two tablets at a time, which would make three grains. I never had a patient to have that much result from a grain and a half of luminal before, and it has been questionable, in my mind, whether or not the luminal had anything to do with it, and she was not relaxed, the eyes, in pulling the lids back, there would be a tension, you know- no relaxation of the lids, and I thought it was her condition more that the luminal in her that caused that condition- that caused the appearance of sleep, you know, and slumber.

Q.   Doctor, was that condition characteristic of her- I mean that stupor you found there- was that characteristic of her condition?

A.   Yes, yes, I found that very characteristic.

Q.   What particularly?

A.   Well, the stupor there is really a condition of the trouble from which she is suffering?

Q.   What is that trouble?

A.   Insanity.

The complainant in support of her cause introduced the following evidence. Dr. J.B. Jarvis introduced as a witness, being duly sworn to tell the truth, the whole truth and nothing but the truth, testified as follows, to-wit. Dr. Jarvis is being direct examined by Mr. Cooper and Dr. Jarvis' qualifications are admitted.

Q.   Doctor, do you know Miss Ouida Keeton?

A.   Yes.

Q.   Have you attended her in the last few days?

A.   Yes.

Q.   When was the last time you saw her?

A.   This morning.

Q.   I will ask you to state to the Court whether or not she is able to come into the court room here and attend to the details of this hear of a writ of habeas corpus?

A.   I don't think she could come to court. I don't think she could stand.

Q.   Describe to the Court her strength or her lack of strength?

A.   She is very weak. I found her very weak yesterday. I have seen her two or three times since last Saturday. I found her very weak yesterday. She told me she fainted sometime during the morning. She made no effort to talk, whether she heard what I said I don't know. She had a weak pulse, a little over ninety-six. She was not able to retain anything on her stomach. The nurse told me she had retained most of a glass of tomato juice, but had vomited most everything she had taken. She made no effort to talk, A few times she took a pencil and wrote words and answers to questions I put to her. I think it is just a nervous condition and dehydration. She can't retain water, she vomits it up as she swallows it.

Q.   What is that due to, in your opinion?

A.   I think her digestive system is upset by metal worry.

Q.   Is she able to walk?

A.   I don't think she could stand up, that is my opinion.

Q.   Now, is there any way for you to feed her so as to give her nourishment except through the digestive system?

A.   You can give it to her through the tissues or veins.

Q.   With reference to hospitalization, what do you say?

A.   I think she is in need of hospitalization at the present time. I don't see how we could give her the treatment she needs, it would not be fairly safe in the jail.

Q.   Would she be in any position to testify?

A.   She would not in my opinion.

Next you will note the copy of the Subpoena Duces Tecum.
Subpoena Duces Tecum
THE STATE OF MISSISSIPPI

TO THE SHERIFF OF Jones COUNTY--GREETING:

By order of the   Circuit Court of said County, first made in
this behalf, we command you to summon:
Jack Deavours and Alexander Currie
to be and appear before the Judge of our said Circuit Court, at the Courthouse
thereof in the town of Laurel at the February term, 1935 thereof, and on the 14th
day of said Term, being the instanter day of 1935, and bring with them into said
Court certain written confessions made by the defendant in the case of The State
vs. Ouida Keeton or alleged to have been made by the defendant.
The _____ named in the aforesaid order of Court, there to testify and
offer the said confessions in evidence on behalf of the defendant in a suit
pending in said Court, wherein The State of Mississippi is, Plaintiff and Ouida
Keeton is defendant. And this you shall in nowise omit under the penalty of One
hundred dollars, and the consequences that may thereby befall.
And have you then and there this Writ.

Given under my hand and seal of office, at my office in the town of
Laurel this the 6th day of March, 1935.

Q.   Now Mr. Currie state whether or not Ouida Keeton made statements in your presence with reference to this matter that were taken down in writing?
A.   The defendant did make a statement which I understood was being taken down by a stenographer in shorthand.
Q.   State whether or not, Mr. Currie- did you hear the statement- state whether or not you heard the statements that were taken down by a stenographer as made by this defendant?
A.   I did.

Now Mrs. Paula Richeimer was introduced on behalf of the defendant and is being directly examined by Mr. Collins.

Q.   Now you are Mrs. Paula Richeimer?
A.   I am.
Q.   Where do you live, Mrs. Richeimer?
A.   614 Cross Street.
Q.   What relation are you to Mrs. Daisy Keeton?
A.   A sister.
Q.   What relation are you to the defendant, Miss Ouida Keeton?
A.   An Aunt.
Q.   Where do you live, Mrs. Richeimer, with reference to her- to the Keeton home?
A.   Diagonally across the street.
Q.   Mrs. Richeimer, living close to the Keeton home where you live, how often did you visit the Keeton home?
A.   For the last two years I was in my sister's home practically every day.
Q.   What about when the defendant here was a girl, how often would you see her?
A.   We played together as children.
Q.   Now, Mrs. Richeimer, state to the court and jury, as you were a girl and the defendant were a girl, whether or not the defendant played with the children like the other children, or what if anything she did?
A.   My niece Maud and Ouida and myself played together a lot, but she would often refuse to go out and play with us, she would stay in the house with her mother, or at times she would go out and play with us and then go in the house and leave us for no reason at all and we would go in and find her playing around her mother with her toys and things, and after school we would come home in the afternoon and play out on the lawn and she would quit often and sit upon the porch and sing, she didn't care about getting out with the other children and romping around, then when she was in high school she didn't care to get out with the boys and girls- she never went to parties.
She was very, very close to her mother from a mere infant. Anyone else would want to get out and go places at night, or go places in the afternoon, but she

147

didn't, she never wanted to go with us, she stayed with her mother and was very, very attached to her.

Q.   Mrs. Richeimer, you said something about her refusing to go out to parties and go out the young men and boys, what did you notice, if anything with reference to this?

A.   Well, when she finished high school, she and my sister were practically in the same class, and of course there were a lot of parties the senior year and for the graduating class and Ouida wouldn't go to any of them, she never would go out with boys, just stayed at home, and when she finished school she went to New Orleans for a short time and took a business course at Soule Business College.

Q.   State if you know what about her work in school and her grades in school?

A.   She made very good grades, I think.

Q.   State with reference to her being a bright or a dull student?

A.   Well, I think she was a bright student- I know I talked to Mr. Ed Soule, president of Soule Business College, and he said she was one of the most brilliant girls that ever went through the school, and when she finished her course he gave her a chance to be his secretary and she wouldn't stay, she declined, saying she wanted to stay at home with her mother who had some small children, and she came back to Laurel and went to work for Mr. W.M. Carter. I believe she came back in 1920 or 1921, and she worked off and on, I would say, around ten years, steady, for Mr. Carter, and off and on for a couple of years since.

Q.   Mrs. Richeimer, what about the defendant's condition with reference to her health, and with reference to her being a slender girl or a stout girl up until about two years?

A.   She was stout- well, I think when she went to Washington she weighted around 126 pounds, when she came home she had lost considerable weight. She has put forward every effort to gain even a pound in the last two years, and ate from five to seven meals a day to gain, she ate at meal time and between meals and would take all the nourishment she could take to put on a few pounds.

Q.   Mrs. Richeimer, what about her condition as to whether during the past two years- as to whether or not she has appeared to be nervous?

A.   She has been highly nervous. Well, I can remember back several years ago when she was working she would shut herself in her room, she would always spend her two weeks vacation in her bedroom, bring her meals into her room and eat, and she would just live her life alone, and during the last two years that I have been with so closely, she would stay in her room alone other than getting out and taking a ride and getting a little air, other than that she would always spend her time in the house.

Q.   Mrs. Richeimer, how often would you see her close herself up in the room and stay those long periods?

148

A.   Well, over a number of years. She would always spend that vacation in her room, and during odd times, in the evenings when she would come home from work she would go to her room and stay and go to her work next morning without anyone seeing her.

Q.   Well, during the past two years state whether or not she has secluded herself?

A.   She has, but not for such long periods because she has been sick and she had to have attention.

Q.   You say she has been sick- about how much has she been sick during that time?

A.   Well, she has had a number of very bad spells, I should say at least ten or twelve, and she was sick for a year almost straight through, she would only get up from the bed for a short period of time and then she would get so restless she would go back to bed.

Q.   Now, Mrs. Richeimer, state whether or not you have taken a trip with her in the last year?

A.   I have, I went to New Orleans with her around the first of December.

Q.   For what purpose, Mrs. Richeimer?

A.   We went down to look over some boarding houses.

Q.   Why were you looking over some boarding houses?

A.   She felt that she wanted to get into something, and she wanted us to go into a boarding house with her.

Q.   Mrs. Richeimer, on that trip to New Orleans, what other thing, if any, did you notice peculiar about here?

A.   Well, she would leave me alone a lot- go out on little trips. I knew she was meeting real estate men and meeting John P. Sullivan, Col. John P. Sullivan, and I knew he was a friend of the family, and she had a letter of introduction to him, and he offered to give her a job if she wanted one, I didn't accompany her to see him; and she also went to see a doctor, and I didn't accompany her. And one afternoon we went to a beauty parlor, she wanted to get her hair cut, and he told her she had such beautiful hair, he told her most women would give thousands of dollars for hair like hers, and told her she was making a mistake to cut her hair and she got a shampoo and a finger wave and he gave her a mirror to look at her hair, and Ouida just walked out and said, "I'm gone" and I said "Wait a minute and I will go with you, but she left out and went to my brother's apartment and when I got there she was almost in a hysterical condition and she had gone in the bathroom and had the water running and had combed out this finger wave they had just put in her hair, and she just went into a real hysterical condition on account of the way she looked with a finger wave.

Q.   Mrs. Richeimer, you say she talked so much about it- explain to the jury what you mean by her talking so much about the apartments, ect.?

A.   Well, she continued to repeat over and over about this boarding house,

"I'm sure we could do well in it" and just kept repeating about the boarding house, just over and over.

Q. Now, Mrs. Richeimer, you needn't tell what was said, but state whether or not it has been discussed in the family about her mental condition?

A. It has.

Q. When was that, Mrs. Richeimer, that it was discussed?

A. Well, between out immediate family, what I mean by that, my sister, Mrs. Sherrill, and my sister Laura, I first discussed it with them, but I told her sister, Mrs. McRae, the day before Thanksgiving that I thought there was something radically wrong with Ouida. She would come to visit my house and sit down and if she was sitting talking to you and had a paper or magazine in her hand, she would keep tearing up little bits of it, and she had me to dress to go down town with her to buy some crepe to make some underwear, and by the time we got down there she had changed her mind and wouldn't even want to look at it-

Q. You spoke about her tearing up bits off of a magazine, what if anything did she do with those bits she would tear off?

A. She would scatter them over the floor.

Q. Well, have you noticed anything about her use of matches?

A. Well, her mother kept matches on the mantel piece, and I have sat and watched her break them up.

Now Dr. Cranford will be questioned by Mr. Collins.

Q. Tell the jury how she appeared?

A. I met up with her and her mother and shook hands with them both and she said Doctor, I've been wanting to see you quite a while, I didn't know where you were, I'm sick, I'm all to pieces, and I want you to treat me, I want you to see me and I said "I'm not practicing, I have been sick, and I haven't opened my office yet" and she said "I want you to see me, I've lost between thirty-five and fifty pounds, I'm all to pieces and I want you to see me" and her mother had walked on and got about half way from here to the door from her and she walked back and got her by the arm and said "Come on Ouida, let's go."

Q. Tell the jury whether or not you noticed any difference in her then?

A. Oh, she wasn't the same girl.

Q. Tell the jury what you mean by that?

A. I mean by that in place of the robust, hale, hearty looking girl she had been, she was then very nervous, had a staring, glassy look out of her eyes, and just looked sick.

Q. Have you seen her since January 19th?

A. Three weeks ago last Tuesday, Dr. Jarvis called me up and says "I have a patient at the hospital--"

Q. I will ask you this way, Doctor, were you called in as a physician to

150

examine this patient and tell the jury what you have done with regard to an examination?

A.   After I was called in the case I set about then, having this picture before me of the atrocious and hideous crime that had been committed, and her actions, and the fact that I saw her in the fall in ill health, the first thing that occurred to me was that the whole picture and act was the work of a crazy lunatic, and I say about in the usual methods and manner to ascertain whether she was a maniac or to whether she had a normal mind, I had been told--

Q.   You can't tell what you had been told, Doctor.

A.   Well, first I commenced trying to get the family history--

Q.   Did you obtain the family history?

A.   I did later, I couldn't do it that day. It was difficult to obtain. I wanted to find out the condition of her health in the last few months or years. We carried her through, or at my request, Dr. Jarvis and I made a spinal puncture to get some spinal fluid, he had made a blood test, but there were so many other things we wanted cleared up, in examining the spinal fluid the patient gave a history of having a very sore spot in the back of her neck, very sore, considerable headache and--

Q.   Well-- all right, go ahead.

A.   And we wanted to ascertain from the spinal fluid as to what it contained, the spinal fluid will reveal things you can't find in the blood stream and can't find elsewhere, for instance if there is a cerebral spinal disorder or an inflamed condition there, there would be a difference in the spinal fluid, it may contain red blood cells, or may contain pus, to take a specimen of blood from the blood stream doesn't every time reveal syphilis, as no one would be exempt that drinks at public drinking fountains. We wanted to clear that point up and wanted to make that test also, so we made the spinal puncture and went to examining the patient. I found the back of her neck very touchous, I discovered then that she has an inguinal glandular disturbance, she hasn't developed a particle with reference to her glandular system since she was two years old, there isn't a gland in that woman's body as big as a pea, the thyroid gland is absent, the gland under the arms and in the groin, the whole glandular structure is undeveloped, then it began to confront us, the kind of insanity- in dementia praecox- we know a person is crazy lots of times, but it takes going into these minute symptoms to find out what kind of insanity it is. Insanity affects people just as differently as whisky affects them, or any other derangement or nervous sickness or disorder, and in examining that girl it struck me, now she's either insane or she's feigning- she's faking- she's insane or she couldn't present the symptoms she presents. We found that the entire reflex was gone, it would return next day probably a little bit, but never to normal, I sat on the side of the bed and drew her foot up this way, and gave it a little twist this way, and held it up to where she couldn't see me, and I put a pin into it and she didn't flinch any more that if it had been a wooden foot. The other symptoms were just as

151

marked, that vacant stare that you notice, and you could tell her to stick her tongue out and she couldn't seem to stick it out, but you could stick a pin in it and take it out and go to stick it again and she wouldn't even flinch. She presents every symptom of catatonia dementia praecox, cataleptic type. Some people have a nervous disorder called epilepsy, or catalepsy, and different forms of nervous diseases, in all cases of catatonia of the cataleptic type, there is an infallible test, and I would like to demonstrate to the jury what I mean by that.

Q.   You may, Doctor.

As Dr. Cranford is about to demonstrate beyond a question of doubt Ouida's form of insanity Mr. Currie would like for the jury to step out of the courtroom. At this time the Judge requests that the jury retire from the room. Now that the jury absent Dr. Cranford continues with his demonstration.

BY THE COURT:

Q.   Go ahead, Dr. Cranford.

A.   I wanted to show you that you can poke anything down her throat and you can't gag her, and to show you that you can put her in this shape(lifting her arm up) and she will probably stay there an hour if you didn't go take her arm down- that is a symptom of catatonic type of dementia praecox- that kind of symptom they cannot feign, they cannot fake. It is the infallible test in those kind of cases.

Q.   Have you made those tests?

A.   I have, repeatedly.

Q.   Doctor, would that be taxing or exhausting or cause any unnecessary pain to the patient?

A.   Well, I believe she would stay in that position until she collapsed.

Q.   We don't want to do anything that would make her uncomfortable.

BY MR. CLARK:

Q.   Doctor, from your observation and from your examination, historically and otherwise, tell the jury whether or not in your opinion that the defendant was sane or insane on January 19th, 1935?

A.   Incurably insane.

Q.   Tell the jury, whether or not in your opinion, taking in consideration all that you know of this case, from the history of the patient and other wise, whether or not the defendant is capable of recognizing right from wrong?

A.   She cannot.

Q.   Tell the court and the jury whether or not in you opinion- or just tell them in your own words, the condition of that defendant at this moment?

A.   She's insane.

Q.   Tell the jury whether or not in your opinion she will live long?

152

A.   That will depend.

BY MR. CURRIE:

Q.   Doctor, I believe you have stated on many occasions that Mr. Carter is not guilty of this alleged offense?
A.   I said that she was so susceptible to suggestion that probably on account of her mental condition, if the same suggestions had been made about you or about me, she probably would have indicted one of us. I said that to you-
Q.   That's right-
A.   And I said that her state of sanity was such that her perceptibility to suggestion was such that if it had presented to her she would have involved you or me in the place of Mr. Carter- It is probable we would have been involved in the place of Mr. Carter.
Q.   That's right, and you further said that Carter was no more guilty of the crime than you or I, in your opinion?
A.   That's right, in my opinion, under those circumstances.
Q.   Doctor, discussing your knowledge of the case, you said that you traded with Mr. Carter back yonder years ago?
A.   I bought some stuff from him, yes.
Q.   And you knew the defendant then?
A.   Very well.
Q.   You sought to employ her as your secretary, did you Doctor?
A.   Yes.
Q.   She was then employed by Mr. Carter?
A.   Yes.
Q.   And just as a matter of touching her qualifications as secretary- her mental capacity- how much did you offer her?
A.   I offered her $150.00 a month to go down to my hospital and keep my books and be my secretary.
Q.   What did she say to you about accepting the position?
A.   "Come back by here tomorrow and I will give you my answer."
Q.   Well, did you go back then?
A.   I did.
Q.   Did you get the answer?
A.   I did.
Q.   What was the answer?
A.   She said Mr. Carter said "If I'm worth $150.00 to you, I'm worth $175.00 to him" and I understand he kept her at that salary for seven years.
Q.   Now touching further phases of the matter, what knowledge if any do you have as to the frequency of the visits of Mr. Carter to her home?
A.   I know nothing about it.
Q.   You know nothing about that?

A. Nothing about it.

Q. And any statement you made about the case was made without that knowledge?

A. It was made with reference to her state of nervous disorder.

Q. Well, was I made without reference to that knowledge?

A. Absolutely.

Q. You didn't know that he visited that home with such regularity that he came in unannounced, did you?

A. I did not.

Q Doctor, you day this type is very cunning?

A. Very cunning.

Q. And so one is likely to be deceived, isn't one?

A. Repeat the question.

Q. So one is likely to be deceived?

A. With reference to what?

Q. To their condition?

A. I mean in covering in covering up their acts.

Q. Doctor, why would they be cunning in covering up their acts?

A. Because in this kind of insanity, they are great schemers.

Q. Schemers?

A. Yes, just as ordinary people, or sane people.

Q. Scheme as ordinary people- why would ordinary people scheme to cover up their acts?

A. To cover guilty, I presume.

Q. Doctor, you said you performed certain tests, I presume someone assisted you in making your tests, did they?

A. Dr. Jarvis and I made them.

Q. Who else was present?

A. The psychiatrists from Memphis and Jackson at times.

Q. Do you know when you performed them?

A. Hunh?

Q. Do you know when you made your tests?

A. Sunday a week ago was one time, and Monday was a week ago was another time.

Q. What test did you make Sunday a week ago?

A. The different tests of sanity and insanity.

Q. I know, but I want to know what they are?

A. Well, we carried her through the knee reflex test and then carried her through the questioning, asked her time and again who killed her mother for instance, to see if there was any emotional expression on her fact.

Q. Was there any?

A. None whatever.

Q. What was the expression and condition on her face?

A. Just as blank as today.
Q. And no blanker than today?
A. Jus the same- just staring.
Q. Same as today?
A. Staring, yes, sir.
Q. And how about her eyes on that occasion?
A. No difference.
Q. No different from now?
A. No.
Q. And so you asked her who killed her mother?
A. A number of times.
Q. I see-
A. In taking her through those tests.
Q. You also asked her other things, didn't you? What did she tell you about who killed her mother?
A. She said she did not know, she told Dr. Mitchell that too, or wrote it to him rather, she couldn't speak, but she did write it to him.
Q. That she did not know?
A. Yes. She also has told up that God and her mother would visit her daily, come every day to see her, and I asked her how her mother looked and she said "Happy and beautiful."
Q. I see- that would be the normal remembrance to have of her mother, wouldn't it? That is how you remember your mother, isn't it? You remember your mother that way?
A. Well, she is still living.
Q. But that is how you would remember her, isn't it?
A. Sure.
Q. That is how I remember mine- she said her mother visited her daily, didn't she?
A. Comes to see her daily now.
Q. Yes- and that God was with her?
A. God was with her- God comes with her.
Q. All right, who else was there when she said that?
A. Dr. Mitchell, Dr. McCool and Dr. Jarvis.

Now Comes Mrs. Leila Mae Martin, On Behalf Of The Defendant To Be Directly Examined By Mr. Collins.

Q. What is your first name, Mrs. Martin?
A. Leila Mae.
Q. Mrs. Martin, were you called- are you a stenographer?
A. I am.
Q. State whether or not you take shorthand?

155

A.   I do.

Q.   Were you called upon to take certain statements of this defendant while she was in jail?

A.   Yes, sir.

Q.   When you went up into the jail to take these statements, tell the court and jury who was present?

A.   Mr. Deavours, Mr. Van Valentine and myself, and as I recall, Mr. Jim Brown- but I won't be sure about him.

Q.   Mr. Jim Brown- all right, did you take a statement of hers there in the jail in short hand?

A.   Yes.

Q.   How many pages of that did you take down, if you remember, Mrs. Martin?

A.   I don't remember.

Q.   Did you transcribe that- those notes?

A.   Yes.

Q.   In all how many typewritten pages were there if you remember?

A.   Well, I don't remember as to that particular.

Q.   Well, about how many, Mrs. Martin, if you remember?

A.   That was a very short statement, not over five or six pages in that particular statement.

BY THE COURT:

Mr. Collins, may the Court ask you sir, if it is your purpose now to introduce an alleged admission or confession? If so, there are certain preliminary inquiries that the Court must make, and as you know, under the recent ruling of the Court it must be done in the absence of the jury.

BY MR. COLLINS:

I will state to the Court, and I want this to go into the record, I am unable to tell at this juncture whether it will be my purpose to introduce the statements or not, because I do not know what is in the statements, but I am offering this evidence to show that there were written statements and to further show that these statements were made in connection with her guilt or innocence in this particular charge, and to further clarify the record on the showing made on yesterday on an application for a writ of subpoena duces tecum, and to further clarify the record in order to require the State to produce the written statements made by the defendant at that time, and for the further purpose of contradiction the testimony of Jim Brown, witness for the State, and for the further reason that there is testimony in this record now that the defendant is unable physically and mentally to testify on her own behalf.

Now Mr. Collins resumes the questioning of Mrs. Martin.

Q.   Now, Mrs. Martin, you say you took down those written statements?
A.   I did.
Q.   Made by this defendant in the presence of the parties you have just names?
A.   Yes.
Q.   Now, Mrs. Martin, was she- state whether or not at that time she was questioned with reference to her guilt or innocence in the case or charge now being tried?
A.   Well, she was asked certain questions- I don't hardly know how to answer that question Mr. Collins.
Q.   Well, state whether or not it was relative to the incident about which she is now being tried?
A.   Oh, yes, it was.
Q.   How many more statements of the defendant did you take, Mrs. Martin?
A.   I took her statements in Mr. Deavours' office on Friday preceding that Saturday that you are talking about, and one at the State hospital on Friday following that Saturday.
Q.   And did you take those down in writing?
A.   Yes.
Q.   And all the statements you took of this defendant, Mrs. Martin, how many pages did it cover? If you remember, how many written pages would it cover?
A.   About eighty.
Q.   About eighty shorthand pages or typewritten pages?
A.   Typewritten pages.
Q.   Who has those typewritten pages in their possession?
A.   I turned them over to Mr. Deavours.
Q.   That is Mr. Jack Deavours, the County Attorney?
A.   Yes.
Q.   To whom- where are the shorthand notes?
A.   Mr. Deavours also has those.

Now Mr. Deavours will cross examine Mrs. Martin.

Q.   Mrs. Martin, you took a statement on Friday night?
A.   Yes.
Q.   The day Miss Keeton was arrested?
A.   That's right.
Q.   You took a statement on Saturday afternoon?
A.   That's right.
Q.   And you took a statement about ten or twelve days later at the State Hospital?

A.   That's right.

Q.   Now did you take any statement in writing- any statement made by Miss Keeton to Mr. Brown, Mr. Currie and Mr. Valentine on Sunday following the Saturday when you said you took the second statement?

A.   No.

Q.   You did not?

A.   No.

Q.   You did not take a written statement of the statement that Mr. Brown referred to in his testimony when he was a witness?

A.   No.

Now Comes Dr. D.C. Mccool On Behalf Of The Defendant Being Directly Examined By Mr. Collins.

Q.   What are your initials, Doctor?

A.   D. C.

Q.   Where do you live, Doctor?

A.   Jackson.

Q.   Doctor, what medical colleges if any have you attended?

A.   The college of medicine of the University of Mississippi and the college of medicine of the University of Illinois, Chicago.

Q.   What particular phase of the treatment of the human body have you specialized in?

A.   Neuropsychiatry, or mental diseases and nervous diseases.

Q.   What examination have you done on the defendant?

A.   Psychopathic and neurotic examination- I examined her mental state and also her nerve state, that is, for the benefit of the jury.

Q.   Doctor, would you mind telling the jury just what you found in that examination- what examination you made and what you found in that examination, in detail.

A.   In detail?

Q.   Yes, the best you can.

A.   I found the defendant in such a state as she seems to be in now, the essential findings in the neurotic examination was the absence of certain reflexes, particularly with reference to the corneal reflex, which we term the batting of the eyes when some object is touched into the eye, the failure to gag when a swab is placed in the throat, and a great diminishing of each reflex, the grip of the elbow and the various muscles, and also the patellar or knee reflex, and the abdominal reflex, and so called reflex of the foot, those were the essential findings. Neurologically. Then as far as the psychiatric or mental examination is concerned, we found her in what is commonly called a cataleptic or perhaps a catatonic stupor, she was apparently without emotion, no suggestion of any emotion, I would say she was devoid of same, and she molded, that is to say, if she was placed in a certain position, she would maintain these positions, however awkward, as long as one would care to have her. It is my opinion that the defendant is insane with the qualifications of the use of the word which you have heard, Mr. Collins.

Q.   Now, Doctor, from your examination and what you have heard testified to here, and taking all that into consideration, what is your opinion as to whether the defendant was sane of insane on January 19th, 1935?

With Mr. Deavours objecting to this question, the court asked Mr. Collins to reform the question to include the facts that have already come out in the trial.

Q.   Now, Doctor, you heard the testimony by Mrs. Richeimer, did you?
A.   Yes, sir.
Q.   You heard the testimony of Mrs. Sherrill, did you?
A.   Yes.
Q.   And it has been testified to here on behalf of the State, by one of the State's witnesses, Mrs. Cook, that the defendant here, during all the time that Mrs. Cook has known her, was extremely affectionate to her mother, noticeably affectionate to her mother; and it has been further testified to by witnesses for the State, Doctor, that during the last two years the defendant here has greatly emaciated in her physical appearance and lost a good deal of weight, and it has been testified to here, Doctor, that she has been sick a great deal of the time for the last two years by witnesses for the State; and it has been testified to here, Doctor, by witnesses for the State, that they noticed a blank and peculiar state in her eyes- now taking all those things into consideration, and your examination of her, Doctor, what is your opinion as to whether or not she was sane or insane on January 19th, 1935?
A.   My opinion is that this condition- that this disease started approximately definitely two months before this alleged incident occurred, and in view of the findings and history at that time, the findings which I made in my first examination and the findings as I see them now, I conclude at the time this incident occurred she was insane.
Q.   Doctor, what is your opinion as to whether or not at that time she was capable of judging right from wrong?
A.   I believe that is understood in the conception of the term insanity- I do not believe that she was able at that time to distinguish right and wrong, where the intent occupied entirely all the conscientious ability to distinguish between right and wrong, there could not be room in the field of consciousness to distinguish between them.
Q.   You mean by that, Doctor, that this delusion or state of mind excluded other things from her mind?
A.   That is my idea and opinion.
Q.   Now, Doctor, I believe you stated that she was suffering from what is

known as catatonic type of insanity, or dementia praecox?

A.   That is correct.

Mr. Collins will now direct examine Dr. O.A. Schmidt on behalf of the defendant.

Q.   You name is Dr. Schmidt?

A.   It is.

Q.   Doctor, did you specialize in any special branch of the study and treatment of human ailments?

A.   Yes.

Q.   What particular branch of it?

A.   In psychiatry.

Q.   From your examination of Ouida state whether or not she- you found her to be afflicted with any form of psychosis?

A.   I would say that she is.

Q.   What form is that, Doctor?

A.   A dementia praecox of the catatonic type.

Q.   Explain to the jury what you mean, Doctor, in your own words, by catatonic dementia praecox?

A.   Praecox means- dementia praecox means dementia young- at the young age, from adolescence on up- it may occur at any age. It is characterized principally by various symptoms, symptoms which are very complex and vary with each individual which is characteristic of all diseases, it usually is childhood, usually what we call a shut in personality, secondly, by a fixation, family fixation. What I mean by that is an unnatural, abnormal attachment to a mother or father or some member of the family, then there is a beginning of reclusiveness', they are intelligent as a rule, It is said that an idiot or an imbecile cannot be a praecox. Following that, we have stages of excitement, unusual activity, impulsive outbursts- they are usually unnoticed, nothing is noticed as being wrong with the individual until he commits some act or he becomes unsocial, that is, he doesn't fit in with the social activities and he is found to be insane, probably his relatives haven't noticed it, they have noticed peculiarities perhaps, but nothing beyond that- then they commit acts of violence, they begin to hallucinate, as we call it, hear imaginary voices, voices of God, voices of those not present, various noises, frequently they have delusions, they have conceptions- ideas based on false conceptions, later they assume what we call the catatonic stage, the state where they become mute, clouded, sometimes, that is, they have a period that lasts from a few minutes to several hours, or several days, that they are oblivious to what is going on about them, just the same as in other diseases, same as in delirium of various diseases, they gradually emerge from that and sometimes become fairly normal and the average man can't see what is wrong with them, they have these attacks frequently, more frequently as take no notice of what is going on about them.

Q.   Doctor, you said that they were intelligent?

160

A.   Yes.

Q.   State, Doctor, whether as a general rule it is the most intelligent who are afflicted with this disease or the least intelligent?

A.   Not always, it varies with the individuals, the same as you have variations with the physical diseases, but ordinarily they are intelligent. I have seen one case of praecox or psychosis that developed in the engineering department in the Louisiana University, the psychologist had advised his family to remove him, but they insisted that he stay, he graduated with high honors, later he drove from Boston to Meridian, Mississippi, without eating, stopping or sleeping, and was admitted next day, or the following week, to the East Mississippi State Hospital, he has no recollection, cannot tell you what took place on his trip or when he started on his trip, that is, in the period when he became fairly normal.

Q.   Doctor, you say that sometime they commit acts or violence?

A.   Yes.

Q.   Doctor, are they mentally responsible for those acts?

A.   Yes.

BY THE COURT:

Q.   "Doctor, having answered that question yes, what do you say with reference to her ability at that time to judge right from wrong?

A.   I would say she was unable to judge right from wrong.

Q.   All right, Doctor, there has been some question raised here about the extraction of some spinal fluid, what effect, Doctor, would that have had upon the defendant?

A.   No effect whatever- the extraction of spinal fluid and other tests are part of the general examination of all patients.

Q.   Why are they made, Doctor?

A.   To determine the nervous system- the condition of the nervous system and to determine the presence of syphilis or other organic diseases, or the presence of a brain tumor and other things, to eliminate other diseases, diagnosis is always made by elimination.

Q.   Doctor, something has been said about melancholia- just explain to the jury what is meant by that and whether this defendant is afflicted with that type of insanity- or is she melancholy?

A.   Melancholia is a symptom of a melancholic condition, a melancholy or depressed state, she is not melancholy, she is unable to be melancholy, that is one of the symptoms of the disease, her emotions are destroyed.

Q.   Have you examined her along that particular line, Doctor?

A.   I have.

Dr. C.D. Mitchell, Introduced On Behalf Of Defendant, Having Been First Duly Sworn, Testified As Follows:

161

BY MR. CLARK.
Q.   Give your name to the stenographer?
A.   Dr. C.D. Mitchell.
Q.   Doctor, where do you live?
A.   I am now living at Gulfport.
Q.   And how long have you been practicing, Doctor?
A.   I practiced general medicine in the town of Pontotoc until 1918 then I went to Jackson, Mississippi as Superintendent of the State Insane Hospital, I am going to use the word insane.
Q.   How long did you serve as superintendent of the insane hospital at Jackson?
A.   Something over seventeen years, until June 1st, last year, I was superintendent.
Q.   Doctor, have you specialized in any one branch of the practice?
A.   Since I have been at Jackson as superintendent, that has been my only work.
Q.   What sort of work, Doctor?
A.   The treating- study and treating of mental diseases, cases of insanity, insane people.
Q.   And after you obtained all the historical information you could concerning this patient, and after your examination while in the hospital, did you come to a conclusion of the condition of this defendant?
A.   Yes, I have.
Q.   Will you tell the jury what that condition is?
A.   I believe she is insane now and was at the time the act was committed.
Q.   Tell the jury whether or not in your judgment, Doctor, that a person suffering with the sort of disease that you have concluded that this defendant is suffering from, would have been, on January 19th, capable of recognizing right from wrong?
A.   I don't think she would. That is my opinion.
Q.   Will you tell the jury what sort of insanity she is suffering from?
A.   She is a dementia praecox of the catatonic from.
Q.   I wish you would tell the jury in your own words the symptoms of the catatonic type of dementia praecox?
A.   As a rule nearly all of them are peculiar and eccentric all their life, as children they are unsocial, and as the doctors have said to you before, are shut-in personally, they don't play and romp around as other children would, they would prefer to be to themselves rather than be out playing, they had no beaux or sweethearts, they made few friends and never confidants. They are ordinarily shut-ins, they are peculiar, they are eccentric, most of them are bright, nearly all of them making high grades in school, some of them even brilliant, that is the type of personality, then we have these symptoms that come on, such as

162

cloudiness, sluggishness, want of interest in their surroundings, want of pep, loss of flesh and such as that, and in many of them, I want to say, they have a severe pain, in some of them you will find a severe pain in the head or back, and other parts of the body, that they complain of seriously, they will go to doctors, from one to another, sometimes they are thought to be neurasthenic, then there comes possibly a period in which they are violent, commit violent acts such as homicide, suicide or violent destruction, after that sometimes there is a period of calm, then you have the stupor us condition such as you see in the patient here today. The catatonic type is very susceptible to suggestion, they have no motive powers of their own, they are easily led by suggestions to do things, they are utterly helpless or powerless to not do them.

Q.   Do you mean by that, Doctor, that the things that they do, they can't refrain from doing?

A.   They can't help doing them, they are powerless, they follow suggestions because they have no motive power of their own.

Q.   Now while a person is suffering with this type of insanity, might they not, at times, Doctor, say they did things that they didn't do?

A.   That is often the case- I have seen these people in the Institutions who are catatonic praecox, when they are able to talk will tell you today one set of facts, and tomorrow it will be an entirely different set, they don't know just why they do that, and I don't, they don't know any more why they do these things that a person knows the different persons that come to him while in a dream.

Q.   Are they able, Doctor, to pursue any course of action, or any sort of logic while in that state?

A.   There are times when they outwardly assume a natural appearance, and sometimes are able to give good account of themselves.

Q.   Then do I understand from you they are unable to resist--

A.   Oh, they are utterly helpless- now most of these people, I want to say- most of these patients have hallucinations, hear voices, have ideas, most of them hear voices from God, and they are going to follow out whatever those voices tell them to do, they are controlled- they are dominated by hallucinations.

Now the court will question Dr. Holbrook for the State about the mental condition of the defendant in his opinion. The Doctor answers...

A.   One expects that sort of behavior in the catatonic patient who doesn't talk, and her writings, by the way, are entirely relevant, usually. They show no signs of delusions, none of the bizarre or unusual ways that a dementia praecox writes. If one examines the writings of a large number of patients, I mean patients from hospitals, you can often make a diagnosis of the type of mental disturbance that the patient is suffering from by examining the writings of these patients. This individual shows no such evidence- I see no evidence of hallucinations or delusions or any of the things that characterizes the writings of patients with dementia praecox. Those things and probably some other observation that I fail to mention now, lead me to the conclusion that she is not suffering from dementia praecox.

Q.   Then, Doctor, what is your opinion of her condition?

A.   I think she is suffering from a minor mental disorder which is very closely related to hysteria and is a result of the situation in which she finds herself.

Q.   What is that commonly called?

A.   That is known as prison psychosis.

Q.   And what are the symptoms of it?

A.   This condition generally begins in people who are arrested for some serious crime, people who are somewhat different from the ordinary individual, and it develops generally while they are waiting for trial or during the course of a trial. It may simulate several things. It may take on a very marked confusion in which the patient doesn't know, apparently, anything, becomes excited, distracted, and gives the impression of being demented, It may take on other maniacal states which resemble dementia praecox or hysteria. It is difficult to differentiate from hysteria, I meant to say from dementia praecox, especially the catatonic type, they have many things in common, The characteristic thing is the way it develops in one who is charged with a serious crime and who is waiting trial, and the reason for the psychosis and the reason for the reaction is that it is an escape from, or an attempt at escape from the serious situation in which the defendant finds himself.

Q.   Then who does it come on, Dr. Holbrook?

A.   It comes on as an escape, as a way out, finding themselves in a situation from which they cannot extricate themselves, realizing the seriousness of their predicament, they develop this hysterical state.

Q.   Now is hysteria and insanity the same thing?

A.   Well, I much prefer--

Q.   Let me ask you this way- basing your opinion upon the history of this defendant, as you have ascertained it, the examinations of her as you have made them, and your observations of her here in the court room, in your opinion is the defendant at this time, and was she able on the 19th day of January, 1935, able to distinguish right from wrong, or realize the responsibility of her actions?

A.   I see no reason to believe that in January, the 19th or 20th, that there was any evidence that she was suffering from a mental disorder, and I believe that she was able to- I believe she was responsible- she was occupied, she was doing work in the usual way and conducting herself in such manner that not any notice was paid of any unusual behavior on her part. I believe at the present time that she is not suffering from any serious mental disorder, that she is probably responsible at this time- I believe she is responsible.

Q.   In your opinion she is responsible?

A.   Yes, people who suffer from hysteria are usually considered

164

responsible, hysteria, shell-shock and similar cases are not considered as productive or irresponsibility.

Now Mr. Collins will recall Mrs. Therrill and cross examine her.

Q.   You haven't seen her since she has been arrested, have you, Mrs. Therrill?
A.   No, sir.
Q.   Now, Mrs. Therrill, you say you were reared with her?
A.   Since 1914.
Q.   In other words, you live in the house with Mrs. Cook now?
A.   Yes, sir.
Q.   And that is where you were practically reared?
A.   Yes, sir.
Q.   You have known Miss Ouida practically all of her life?
A.   Yes, sir.
Q.   Mrs. Therrill, did you ever see her have any beaux?
A.   No, sir.
Q.   Did you ever see her out with any young men?
A.   Jus one time.
Q.   One time- you have known her all your life?
A.   Yes, sir.
Q.   All right, now Mrs. Therrill, you have seen her and her mother around the home there?
A.   Yes, sir.

Now Mr. Deavours will direct examine McWhorter Beers.

Q.   Your name is McWhorter Beers?
A.   Yes, sir.
Q.   Mr. Beers, what official position if any do you hold in connection with the First National Bank of Laurel?
A.   Cashier.
Q.   I will ask you, Mr. Beers, whether or not the defendant, Ouida Keeton, has a bank account in that institution?
A.   Yes, sir.
Q.   How many bank accounts?
A.   Has three.
Q.   Three bank accounts. I will ask you whether or not she has a safety deposit box in that institution?
A.   Yes, sir.
Q.   What is the total of her bank accounts, Mr. Beers?
A.   Well at the present time she has no checking account, but she has two saving accounts. The balance in one is $20,645.00- and the balance in the other

is $2,060.45, and the balance in the other is $17,923.14.

Q.   That is at the present time?

A.   Yes, sir.

Q.   Is there any difference in the name they are carried in?

A.   One is carried in the name Ouida Keeton and the other is carried in the name Miss O. Keeton.

Q.   Which is the larger account?

A.   The one carried in the name of Ouida Keeton.

Q.   The larger account, that is, the $17,000.00 account; now Mr. Beers, when was that account opened?

A.   January 15th, 1927.

Q.   And has it been active since that date?

A.   Well, I wouldn't call it active, it has been semi-dormant, some deposits and some withdrawals.

Q.   Some deposits and some withdrawals. Has that account increased and decreased from time to time?

A.   Yes, sir.

Q.   With what amount was it opened?

A. $500.00.

Q.   And that was when?

A.   January 15th, 1927.

Q.   And when was the next increase in it?

A.   January 15th 1929.

Q.   And what was the deposit at that time?

A. $1104.02

Q.   And when was the next increase?

A.   May 3rd 1929.

Q.   What was that deposit?

A. $8510.00.

Q.   So from time to time there have been deposits?

A.   Yes, sir.

Q.   What was the largest or maximum deposit in there at one time?

A.   In this particular account?

Q.   Yes.

A. $21,302.71.

Q.   And you say that account was opened when?

A.   January 15th, 1927.

Q.   Now take the other account, when was it opened?

A.   May 3rd, 1927.

Q.   And what is the greatest amount it has at any time had in it?

A. $12,200.00

Q.   Now when was it opened?

A.   May 3rd, 1929.

Q.   What was the amount in that account, Mr. Beers, say January 1st, 1935?
A.   2,060.45.
Q.   That was on January 1, 1935?
A.   Yes.
Q.   So that account has also been active?
A.   Yes.
Q.   There being withdrawals and deposits from time to time?
A.   Yes.
Q.   Now, Mr. Beers, I will ask you, during the period of time in which those accounts have been in your bank, who signed the checks?
A.   Miss Ouida Keeton.
Q.   Miss Ouida Keeton signed the checks?
A.   Yes, sir.

DEFENDANT RESTS.
STATE RESTS.
BOTH REST.

I hereby certify that the above and foregoing is a true and correct transcript of all the testimony taken by me on the trial of the above styled case; I further certify that I have filed this record with the Circuit Clerk of the Second Judicial District of Jones County, Mississippi, and that I have advised Mr. Alexander Currie, District Attorney, and Mr. Jack Deavours, County Attorney, Representing the State and Judge F. Burkitt Collins and Mr. Frank Clark, Representing Defendant, of the filing of same.

WITNESS MY SIGNATURE, on this the _5_ day of July, 1935.

Mrs. Hettie Belle Stevens
Official Reporter, Circuit Court.

THE STATE
VS
KEETON

The court charges the jury that in considering whether the defendant was able to distinguish between right and wrong at the time she is alleged to have committed the act with which she is charged, you may consider not only the evidence offered in the case which bears directly on this question, but all other facts and evidence introduced in this case which bear or touch on this question in any way.
Filed March 11, 1935   GIVEN.
T.L. Sumrall, clerk
By Mrs. L.M. Martin, D.C.

....

In cases where the defendant offers insanity as a defense to the crime with which he is charged, the court charges the jury that it is the law of this state that the test of criminal responsibility is the ability of the defendant at the time of the alleged commission of the crime with which he is charged to distinguish between right and wrong and realize and appreciate the nature and quality of the alleged criminal act.

GIVEN.

Filed March 11, 1935
T.L. Sumrall, clerk
By Mrs. L.M. Martin, D.C.

THE STATE

VS.

KEETON

    The court instructs the jury for the defendant that the law is that in the crime of murder one of the necessary elements in said crime is the presence of a criminal intent, and criminal intent involves two things; first, the exercise of the reasoning powers in which the result of the criminal act is foreseen and (clearly) understood; second, the exercise of reasoning power in which the result of the Criminal act is recognized as being contrary to the rules of law, *(and justice, and if a person is mentally unsound, one or both of these elements may be and usually are wanting) and if you believe from the evidence or lack of evidence or have a reasonable doubt in your minds created by the evidence or lack of evidence that this defendant at the time of the alleged crime was mentally unsound, and could not therefore fully in possession of the exercise of such reasoning powers to fully comprehend each of there elements of intent, then you must under your oath find her not guilty because of insanity.

GIVEN.

    Modified as indicated in pen. Not used after being modified and Given.

W.J.

Pack, Judge

(*Clerk's note: That part of the above instruction that is underscored and enclosed in parenthesis was marked out on the original instruction by Judge Pack.)

Filed March 11, 1935
T.L. Sumrall, clerk
By: Mrs. L.M. Martin, D.C.

THE STATE

VS.

KEETON

The court instructs the jury for the defendant that the law is that before there can be a crime, there must be an intelligence capable of comprehending the act prohibited, and the probable consequence of the act, and that the act is wrong, but that this is not so with an insane person whose power to reason has been dethroned, and if, from the evidence in this case, you have a reasonable doubt as to whether or not this defendant at the time of the alleged slaying was mentally capable of comprehending the consequences of her own act and recognizing the wrongfulness thereof, then it is your sworn duty under your oath to find the defendant not guilty because of insanity, and in so doing you will be enforcing the law as much as you would if you found her guilty provided you believed beyond a reasonable doubt that she was guilty.

GIVEN.

....

The court instructs the jury for the defendant that so sacredly does the law regard the life and liberty of its citizens that it will not permit the conviction of one of then unless the facts of the case, as given in testimony, upon the trial of this case, prove the guilty of the defendant by competent, believable, credible and trustworthy evidence, so accurate, clear and convincing as to remove from the minds of the jury every reasonable doubt of the guilt of the defendant.

GIVEN.

Filed March 11, 1935

T.L. Sumrall, clerk

By: Mrs. L.M. Martin, D.C.

171

THE STATE

VS.

KEETON

        The court instructs the jury for the defendant that the defendant is entitled to the verdict of twelve jurors, each and severally convinced beyond all reasonable doubt and to a moral certainty that the defendant is guilty of the crime charged in the indictment, and if there is a single juror whose mind wavers, or who has a reasonable doubt as to defendants guilt, either from the testimony then that juror, under his oath, must vote for an acquittal, first, last and all the time, until he is satisfied beyond all reasonable doubt and to a moral certainty, from the testimony, that the defendant is guilty as charged in the indictment.

GIVEN.

....

        The court instructs the jury for the defendant that if you should find the Defendant not guilty because of insanity and at the same time believing that she is dangerous, then the form of your verdict will be:

        "We, the jury, find the defendant not guilty because of insanity and certify that she is dangerous."

        In which event it will become the duty of the court to order her confined in the insane asylum.

GIVEN.

Filed March 11, 1935
T.L. Sumrall, clerk
By: Mrs. L.M. Martin, D.C.

THE STATE

VS.

KEETON

The court instructs you for the defendant that the words "aid" and "abet" mean pretty nearly the same thing, and before the defendant can be Guilty of murder by aiding and abetting, you must believe beyond a reasonable doubt and to a moral certainty from the evidence that the acts of the defendant while acting willfully and with malice aforethought at the time of the alleged slaying took the life of Mrs. Daisy Keeton or contributed thereto.

GIVEN.

Flied March 11, 1935

T.L. Sumrall, clerk

By: Mrs. L.M. Martin, D.C.

173

THE STATE

VS.

KEETON

     The court further tells you that any and all acts done by the Defendant after her mother was slain, if she has been slain, do not constitute murder within themselves, and that is true regardless of the atrociousness and brutality of the acts.

GIVEN.

. . . .

     The court instructs the jury for the defendant that if you believe from the evidence that the defendant had nothing to do with the slaying of her mother, if she was slain, but further believe that her mother was slain before her eyes and that the slaying if she was slain, dethroned the reason of this defendant, and caused her to act as she has acted, then under the law she is not guilty of murder,
and it is your sworn duty to find her not guilty.

GIVEN.

Filed March 11, 1935

T.L. Sumrall, clerk

By: Mrs. L.M. Martin, D.C.

THE STATE

VS.

KEETON

        The court further charged the jury for the state, that the gist of a conspiracy is the planning and agreeing to commit an offense, and that the existence of a conspiracy may be established by proof of acts and conduct, as well as by proof of an express agreement.

REFUSED.

Filed March 11, 1935

T.L. Sumrall, clerk

By: Mrs. L.M. Martin, D.C.

                                              ....

        You are further instructed for the defendant that ever though you may believe beyond a reasonable doubt from the evidence that defendant and W.M. Carter planned to kill Mrs. Daisy Keeton, and further believe from the evidence that defendant aided and assisted in carrying away and disposing of her Mother's dead body, this is not murder, but you must further believe beyond every reasonable doubt and to a moral certainty that defendant committed some over act before her mother was killed, if she was killed, that aided and assisted in the death of her mother.

REFUSED.

THE STATE

VS.

KEETON

       The court charges the jury, that should you, acting upon all of the evidence and instructions of the court in this case, believe beyond a reasonable doubt that the defendant committed or aided or abetted the commission of the crime with which she id charged in the indictment, the defendant is not entitled to an acquittal on the grounds of insanity, if you further believe from all of the evidence in the case beyond a reasonable doubt that the defendant had sufficient mental capacity to enable her to distinguish between right and wrong as to the particular offense with which she is charged, at the time of the alleged commission thereof.

GIVEN.

....

       The court charges the jury that if from all of the testimony in this case you believe the defendant to be guilty as charged beyond a reasonable doubt, then the form of your verdict should be:

       "We the jury, find the defendant guilty as charged and fix her punishment at life imprisonment in the State Penitentiary."

Or

       "We the jury, find the defendant guilty as charged, but are unable to agree as to her punishment."

GIVEN.

Filed March 11, 1935
T.L. Sumrall, clerk
By: Mrs. L.M. Martin, D.C.

Laurel, Mississippi

March 12th, 1935

Mrs. Hettie Belle Stevens, Official Court Reporter,

Laurel, Mississippi

Dear Mrs. Stevens:

You will please take notice that an appeal is desired and has been allowed by the court to the Supreme Court of Mississippi in the case of the State of Mississippi vs. Ouida Keeton, tried and convicted of murder in the Circuit Court of Jones County. You will, therefore, transcribe your notes and properly prepare the record for said appeal to the Supreme Court.

Yours truly,
Frank Clark
F.B. Collins

Filed March 12, 1935   Attorneys   for   the
Defendant
T.L. Sumrall, clerk
By: Mrs. L.M. Martin, D.C.

177

THE STATE OF MISSISSIPPI IN THE CIRCUIT COURT OF THE SECOND
DISTRICT OF JONES COUNTY, MISSISSIPPI AT THE FEBRUARY TERM
THEREOF.
THE STATE

VS

OUIDA KEETON

KNOW ALL MEN BY THESE PRESENTS, That we, Ouida
Keeton, Principal, and UNITED STATE FIDELITY & GUARANTY
COMPANY, surety, are held and firmly bound unto the State of Mississippi in
the penal sum of TEN THOUSAND DOLLARS ($10,000.00), for which
payment well and truly to be made, we jointly and severally bind ourselves, our
heirs, executors and Administrators forever.

The condition of the foregoing obligation is such that whereas
in the Circuit Court of the Second District of Jones county, Mississippi on the
12th day of March, 1935, Ouida Keeton, the defendant, was convicted of murder
and sentenced to life imprisonment in the State Penitentiary and to pay all costs,
and said Ouida Keeton feeling aggrieved by said conviction has prayed and
obtained an appeal to the Supreme Court of the State of Miss., to the September
tern thereof.

Now therefore, if the said Ouida Keeton shall prosecute said
Appeal with effect, and if the judgment of conviction be affirmed, said Ouida
Keeton shall surrender to the sheriff of Jones County, Mississippi within one
week after the judgment of affirmation shall be certified to said circuit court, and
shall appear before the said circuit court at the next term after a judgment of
reversal of said judgment and conviction shall be certified to said circuit clerk to
answer the charge of the State, and so to continue until discharged by law, then
this obligation to be void; otherwise in full force and effect.

THE DEFENDANT HAVING BEEN BROUGHT INTO THE COURT ROOM FOR THE PURPOSE OF ARRAIGNMENT, THE FOLLOWING PROCEEDINGS ARE HAD AND DONE:

BY: MR. F.B. COLLINS:

Now comes the defendant, Ouida Keeton, through her attorneys of record, F.B. Collins and Frank Clark, same being case No. 577, the State Vs. Ouida Keeton and W.M. Carter, charged with murder, and objects to the Court at this time bringing the defendant into court and arraigning the defendant at this time, for the following reasons:

That on the 13th day of February, 1935, on a petition sued out by this defendant, through her counsel in the Chancery Court of the Second District of Jones County, Mississippi, same being a petition for a writ of Habeas Corpus, the Chancery Judge of this District found that on account of the serious physical condition of this defendant she should be transferred from the Jones County Jail to the Laurel General Hospital, where she had been confined ever since; a copy of which decree in said matter is prayed to be made a part of this motion as fully as though copied herein; that said defendant has been confined in the General Hospital ever since said date, her physical condition has not improved, is not any better, and that it is dangerous to her health now to bring her into Court, and the act of the Court in bringing her, or ordering her brought into

Court will and has endangered her life;

THE STATE

VS.

OUIDA KEETON

It appearing to the court that the defendant, Ouida Keeton, has been convicted of murder and is now under sentence to the State Penitentiary for the balance of her natural life and it further appearing to the court that the Defendant, Ouida Keeton, has requested an appeal to the Supreme Court and that due to her physical condition, she is entitled to bail until the Supreme Court decides her case, as it is, therefore.

Ordered and adjudged by the court that the defendant, Ouida Keeton, be and she is hereby allowed bail in the sum of $15,000.00, made payable to the State of Mississippi to secure her appearance at the next regular term of the Supreme Court of Mississippi and that said bond be approved by the clerk of this court.

Filed March 12, 1935

T.L. Sumrall, clerk

THE STATE

VS

OUIDA KEETON

     This day came the District Attorney who prosecutes for the State, and the defendant, Ouida Keeton, in her own proper person and by attorneys, who on a former day of this term of the court, to-wit: February 20, 1935, was arraigned and entered a plea of not guilty to a charge of murder, preferred by bill of indictment, and by her attorneys announced ready for trial and issue joined between the State and the defendant; whereupon there came a jury of twelve good and lawful men, composed of A. Blackwell, J.D. Wade, Jess Bynum, Everett Trest, Vernon Bush, A.O. Blue, I.H. Howard, Austin Shows, J.M. Delk, O.R. Flynt, J.L. Davidson, and Matt Byrd................, the jury retired for the consideration of its verdict and this day returned into open court the following verdict, to-wit:

     "We, the jury, find the defendant guilty as charged, and fix her punishment at life imprisonment in the State Penitentiary."

     It is therefore ordered by the court that the defendant, Ouida Keeton, be and she is hereby sentenced to the State Penitentiary for the balance of her natural life.

Filed March 12, 1935

T.L. Sumrall, clerk

By: Mrs. L.M. Martin, D.C.

THE STATE

VS

OUIDA KEETON

We, the jury, find the defendant guilty as charged and fix her punishment at life imprisonment in the State Penitentiary.

Filed March 12, 1935

T.L. Sumrall, Clerk

By Mrs. L.M. Martin, D.C.

****

THE FOLLOWING PHOTOS

ARE OF AN EXPLICIT NATURE.

I APOLOGIZE IF THEY OFFEND OR SICKEN ANYONE IN ANY WAY, BUT THEY ARE A NECESSARY PART OF THIS BOOK, SO THAT YOU, THE READER CAN FORM YOUR OWN OPINION ABOUT WHAT REALLY HAPPENED TO MRS. DAISY KEETON.

****

These photos were copied from the exhibits for the trial of Ouida Keeton.

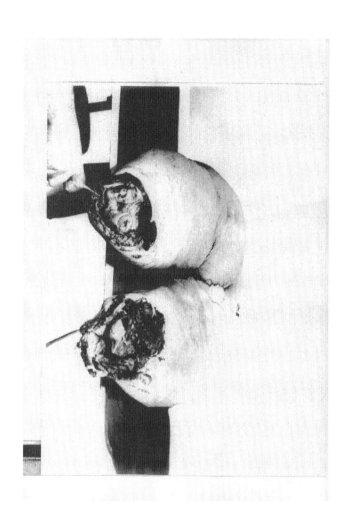

184

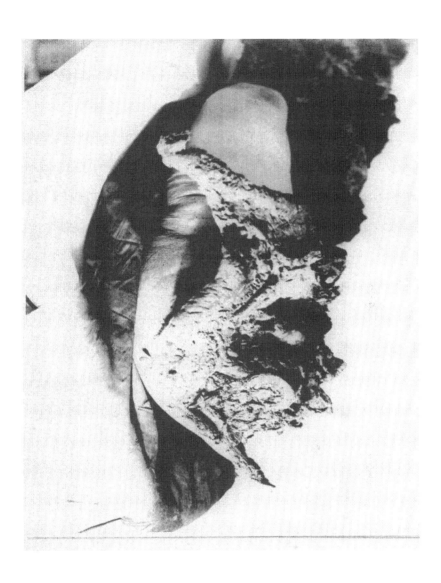

185

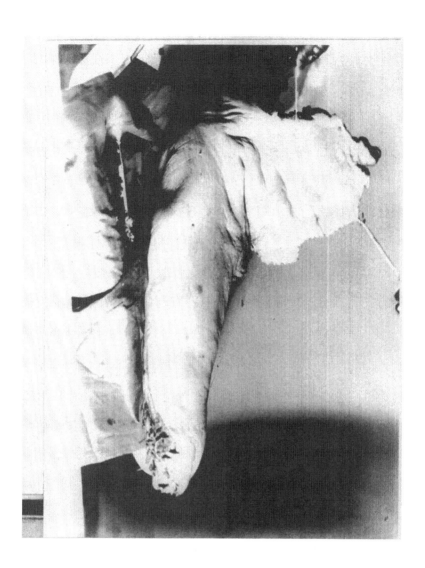

187

The trial of Ouida has brought out a lot about the beautiful young woman. She claimed in a moment of rage Carter struck her mother on the head with the fire poker, as she stood there by the fireplace. Her body fell to the floor in a puddle of blood. Ouida felt her pulse and found none; her mother was dead! Then she changed the confession to Carter shooting her mother in the head. In the catatonic state she was in she did exactly as Carter commanded.

Knowing something would have to be done with her body, she said they decided to cut her up and dispose of her in different places. Using the butchery tools she had purchased for her Hotel Schooling. Her head was cut off first and thrown in the fireplace to burn. Ouida could not stand to look at her face, her eyes open, looking at her in an expression of horror. She felt she was still alive and staring at her with her evil eyes. She even thought her mother was screaming at her, she covered her ears and shouted for her to shut up!

The smells emanating from the fireplace was unbearable, Ouida threw-up as she bent over the tub cutting her mother's body up. Carter with no training in butchery hacked at the body making deep cuts in the bathtub. As they went about the ghastly task of cutting her all up. She threw her pajamas and kimono in the fire along with her pillow and rug. As they worked into the night about their monstrous job. Flushing some small parts in the toilet.

As the ashes began piling up in the fireplace, they has to get the coal hod and shovel the ashes out into it and dump them outside the back door. Continually adding coals to the fire to keep it hot enough to burn the bones.

Finally coming to a point where *THE REST OF HER MOTHER* couldn't be burned. Her upper half and her pelvic and thighs. Carter decided they would each take half and dump it out in the country. He took the upper half and left in his car sometime in the late night, returning after a short time. She said he told her she would have to dispose of the other parts. She was so weak she couldn't do it that night or even the next day, Sunday. She waited until Monday morning. Carter left in the dark hours of Sunday morning for Mobile, to have an alibi. Ouida had a difficult time lifting her mother's pelvic and thighs to put in her car. She had to drag them across the back yard to the garage and into the car. The morning was very cold and rainy, she wasn't dressed as warm as she should have been. She wasn't able to wear her stockings, because she got pieces of intestines on them and on her shoes, the smell was sickening. She put on her short mink coat and high heels along with a dress and drove out Highway 11 North towards Sandersville. She was shaking all over as she looked at her side and saw the lower half of her mother. Her stomach and pelvic had come uncovered as the car drove down the slippery roads. As she reached over to cover the remains, the sight of the open end with intestines showing made her feel very sick. Her mind in a daze she wondered how could anyone do such a terrible thing. As she tried to remember the weekends events she couldn't remember anything other than Will coming to visit Saturday night and all three of them talking around the fireplace. She remembered being very tired and sleeping a lot. Then Monday morning she got up out of bed, dressed and did the job she was told to do. She acted as though she was in a trance completely unaware of her surroundings. As she drove the car, the cold rain was coming down in torrents, occasionally the car would slide and she would jerk the wheel back to keep from going off the highway. Finally she saw a road that seemed to be a good place, so she turned off the highway onto the dirt road. Almost immediately she realized it came to someone's house, as she passed the front of the house a man was standing up on the porch and stared at her, she was petrified, she just knew he was aware of her business out on that cold, rainy morning. Her eyes locked in on his, she suddenly reached over to her side and adjusted the covers on the body parts. Driving past she could feel his eyes on her, she turned the car around at the gate of the barn almost running into it. The road was so muddy. She drove back past the house slipping and sliding the whole way. Her heart was pounding with fear of being discovered. She got back on the highway and continued on her way. Finally she saw another road that looked deserted so she turned onto it. She only went a short distance, then stopped the car; got out and walked around to the passenger side. The rain was cold, but it wasn't the cold that made her shiver. She opened the door and grabbed the first bundle and drug it out of the car, then the other bundle, they were heavy so she could only drag them just a few feet from the car. She got back into the drivers seat and put the car in reverse, she backed into a small sapling and caught the bumper. She tried to go forward, but the wheels started spinning. She was gripped with terror. She got out of the car and walked to the highway. All she could think of was to get away from the evidence. She walked in the freezing rain on the side of the highway trying to think of what she would say if someone saw her. After walking, about twenty minutes, what seemed like an eternity; a car pulled up beside her. The man driving opened the door and asked her if she needed a ride. She said she did and got into his car. She asked to go to the nearest phone. He asked why she was walking in such cold bad weather. She told him she got stuck trying to do a good deed by giving an old lady a ride to her home. She said she was a nervous wreak from everything. He told her the nearest phone was Sandersville, then she asked if he was going through Laurel and if he was she would like to go there. He said he was and he took her to her house which he would have to pass on highway 11 into Laurel. He dropped her off and she offered to pay him, but he declined saying he didn't mind helping her. Mr. Kennedy(the man that gave her a ride) noticed a short mink coat, a thin dress, no hat, no stockings and high heel shoes. He couldn't help noticing she was a beautiful woman as well. When Ouida got into the house she went to her room. She stripped off all of her clothes, as she stood there naked she looked in the mirror, her hair was dripping wet, her face was pale, she looked at the reflection of the woman. She thought she was going to see someone else, but she only saw Ouida. Her mind confused; she dressed warmly and called Mr. Duckworth's garage, she knew he had a wrecker. He said he would be there shortly. He drove Ouida out to her car, got it unstuck and she drove it home. As he followed in his wrecker, she pulled into her driveway and he went back to his garage without stopping. She went to Maude's house to spend the night, saying Ma went on the train to New Orleans to see Eloise.

Ouida's fate was doomed from the beginning, her destiny preordained. It was not God's will for her to go unpunished for the evil she had done. She had to face the consequences of her actions, even though we will learn she was not completely responsible for her act of matricide. Her mother played a major role in the mental condition of Ouida's mind. It was being formed at an early age from the traumatic situations she was exposed to the physical abuse she suffered as a child and the unrelenting mental abuse her whole life. Whether she deserved what she got is hard to say. Can the human mind endure horrible things and suffer abuse over and over without it having serious effect on the person's mental state, to the point where that person snaps. It has been proven that to escape the real world they live in, the mind puts up a defense barrier and a person slips into psychosis. This behavior can dominate and control the behavior of the person. Their hallucinations even come in a spiritual form they hear God and voices and see people that are dead. Schizophrenia has symptoms of withdrawal reclusive behavior, eating disorders, glazed over expression, trance like moods and violent behavior that can come on in a moments notice. What ever diagnosis has been given to Ouida in her examination's by many specialist. She is most certainly and completely INSANE!
Poor Beautiful Demented Ouida!

Ouida began working part time for W.M. Carter at his lumber business when she was seventeen. With long black hair and big brown eyes and the figure of a twenty year old woman, she was a real beauty. It didn't take Carter long to begin his seduction of this bright young girl.

Carter, fifty-three years old and married with a family, Ouida was easy prey to his sexual advances, never realizing his intensions. Her womanly feelings arousing in her young body with a need for love and affection. Living in her imaginary world she created her first sweetheart, John only losing him to her dominating mother, her insecurities making this romance impossible to continue even in her delusions. Carter took full advantage of her needs. Taking her innocence from her like plucking a rose bud before it has fully bloomed. Her guilt produced another hallucination. Thomas, a young sweet pure man with a Christian soul. Her sinful liaisons' prompted the need to escape into a world of Christianity to try to forget the life she was living then, of course, it could not last, because her heart could not allow this lie when reality hit her in the face. Her only hope was a real father with Luke coming on the scene to rescue her from the fake father she was having an illicit affair with. Her thoughts were so full of shame, but yet she needed Carter. Of course in her dementia Luke would not be with her long. Her delusion of her imaginary father had to die leaving her broken hearted. Ouida's life went from hallucinations to reality she eventually didn't know the difference.

Was Carter's crime against this young virtuous girl a sin? Did his greed go even farther, to lust after the Keeton fortune, as well as Ouida's affections? Knowing the entire estate had been put in Ouida's name, was it too much temptation for him to resist with his own wealth virtually gone at the height of the depression? Was it Carter's idea to enter into a conspiracy with the easily controlled Ouida, to do away with her mother? If he did conspire with her, did he really know how fragile she was mentally and physically? If so, they entered into a "Devil's Deal", with no turning back from the pact that would send Ouida to a hell she could never escape from mentally, for the rest of her life. The murder and horrid mutilation of her mother's body was more than her mind could bear. It was at this point she went completely insane. That's why she had no memory of the events that followed.

And Carter...if guilty, what was his punishment? A couple of years out on bail, then freedom, because Ouida refused or was unable to testify against him two years later at his appeal.

ALL of the above facts were brought out at the trials. It is for you to decide what the truth is.

Now We Will Hear The Testimony In The Defense Of W.M. Carter Charged
With The Murder Of Mrs. Daisy Keeton.
IN CROSS EXAMINATION
BY MR. CURRIE
"This eventful night, he (Carter) was going around to see and saying goodbye to
all of his relatives, wasn't he?"

Miss Carolyn Carter for Defendant made the following statement:
Miss Carolyn the ten year old granddaughter of Carter said that her
Mother and Father had gone to a dinner party. Her brother Matt was in his room
asleep. She played in her room and went to bed. She said Carter was taking a
bath and packing for a trip to Mobile early the next morning. She saw him
dressed in a night gown ready for bed and he was going back and forth getting
things to pack. Her Mother and Father came home and went out again. They left
after 10:00 p.m., she didn't know what time they returned and Carter was gone
when everyone woke-up the next morning. They didn't see him again until
about 6:00 p.m. Wednesday evening.

Miss Rosa Carter for Defendant made the following statement:
Miss Rosa Carter, sister to Carter lived at 714, 7th Ave., Laurel, Ms.
Carter lived on 6th Ave, a few blocks above her. Carter came for dinner between
6:30 and 7:00. Carters brothers, Charlie, Eugene and his wife and Matt all had
dinner together, Carter left about 7:00 p.m.

Mrs. P.H. Decker for the Defendant made the following statement.
Pauline Decker is Carter's daughter, she lives at 846 6th Ave., Carter
lived half a block up from them. Next Carter went to his son's, Newton to visit
with him, his wife and their son who is eighteen. Carter left about 8:00 p.m.

Court stated that Carter's wife died in May of 1933.

Mrs. Walter Bailey for the Defendant made the following statement.
Helen Carter Bailey, daughter of Carter had two children, boys seven
and four years old. Carter came to visit at about 8:00 p.m. and left at 9:00 p.m.
with Newton's child, Carolyn. They left and went home across the street.

Miss Massalena Adams for the Defendant made the following statement.
Miss Adams, from Mobile, Carter visited their home from 10:00 a.m.
until 10:00 p.m., he was in and out all day. Carter went to the cemetery with her
to take flowers to a relatives grave.

Mr. Reece Boone for the Defendant made the following statement.
Mr. Boone, constable for Beat one, Jones County, found pieces of skull

and pieces of a finger and human hair in and around the fireplace.

Mr. Ethel Hicks for the Defendant made the following statement.

Mr. Hicks was at Beech's Barber shop when Carter was there at about 6:00. Carter was getting a shave from W.T. Chisholm. Mr. Carter left about 6:30.

Mr. Hamilton continued with the statement as the evidence that was collected from the Keeton home. He cleaned out the fireplace and found pieces of bone. He took knives from the kitchen and also found the pistol. Under the house where the fireplace was located there was found grease about 24 inches long, 6 inches wide and 2 inches deep. The hearth was freshly painted with green paint. The fire poker was found to have blood stains and hair on the handle end. A shoe was found with intestines on them and they had an odor of a dead body.

Ouida asked Carter when she saw him in the Jackson Jail, "What did you do with the rest of my Mother?" Carter denied, in front of authorities any guilt to the crime.

Mr. J. C. Jordan, garage attendant, testified for the Defendant with the following statement.

Mr. Carter was in Mobile at the St. Andrews Hotel, where I parked his car in the garage on January 20th and on the 26th. He checked in at 11:00 p.m., January 20th. His car was not there Saturday night January 19th.

Mr. P.J. Wallace for the Defendant made the following statement.

Mr. Wallace was Chief Clerk at the hotel and stated that Carter checked in the hotel at 11:30 p.m. on Sunday, January 20th.

Mrs. Phil Cook testifies for the State and made the following statement.

I saw Carter Wednesday with Ouida sitting in the car, they stayed there until 5:00. I shared the driveway with the Keeton's, I live across the alley. Ouida and her Mother looked as though they loved each other. I have knew the family since they moved here in 1912. I thought I saw Carter again Thursday morning. The Keeton's also owned a German Police dog that would bite.

Mr. C.A. Rowell testified for the State and made the following statement.

I heard three shots fired between 12:00 a.m. and 1:30 a.m. Sunday morning.

Mr. Hamilton testified for the State and made the following statement.

Back at the Keeton home in the Mother's room the floor had been painted, but around the hearth paint had been scrubbed off. It was a spot about 6 feet long by 4 ½ feet wide. Blood was on the head post and on the wall in back of bed. A spot that looked like blood was on the mattress, 12 to 14 inches wide. We found blood on the door casing in the bathroom. In the kitchen we found part of burned shoes and stocking in the fireplace.

Mr. Ethel McNair testified for the State and made the following statement.
I smelt an unusual smell burning from the fireplace of the Keeton home. It smelt like rubber and wool, it was Sunday night.

Mr. J.W. Smith testified for the State and made the following statement.
I smelled an odor burning Sunday morning. It smelled like hair and horn. I live about 178 steps from the Keeton home, North on Cross Street.

Mr. L.S. Brown testified for the State made the following statement.
I passed the Keeton home about 6:00 in the evening on Friday and saw a black Pontiac coupe was there. I also saw the same car at the Keeton home late Saturday evening after 12:00 p.m.

R.C. Buckalew (a negro) testified for the State and made the following statement.
I saw Carter on Front Street in front of his business talking to two Negros, between 2:00 and 3:00 a.m. Sunday morning. I caught the 3:00 morning train to Ellisville, where I work for the County home. After I heard about the murder I told the policeman what I had seen. I have know Mr. Carter since 1917.

Ouida admits her Mother was shot after midnight, instead of hit in the head with the fire poker at 8:00 p.m.

W.T. Trigg testified for the State made the following statement.
I went to the Strand Theater to see a movie, got out at 8:30, then went coon hunting at Tallahala Creek and came back at 1:30 a.m. I heard a pistol shots, three, it sounded muffled. I saw a one seater black coupe at the Keeton home, with the full moon I could see plain as day and the electric street light shined on the car.

Mrs. Trigg testified that she heard shots too, they lived 100 yards from the Keeton house.

Mr. George Quinnely testifies for the State and made the following statement.
I have known Ouida twelve to fifteen years and I also know Mr. Carter. I saw Mr. Carter visit the Keeton home two to four times a week. I saw Carter Wednesday at Ouida's. I saw him bring a plumber, Mr. McLeod, to the house to unstop sewage.

Facts were brought to light about the family. Eloise got married a week after Mrs. Daisy Keeton's death.

Mrs. Daisy Keeton's estate put up 10,000.00 in Ouida's defense.

Carter's lawyer presented to the court the training of butchering beef in an itemized program.

Jesse Woods testified for the State and made the following statement.

I passed the Keeton house around 11:00 after going to see a movie at the Jean. I saw a black Pontiac coupe in the driveway of the Keeton home.

R.H. Morrison testified for the State and made the following statement.

I saw Mr. Carter in his car Wednesday with Ouida for hours. Mr. Carter also visited the Keeton home two to three times a week.

More facts about the Keeton family were stated.

Mrs. Daisy Keeton's money was divided after her death, $2368.00, four ways, Ouida's was put in the bank, because she refused it.

Ouida also stated that she never had intimate relations with anyone other than Carter.

Now Ouida Keeton will state facts about what she remembers about her trail and about what was said. We will also see Ouida's testimony for the State in W.M. Carter's trail.

Ouida talks of how she has suffered since the death of her Mother. She says she was not guilty of killing her. She talked of how she was unable to speak at her trial, but remembered everything said. She said Carter asked for $10,000.00 for her defense. Ouida stated that Mr. Carter said that they wouldn't be able to prove anything about the murder on him. She talked about sitting in the car with Carter on Wednesday. She also said she did not learn how to butcher a cow in her training course in Washington.

Mrs. Daisy Keeton's estate was settled after her death and during trail. Earl got the house, David McRae got Ouida to deed the house on the Boulevard to his daughter, Maude Louisa. Ouida loved her niece, Maude Louise. Earl and David got in a fight about David trying to get Ouida's money, Earl threatened to kill David.

The following is the testimony of Miss Ouida Keeton, offered by the State, she is being questioned by Mr. Currie.

BY MR. CURRIE:
Q.   You are Miss Ouida Keeton?

A.   Yes.

Q.   Miss Keeton, you are co-defendant with W.M. Carter, charged with murder of Mrs. Daisy Keeton?

A.   Yes.

Q.   Under the law you are not required to give any testimony that would incriminate yourself and under the guidance of the court I am advising you of your constitutional rights, to claim that if you wish. Are you willing and do you desire to testify in this case?

A.   I do.

Q.   Miss Ouida, where did you live on an prior to January 19th of this year?

A.   At my mother's home, 539 Cross Street in the city.

Q.   That was on Cross Street here in the city of Laurel?

A.   Yes, sir.

Q.   How long had you lived there, approximately how long?

A.   20 years.

Q.   Is your father living or dead?

A.   Dead.

Q.   And how long has your father been dead?

A.   A little better than 20 years.

Q.   Something over 20 years?

A.   Yes, sir.

Q.   When, if at all, did you begin to work for this defendant?

A.   Around 15 years ago.

Q.   You are now 33 or 34 years of age?

A.   33.

Q.   So you began working with him when you were a girl of approximately 17 years of age?

A.   Yes, sir.

Q.   What business was he engaged in at that time?

A.   Lumber and real estate.

Q.   Where did he maintain his office, where was his place of business?

A.   Across from two filling stations, I think they call it Magnolia Street.

Q.   Miss Keeton, how long did you continue in the employ of this defendant?

A.   Up until about close to three years ago, I think.

Q.   Where was his place of business situated when you last worked for him?

A.   On Front Street.

Q.   The same as it is situated now?

A.   Yes, sir.

Q.   Prior or shortly prior to January 19th of this year, where have you been working?

A.   McRae's Filling Station.

197

Q.   Now, where is McRae's Filling Station located?
A.   On the Ellisville Boulevard.
Q.   Did the defendant, W.M. Carter, trade or come to that filling station while you were there?
A.   Yes.
Q.   State whether or not on the afternoon of January 19th, 1935, you saw him at that station?
A.   On Saturday afternoon, January 19th.
Q.   State to the Court and jury whether or not on January 19th you saw W.M. Carter at the McRae Filling Station?
A.   I did see him at the station.
Q.   Did you have any conversation with him there at the station?
A.   Yes.
Q.   During the time that you worked for Mr. Carter, the defendant, I will ask you whether or not, or what his custom was with reference to visiting and coming to your mother's home and you home. State whether or not he frequently came there.
A.   He came unannounced. He called often.
Q.   Was Mr. Carter at that time married or a single man?
A.   Married.
Q.   Miss Ouida, tell the court and jury whether or not in the period of your early employment with him there was established an intimate relationship between the defendant Carter and yourself?
A.   There was.
Q.   Was that intimacy-- how soon after you began or was in his employ that this relationship was established?
A.   A little over a year.
Q.   And you were a girl then about 18 years of age?
A.   Yes.
Q.   Along about September of this year, did you have a sister that went to New Orleans?
A.   In August I had one that went to New Orleans.
Q.   That was Eloise?
A.   Yes.
Q.   When Eloise went to New Orleans who did that leave in your mother's home?
A.   Mother and myself.
Q.   What was your mother's attitude toward that relationship and conditions?
A.   She did not approve of his coming to the house as often as he did but she did not know of the relationship.
Q.   Did the defendant Carter know of this disapproval?
A.   Yes.

Q.   State to the Court and jury what, if anything, was ever said between you and the defendant or by the defendant with reference to her objections and what threat, if any, was made-- just tell the court and jury the facts about it.

A.   Well, after my sister went to New Orleans it was very difficult for Mr. Carter and I to see each other. He said if I didn't make frequent trips out of town with him and agree with all plans that he made and agree to leave my mother on every occasion that he could arrange to leave his business that he would kill my mother.

Q.   State whether or not you agreed to go with him and make these trips as he suggested?

A.   I told him I could not leave mother.

Q.   And state whether or not you were willing to leave your mother under the circumstances?

A.   I wasn't willing to leave her there in the house alone.

Q.   When did this conversation first take place with reference to the death of your mother?

A.   The latter part of September, 1934.

Q.   Miss Ouida, what conversation, if any, did you have with the defendant on the date of January 19th of this year?

A.   I told him I wouldn't be working at the filling station after that Saturday for two weeks, and this trip to Mobile was discussed and he asked me to go with him, and in this same conversation all the threats were renewed at that time, and I told him I couldn't go with him.

Q.   You said the same conversation took place--similar--state whether or not you did or did not consent to go to Mobile with him?

A.   Not and leave mother alone.

Q,   State the place and when it was?

A.   The conversation was at the filling station on Saturday afternoon.

Q.   At about what time of the afternoon?

A.   About the middle of the afternoon.

Q.   How many automobiles did the defendant Carter own or sometimes use?

A.   Lincoln, Buick and Pontiac.

Q.   And what was the color of the Pontiac?

A.   Black.

Q.   And how many seats in the Pontiac?

A.   Coupe with a rumble.

Q.   A single seated car with a rumble seat?

A.   Yes.

Q.   After you saw the defendant Carter at the filling station Saturday afternoon on the 19th, when did you next see him?

A.   At night at home around six o'clock.

Q.   Now did he come to your home-- I will ask you this: What time did you

leave the filling station on that Saturday afternoon?
A.   Five o'clock.
Q.   And where did you go?
A.   Home, and took mother for a ride.
Q.   When you reached home did you find your mother there?
A.   Yes.
Q.   Approximately how long were you gone?
A.   Less that a half hour.
Q.   State to the court and jury how Mr. Carter came to your home, at about six o'clock, if you know, and just tell what transpired at that time?
A.   He brought a pint of vanilla ice cream but he didn't come in.
Q.   State whether or not he went into the house at that time?
A.   No.
Q.   When, if at all, did you next see Mr. Carter on that night?
A.   It was somewhere around 8 o'clock.
Q.   Where did you see him?
A.   At the house.
Q.   Who was at your home at that time?
A.   Mother and myself.
Q.   Any other persons there at that time other than your mother and yourself?
A.   No.
Q.   Have you a garage on that place?
A.   Yes.
Q.   Where is the garage built with reference to the house?
A.   About the distance from here in that post there, it's very close to the house.
Q.   It is in the back of the house, you say?
A.   Yes.
Q.   You said that the defendant Carter came to your home on that night, I believe you said somewhere around 8 o'clock?
A.   Yes.
Q.   How long did he stay there at that time?
A.   Something over an hour.
Q.   Where was he entertained, in what part of the house did you all occupy while he was there?
A.   Mother's bedroom.
Q.   State whether or not your mother remained present during the time he was there?
A.   She was present during the entire time.
Q.   After he had gone away that time state whether or not he again returned on that Saturday night?
A.   Something after midnight.

Q.   How do you know it was somewhere after midnight?

A.   The one o'clock train going north had gone up.

Q.   Miss Ouida, by what means did he enter your house on this late visit?

A.   I let him in the side window.

Q.   Tell the jury what transpired when he came back on this last visit and you let him in by the side window?

A.   He had only been in my room a very short time when we heard a slight noise in Mother's room and he ran in there and I heard shots fired and I went into the room and Mother-- I sat down on the side of Mother's bed and tried to get her to speak to me and she wouldn't , and while I was sitting there holding her, the man I thought was always my friend started abusing me and said, "Get up or I will do to you just what I did to your mother." I went all to pieces and I don't remember anything else.

Q.   You said that after the defendant had entered your room and was there a short while you heard there was a noise in your Mother's room? Miss Ouida, where was your mother when you entered the room and first saw her?

A.   She was in bed.

Q.   Where was she shot?

A.   The right side of her head.

Q.   Who shot and killed your mother, Mrs. Daisy Keeton, if you know?

A.   Mr. Carter.

Q.   What date was it?

A.   After midnight, making it January 20th.

Q.   After you saw him on this Saturday night, the 19th, or the morning of January 20th, when did you next see Mr. Carter?

A.   No more until Wednesday afternoon.

Q.   Where did you see him on Wednesday afternoon?

A.   In front of our home.

Q.   What automobile was he driving when he came there on Wednesday?

A.   No I remember it, the Pontiac.

Q.   State whether or not you talked to the defendant Carter there at your place on that date, Wednesday?

A.   I did.

Q.   And during your conversation with him there state whether or not the two of you discussed the means of escape for the killing of you mother, Mrs. Daisy Keeton?

By Mr. Riley, By Mr. Collins, We object that is leading.
By the Court: Sustained.

Q.   Miss Ouida, while the defendant was there state whether or not he asked you to give him a check for money?

By Mr. Riley, By Mr. Collins, We object as leading.

By the Court: Sustained.

Q.   What did he say to you there, tell the conversation to the jury?

By the Court: Was that on Wednesday that you are talking about?
By Mr. Currie: On Wednesday afternoon, the first visit there.
By the Court: All right, proceed.

A.   He wanted a check to help out in my defense.
Q.   How much did he want a check for?
A.   Ten.

By Mr. Riley: We ask the stenographer to read the answer.

A.   Ten thousand dollars.

By the Court: Ten thousand dollars do you say now, Miss Keeton?

A.   Yes.
Q.   State whether or not you gave him any check for ten thousand dollars?
A.   I did not.
Q.   What other conversation did you have with him there at that time, tell the jury about it?
A.   He told me some of these things that I was to relate.
Q.   What were some of the things he told you to relate?
A.   This kidnapping story principally as I recall it.
Q.   Why were you to tell the kidnap story?
A.   Why was I to tell it?
Q.   What was the purpose of his having you to do that?
A.   I don't know how to answer that.
Q.   After the time he was there the first time on Wednesday, did he come back later?
A.   Yes.
Q.   What time that afternoon did he again came back?
A.   It was late in the afternoon.
Q.   What automobile was he driving when he came back the second time?
A.   As I remember he was in the Buick at that time.
Q.   Tell the court and jury what his object or purpose of slaying your mother was?
By Mr. Collins: We object.
By Mr. Watkins: We object to that; that is a conclusion of law and a matter of opinion.
By the Court: Overruled, if she knows.
By Mr. Riley: We except.

A.   So that we could have more privileges.

Q.   State whether or not, if you know, the defendant, W.M. Carter, was personally familiar with every item and detail of the personal affairs of Mrs. Daisy Keeton?

A.   He was consulted on all business affairs.

Q.   Miss Ouida, is your mother now living or dead?

A.   She is dead.

Q.   During the course of you acquaintanceship with the defendant Carter, I will ask you to state to the court and jury whether or not you carried on a correspondence between the two of you and how it was done?

A.   There were some letters written while I was in his employ but not very many. Most of the letters were written after I was at home.

Q.   How did you receive those letters?

A.   I was usually the one to go to the front door, if I wasn't I would always see him to the door and he would bring letters to the house and hand them to me.

Q.   Did you hire Dr. Mitchell to testify for you?

A.   I did not.

Q.   Do you know Dr. Schmidt who testified in that case?

A.   Yes.

Here the jury is excluded and the following proceedings are had and done in the jury's absence.

BY MR. WATKINS:

If your Honor please, come days ago the defendant filed written application with the Court to require the prosecuting officers to produce for examination by the defendant, a stenographic transcript of the examination on various and sundry occasions of Ouida Keeton, by the prosecuting office's in reference to the death of her mother. We now desire, if your Honor please, to renew that application with the affidavits thereto attached. And we state to the Court that the prosecuting witness upon the stand has according to all information, her twelfth different account of this killing and the stenographic notes of the examinations had by the prosecuting officers will reveal this and enable us to lay proper grounds for impeachment, which we are not able to do with entire accuracy without them.

Upon presentation of the motion at a former day of this Court, after a hearing on the name, the Court withheld its decision until it was definitely ascertained whether or not Miss Keeton should take the stand and testify--

BY MR. CURRIE:

If the Court please, 1st the representatives of the State dictate and objection into the record before your Honor rules.

BY THE COURT:
Very well.

BY MR. CURRIE:
The County and District attorneys deny the right of the defense that they have delivered to them any statement that may have been taken in the course of the investigation of this crime, for the reason that their motion discloses and the record discloses that any purported statement that they are now asking for was made, if at all, by the co-defendant, Ouida Keeton, who has now been introduces as a witness, subject to full cross-examination, and the defendant likewise all through the trial, has had access to her, and that it is and unwarranted invasion into the prerogative of the investigators for the State, to require us to deliver any such statement, if any we possess, to the defense, and it is not competent or relevant evidence in the case.

BY THE COURT:
The Court now holds and directs the prosecuting attorneys, if they have in their possession any of the alleged documents set out in the motion, to produce the same instanter for the investigation of the defendant and defense counsel.

BY MR. CURRIE:
Let the record show, if your Honor please, that the County and District Attorneys, deliver into the keeping of the Court, the only signed copy of the only statement we now possess of Ouida Keeton.

BY THE COURT:
The Court receives it from the District Attorney, and in turn hands it to counsel for defense for inspection and examination.

BY MR. RILEY:
If your Honor please, we desire to take a little proof, in view of the statement just delivered to us, and we call Mrs. Leila Mae Martin as a witness. The following testimony was taken on motion of defense to require prosecuting attorneys to produce statements or confessions of Miss Ouida Keeton.

Now the defense calls Mrs. Leila Mae Martin to testify as follows.
By Mr. Ross:
Q.   You are Mrs. Leila Mae Martin?
A.   Yes.
Q.   What official position if any do you hold in Jones County?
A.   Deputy Circuit Clerk.
Q.   You were deputy Circuit Clerk in and during the entire month of January, 1935?
A.   Yes, sir.

204

Q.   Are you a stenographer? Do you write shorthand?
A.   Yes.
Q.   I will ask you, Mrs. Martin, if you were called on in January of this year, by County Attorney Jack Deavours, to take certain statements, questions and answers propounded by him and other officers of Jones County, to Miss Ouida Keeton?
A.   Yes.
Q.   Did you take those statements?
A.   I did.
Q.   On how many occasions did you take statements fro Miss Keeton?
A.   Three times.
Q.   Where and when was the first occasion?
A.   At Mr. Deavours' office on Friday night.
Q.   What time did you go there?
A.   About seven-thirty, I believe.
Q.   What time did you leave?
A.   Between eleven and twelve.
Q.   Were you during that time, engaged during the entire time in taking a statement from Miss Keeton?
A.   Well, most of the time, a short time I wasn't.
Q.   Where did you next take a statement from Miss Keeton?
A.   In the County Jail.
Q.   How long was that after you took the first statement in Mr. Jack Deavours' office?
A.   That was on Saturday after that Friday in Mr. Deavours' office.
Q.   The following day?
A.   Yes, sir.
Q.   When did you then take the third statement that you mentioned?
A.   At the Charity Hospital.
Q.   When?
A.   On Friday following that Saturday.
Q.   Did you take those statements in shorthand?
A.   Yes.
Q.   Did you later transcribe them?
A.   Yes.
Q.   How many pages did it make, all told?
A.   Around 80.
Q.   Where are the original shorthand notes or the notebooks that you took the original notes in ?
A.   I don't know, I turned them over to Mr. Deavours.
Q.   Did you retain a copy of this matter?
A.   I did not.
Q.   What did you do with all the copies, including the original shorthand

notes you made in this case?

A.   I turned them over to Mr. Deavours.

Q.   When did you turn them over to him?

A.   Immediately after I transcribed them.

Q.   How many different stories did you take?

A.   Well, two of them were entirely different, I would say, and the others differed as to parts.

Q.   Did you take any statement during that time alleging that Mr. Carter shot and killed Mrs. Daisy Keeton?

A.   No, as I recall- I don't remember a pistol being mentioned.

Q.   Mrs. Martin, did you ever take a statement wherein Miss Keeton told you some person other than Mr. Carter killed or assisted in the killing of her mother?

A.   No.

Q.   You didn't do that?

A.   No.

Q.   The last one- and this was taken where?

A.   At the Charity Hospital.

Q.   Who accompanied you when you took this statement?

A.   Mr. Jack Deavours and Mr. Wayne Valentine.

Q.   Did you take these statements correctly as Miss Keeton dictated to you?

A.   Yes.

Q.   Did you transcribe them correctly?

A.   I did.

Q.   If you were in possession of those original notes, could you again correctly transcribe that?

A.   Sure.

Q.   Could you Mrs. Martin, take the witness stand and correctly and intelligently read them to the jury, if you had the original notes?

A.   Yes.

THAT'S ALL.

CROSS EXAMINATION
BY MR. DEAVOURS:

Q.   You say in the various stories told by the defendant she never named any other person as being implicated in the murder except Mr. W.M. Carter?

A.   No.

Q.   An whenever she named a person as being implicated or assisting in it, she named W.M. Carter?

A.   Yes.

Q.   All of the statements agreed in that respect, did they not?

A.   Yes.

Q.   And the statements were turned over to the State long before court?

A.   Yes.
Q.   And the notebooks were also turned over to the State?
A.   That's right.
THAT'S ALL.
BY MR. WATKINS:
Our motion called for all statements whether they were sworn to or not.
BY MR. DEAVOURS:
They called for statements we have got in our possession. Mr. Currie has stated to the Court that he didn't have any statement except this one. If Mr. Watkins wants to put witnesses on the stand to impeach Mr. Currie he can do so, that's up to them.
BY MR. WATKINS:
Our motion in that they be required to produce each and every statement, whether signed or not, and if they can't do that, produce the stenographer's shorthand notes and we will have it transcribed.

BY MR. CURRIE:
You Honor only ordered us to produce in Court such statements as we have, if we have got the notes and the statements, we would have to produce them, if we haven't we can't produce them.

BY MR. RILEY:
If it is true that this lady made a number of statements contradicting what she said on the witness stand, it would be a crime before God and man for this man to be tried for his life and that jury not know what is in the statements, and we have got a right to know where they are or what became of them.

BY THE COURT:
Mr. Ross, the Court asked you to be seated; I will hear you now.
BY MR. ROSS:
Yes, sir. I now call Mr. Jack Deavours as a witness.
Now comes Mr. Jack Deavours, call by the defense to testify as follows.
BY MR. ROSS:
Q.   You are Mr. Jack Deavours?
A.   Yes, sir.
Q.   You are County Prosecuting Attorney in and for Jones County?
A.   Yes.
Q.   You have been since January, 1933?
A.   Yes.
Q.   You were during all the year 1934?
A.   Yes, sir.
Q.   She told the truth about the number of statements and number of pages in the statements, did she not?

A.   Now I wasn't present when all those statements were taken, Mr. Ross, but I understand that is true.

Q.   Who did the other questioning, if you know, other than you?

A.   I don't know, I understand one statement was taken in the jail in the presence of Mr. Currie when I wasn't there.

Q.   How many pages did you have delivered to you by Mrs. Martin?

A.   I can't tell you.

Q.   Does this comprise all Mrs. Martin delivered to you?

A.   No, sir.

Q.   What became of the ones not included in here that were delivered to you by Mrs. Martin?

A.   They were destroyed right after the Keeton case.

Q.   Why were they destroyed then?

A.   Because I had that last one acknowledged by the Circuit Clerk, and that one being the only sworn statement we had, that was the only one I considered of any value, and that last one was left with the Circuit Clerk, and about ten days ago I turned it over to Mr. Currie.

Q.   What became of the original notebooks or shorthand notes?

A.   Torn up and thrown in the waste basket.

Q.   You tore up the notebooks?

A.   Yes, sir.

Q.   And threw them in the waste basket?

A.   Yes, sir, they were of no use to us.

Q.   Why did you see fit to destroy the other statements that were taken down?

A.   Because that statement was signed and sworn to and the others were not.

Q.   Were the others sworn to?

A.   No, sir.

Q.   Were they signed?

A.   Yes.

Q.   Were those questions and answers to questions propounded to her by officers of this court?

A.   Some of them.

Q.   And they were different from this?

A.   Well, yes.

Q.   Telling an entirely different story of this alleged homicide to this one?

A.   Let's see- the first statement made was the story she referred to on the witness stand, about the kidnapping- that was published in the newspaper.

Now Miss Ouida Keeton resumes the stand and testifies as follows:

BY MR. WATKINS:

Q.   And you left Mr. Carter's employ about the year 1932, didn't you?
A.   Yes, about.
Q.   You stayed with him twelve years, that is true, is it not?
A.   Yes.
Q.   Your salary began at $75.00 a month, and during the peak of 1928 it went to $175.00, didn't it? That is true isn't it?
A.   No, $150.00 is all I got.
Q. $50.00- now, Miss Keeton, during all this period Mr. Carter was regarded as an experienced business man?
A.   Yes.
Q.   And when the depression came along it punctured a hole in a good many of what were regarded as good business men, and it got him, didn't it?
A.   Yes.
Q.   You were thoroughly familiar with his business were you not?
A.   Yes.
Q.   You were his confidential secretary and clerk?
A.   Yes.
Q.   Every entry made upon his books, you made it?
A.   Not all of them.
Q.   Most of them?
A.   Yes.
Q.   Miss Keeton, I wish to ask you if from the year 1922 or 1920, when you entered Mr. Carter's service, up until the 19th of January, 1935, if the most cordial relationships did not exist between your mother and Mr. Carter?
A.   On the surface.
Q.   Ma'am?
A.   On the surface, yes, they seemed to be the best of friends, because she was always courteous to him.
Q.   Ma'am?
A.   Because she was always courteous to him.
Q.   I will ask you if during the intervening time between 1920 and the date of her death, if Mr. Carter didn't extent many acts of neighborliness and kindness to your mother and other members of your family?
A.   Up until this--the 19th of January, 1935? We considered Mr. Carter a good friend.
Q.   Later you had a brother- and still have a brother by the name of Earl Keeton?
A.   Yes.
Q.   Is he still living in Laurel?
A.   Yes.
Q.   I will ask you if shortly subsequent to that time, he wasn't wrongfully and unjustly accused of a very serious crime?
A.   Yes.

Q.   In other words, your brother was wrongfully and unjustly accused of a serious crime in connection with a woman in this town?

A.   Not in this town, but he was-

Q.   I mean he was indicted and tried here in town?

A.   Yes.

Q.   Miss Keeton, don't you remember that in order to protect your brother form a mob, they had to take him from here and Mr. Carter protected him by-- that's true, isn't it? You know they had to take your brother away from here to save his life?

A.   All of those kindly acts, Mr. Watkins, is why this relationship existed between Mr. Carter and myself.

Q.   You had no servants? You did your own work?

A.   Yes.

Q.   Mr. Carter would frequently stop by and bring ice cream in the afternoon?

A.   Yes.

Q.   It was no unusual thing for him to do that was it?

A.   No.

Q.   Miss Ouida, when Mr. Carter would come there at night he would talk to the three of you, freely, yourself and your mother and Eloise- he would sit down in that room and talk to you?

A.   It was very seldom that Eloise would come in.

Q.   But I mean you and your mother?

A.   Correct.

Q.   And when Mr. Carter would go there even on the most casual occasion, your mother would sit down with you and he therefore you would talk together?

A.   Yes.

Q.   And that thing kept up until the 19th of January, 1935, isn't that true?

A.   Correct.

Q.   There was never a cross word between them, was there?

A.   Not between Mother and Mr. Carter, no.

Q.   You never heard you mother say a cross word to Mr. Carter, did you, up to that night?

A.   Oh, they would disagree on things, but nothing--

Q.   What I mean is, there was no cross about it- no disagreement?

A.   No, I wouldn't see that.

Q.   Of course Mr. Carter would argue with anybody, wouldn't he?

A.   (no answer)

Q.   He was a great arguer, wasn't he, Ma'am?

A.   Yes.

Q.   You have told the jury about your relationship- your intimacy with Mr. Carter- well, you had a beau by the name of Pearce, didn't you?

A.   I don't know him.

Q.   Who did give you a thousand dollar diamond pin?

A.   Mr. Carter.

Q.   Now when did you go down to work for your brother-in-law Dave McRae at the filling station?

A.   Some time I think the first part of December, or it may have been the latter part of November, I don't recall the exact date.

Q.   1934?

A.   Yes.

Q.   And after you went down there, Mr. Carter frequently bought gasoline there, didn't he?

A.   Yes.

Q.   For his cars-Mr. McRae and his wife at that time did not speak to your mother, did they?

A.   They spoke to her, yes.

Q.   That was all, was it not?

A.   Yes.

Q.   And they were very unfriendly were they not?

A.   Well, they had had family difficulty.

Q.   And one of your purposes in going there was to try to bring your mother and sister, Mrs. McRae, together?

A.   No, my sister noticed the nervous strain I was under, and she felt like if maybe I was busy part of the day, that would help me overcome it.

Q.   But at the same time relations were very bitter- unfriendly between your mother and Mr. and Mrs. McRae?

A.   Not bitter.

Q.   Unfriendly?

A.   But we weren't visiting each other.

Q.   Well, Mr. and Mrs. McRae lived in the home with your mother before then, didn't they?

A.   No, way back there, during the time he was overseas she was over there.

Q.   Well, she left there then, has a falling out with her and their relations have been very unfriendly?

A.   Oh, no, not at that time.

Q.   Well, they had a falling out subsequent to that?

A.   It has been about three or four years ago.

Q.   You had an aunt by the name of McKinstry who died and Mr. and Mrs. McRae were at the funeral and didn't even speak to you and your mother did they?

A.   My grandmother died.

Q.   And isn't it true that at the funeral Mr. and Mrs. McRae didn't even speak to you and your mother?

211

A. I couldn't answer that.
Q. You say Mr. Carter came down to that filling station on Saturday and bought gas on the 19th January, 1935?
A. Yes.
Q. That is true, is it Ma'am?
A. Yes.
Q. What time did he get gasoline there that day?
A. Around the middle of the afternoon.
Q. And when was the next time you saw him?
A. Around six o'clock.
Q. Where did you see him?
A. At home.
Q. That was after your mother had been riding and had come back?
A. Yes.
Q. Well, would you say it was before six o'clock or afterwards?
A. It was around six o'clock, I can't say the exact hour.
Q. Which door did he come in?
A. He knocked at the front door, he didn't come in.
Q. What did he bring with him?
A. A pint of vanilla ice cream.
Q. To whom did he deliver it?
A. To me.
Q. And went on off?
A. Yes.
Q. Then when did he come back?
A. Eight o'clock.
Q. Into which room did he come?
A. Mother's room.
Q. He had to go in through the living room and out of the living room into a little hall and into your mother's room?
A. That's right.
Q. And that bedroom is right back of your room, which you would enter through a door from you room?
A. Yes.
Q. How long did he stay there?
A. Something over an hour.
Q. Sat there and talked to you and your mother?
A. Yes.
Q. You say he came what time?
A. Somewhere around eight o'clock?
Q. And stayed how long?
A. Something over an hour.
Q. Did you have a fire in the fireplace?

A.   I don't recall whether I did or not, I imagine we must have.

Q.   What kind of fire, grate fire?

A.   Yes.

Q.   You sat around it and talked?

A.   Yes.

Q.   And she was perfectly friendly to him?

A.   Yes.

Q.   And then he got up and went out?

A.   Yes.

Q.   Went out the way he came in, at the front door?

A.   I don't remember that.

Q.   And you never saw him any more until about what time?

A.   After midnight.

Q.   What time did you go to bed?

A.   I imagine, Mr. - I don't recall the exact hour, I imagine ten-thirty or eleven.

Q.   Did you shut the door between your room and your mother's?

A.   Yes.

Q.   What time did your mother go to bed? Had she gone to bed before you did?

A.   No, we went to bed at the same time.

Q.   Ma'am?

A.   We went to bed at the same time.

Q.   Pretty good sleeper?

A.   Sound sleeper.

Q.   Ma'am?

A.   Sound sleeper.

Q.   What time did you say Mr. Carter came back there?

A.   Little after midnight.

Q.   Would you say it was around twelve-fifteen?

A.   After that time.

Q.   Would you say it was after twelve-thirty?

A.   After one o'clock.

Q.   I thought you said about twelve o'clock?

A.   It was after the midnight train had gone up and it doesn't go until one.

Q.   The midnight train goes up at one o'clock?

A.   Yes.

Q.   How long after the midnight train went up?

A.   Not very long.

Q.   And he came in your room, did he?

A.   Yes.

Q.   You let him in?

A.   Yes.

Q.   Is that true?
A.   That's true.
Q.   Then after he came in your room what happened?
A.   He had been in my room just a short time--
Q.   Well, a few minutes? Ten minutes?
A.   Something like that.
Q.   What happened?
A.   We heard this noise in Mother's room.
Q.   What kind of noise?
A.   As if though she was turning over in bed.
Q.   There had been no loud talking between you and Mr. Carter?
A.   No.
Q.   If you talked at all you talked in whispers?
A.   That's right.
Q.   There was no light in there?
A.   No.
Q.   The door was closed?
A.   The door was closed, the transom was up is all.
Q.   Transom was up?
A.   Yes.
Q.   He did what now?
A.   He went from my room into her room.
Q.   And did what?
A.   Shot Mother.
Q.   Where were you at the time he shot her?
A.   In bed.
Q.   After you say Mr. Carter shot your mother, you took hold of her head and where did you go from there?
A.   As I said, I went completely to pieces, I was torn up from seeing Mother there in that shape.
Q.   Well, when did you come to yourself?
A.   I have a faint recollection of going- trying to go to Corinth Church.
Q.   When was that?
A.   I don't remember the day.
Q.   What church did you say?
A.   Corinth Church.
Q   The Corinth Church?
A.   Yes, sir.
Q.   Where is the Corinth Church?
A.   That is the McKinstry burial place.
Q.   Well, when did you try to go out there?
A.   I don't recall the date.
Q.   What day was it?

A.   I don't recall the day.

Q.   Was it night or day? Hunh?

A.   I can only tell you what I have been told about that. I have been told that it was day, but I don't remember.

Q.   Who told you you went to the McKinstry Church?

A.   What I have read in the paper.

Q.   I see. Now then, when you went out of that room your mother was laying on the bed shot, wasn't she?

A.   I don't recall even leaving the room.

Q.   What became of her body?

A.   I don't know.

Q.   Who cut her body up?

A.   I don't know.

Q.   Who disposed of her body?

A.   I don't know.

Q.   Who took her body away from there?

A.   I don't know.

Q.   What did you say Mr. Carter told you to tell?

A.   This kidnapping story.

Q.   And what is all he told you to tell?

A.   No, numerous other little things.

Q.   Well, what were the others?

A.   Talking this old woman up there and then the kidnapping to follow.

Q.   And that's what he told you to tell?

A.   Yes.

Q.   All right, I will ask you if on Saturday afternoon- you know Mrs. Nicholson, do you not?

A.   Which Mrs. Nicholson.

Q.   Mrs. C. H. Nicholson?

A.   I know a Mrs. Nicholson that used to live next door to us, if that is the same Mrs. Nicholson.

Q.   You know her, don't you?

A.   Yes.

Q.   I will ask you if she wasn't down at that filling station Saturday afternoon?

A.   Possibly so.

Q.   You say this killing occurred Saturday night a little after one o'clock- where did you spend the night that night?

A.   I presume I was at home, but I don't know.

Q.   Did you sleep in your bed?

A.   After seeing the condition that Mr. Carter had placed my mother in, I was so shocked and nervous and torn up until I couldn't relate just what I did.

Q.   You don't remember anything else that happened Saturday night?

A.   I do not.
Q.   Do you remember anything that happened Sunday?
A.   I do not.
Q.   Where did you go Sunday?
A.   I don't know.
Q.   You have no recollection of anything that happened on Sunday?
A.   No, sir.
Q.   Did you stay in bed all day?
A.   I cannot answer that, the nervous shock was too great for me.
Q.   Who was that you were out riding with Sunday afternoon?
A.   I have no knowledge of taking a ride.
Q.   Will you deny that you were out riding with a man late Sunday afternoon?
A.   I couldn't deny or affirm anything.
Q.   And you are not denying or affirming it?
A.   No.
Q.   Is that true?
A.   That's true.
Q.   Why don't you remember going up the Bay Springs road and passing Mr. and Mrs. Nicholson on the road and waving at Mr. and Mrs. Nicholson?
A.   I cannot deny or affirm it.
Q.   And you are not denying or affirming it?
A.   No.
Q.   That is what you say- do you remember Monday morning, January 21st, 1935?
A.   I have a faint remembrance of that.
Q.   Just tell me what your recollection is of that morning-what do you remember?
A.   I can remember trying to go to Corinth.
Q.   To where?
A.   Corinth.
Q.   Where is Corinth?
A.   It is a place known as Corinth Church.
Q.   How far is it from Laurel?
A.   I don't know.
Q.   Is that in Jones County?
A.   No, I thing it is in Jasper County.
Q.   How did you go there if you don't know where it is?
A.   Oh, I have been there frequently.
Q.   But you don't know where it is?
A.   I don't know how many miles.
Q.   What direction is it?
A.   Well, it is North of Laurel.

Q.   Isn't it a fact that after-where were you that Sunday night? Where did you stay that Sunday night? Do you know?
A.   I don't.
Q.   Hunh?
A.   I don't know.
Q.   Where did you go on Monday?
A.   I have a recollection of making this trip up in the country.
Q.   Don't you remember that about half past seven o'clock Monday morning that you came out of the back porch of your residence and came down the sidewalk and met Mrs. W. C. Therrill? You know Mrs. Therrill, don't you?
A.   Yes, sir.
Q.   And didn't you tell her you were very tired you had worked Sunday night all night?
A.   I have no remembrance of any such statement.
Q.   You don't remember making that statement?
A.   On Monday morning I don't remember making any such statement.
Q.   Well, you recollect taking a portion of your mother's body and going up the road above Sandersville and throwing it out in the woods for the dogs to fight over?

BY MR. CURRIE:
We object, that is a very unkind, unwarranted and insulting remark to this girl, situated as she is, and we ask the Court to expunge it from the record; it is indecent-
Q.   I will ask you whether or not on Monday morning, about half past seven o'clock, you took all the remains of your mother's body that has ever been found and went up north of Sandersville and turned into a small private road and threw it off into the woods?
A.   I can remember trying to go to the McKinstry burial place.
Q.   I don't like to ask you an unkind question, but I will ask you if you didn't carve your mother's body up, either during the day Sunday or Sunday night, burn part of it, throw a potion of it through the commode or bath tub and take the balance up there and throw if off on the side of that little road?
A.   No, Mr. Watkins, I would like to tell you confidentially that Mr. Carter told me on Wednesday afternoon what was done with my mother-

BY MR. CURRIE:
You have the right to do that.

BY MR. WATKINS:
Q.   You have already been asked by the District Attorney on direct examination about that-
A.   You asked me for statements I was to tell, not anything that was said

confidentially.

Q,   All right, what did he tell you he had done with the body?

A.   He told me that that was the part that I carried off, that he gave me there, that it was wrapped right there at home, and he told me I had been most careless in leaving it and exposing of it in the manner that I did.

Q.   Well, I understood you to say you didn't remember about it?

A.   I remember what Mr. Carter told me on Wednesday afternoon?

Q.   Then you had come back to yourself on Wednesday afternoon?

A.   I didn't come back to myself entirely, I was still very nervous and torn up-

Q.   Well, I'm asking you--

BY MR. CURRIE:

        Let her answer the question.

A.   Then I asked him- I said, "Where is the rest of my mother's body?" and he said, "It is just as though buried at sea."

Q.   Coming back to the question I asked you- I will ask you if Monday morning about half past seven you didn't take all that had ever been found of your mother's body, take it in your car up above Sandersville and thrown it out?

A.   He says I carried it there.

Q.   I'm asking you, Miss Keeton?

A.   And I will say that I did, there is every evidence in the world that I did.

Q.   Do you remember doing so?

A.   I remember trying to go to the McKinstry cemetery.

Q.   Have you any recollection now of taking the portion of your mother's body up the road Monday morning and throwing it out on the road?

A.   If it hadn't been that I was so shocked and torn up, my mother's body wouldn't have been taken there.

Q.   You left it there?

A.   It has been proven that I left it there.

Q.   I'm asking you now if you remember it?

A.   No, if I did it wouldn't have been there.

Q.   You wrapped it up in order to take it there?

A.   He says we wrapped it up.

Q.   I'm asking you of your own knowledge, do you recognize the pieces of cloth exhibited before you, which are marked exhibits "1", "2" and "3" to the Evan's testimony?

A.   There are many more like it at home.

Q.   In other words the pieces of cloth came from you home?

A.   There are many more there like it.

Q.   What are they? Pieces of sugar sacks?

A.   I don't know whether they are sugar, meal or what, but there are a number of them there at home.

Q.   Isn't it true that you then drove from there up the road to where nobody lived and threw the portion of your mother's body out?

A.   It has been proven that I did.

Q.   Don't you remember it?

A.   No, sir.

Q.   I will ask you to state then if it isn't true that you got in the middle of the road and started walking to Laurel and walked about six miles when a man by the name of Kennedy picked you up and brought you to Laurel?

A.   I am not denying it.

Q.   Do you admit it?

A.   No, sir.

Q.   Not a bit in the world- just all a stone wall to you - just a blank to you, is that right?

A.   Mr. Watkins, if you were to go to the bedside and pick up your mother's head and see the blood stream out of her nose and see the man that you thought has always been your friend-

BY MR. RILEY, MR. COLLINS, MR. ROSS AND MR. CURRIE;
We object.

BY MR. CURRIE:
Let her answer.

BY MR. CURRIE:
She's got a right to explain.

BY MR. COLLINS:
And we make a motion that the statement be expunged and the jury be instructed to totally disregard it.

BY THE COURT:
Overruled.

BY MR. COLLINS:
Because it is incompetent, irrelevant and immaterial, is based upon supposition, and is entirely for the purpose of stage play.

Q.   What did you do Tuesday?

A.   What did I do Tuesday?

Q.   Yes.

A.   I sat there in that house, went in Mother's room and stayed there in Mother's room a good long time Tuesday morning. I don't know anything I did Tuesday afternoon.

Q.   Well, when was the next time you saw Mr. Carter?

A.   Wednesday afternoon.

Q.   Well, where were you Wednesday? Where were you Wednesday morning?
A.   I was at my aunt's house Wednesday morning.
Q.   You remember that?
A.   I remember helping her prepare dinner.
Q.   Did you tell her Mr. Carter shot your mother?
A.   No.
Q.   Did you say anything to your brother about it?
A.   I hadn't seen my brother.
Q.   Well, you learned that it happened, did you?
A.   I knew my mother was gone.
Q.   Did you know Mr. Carter had shot her Wednesday morning?
A.   Yes, I knew it.
Q.   Why didn't you go and tell your brother?
A.   Because, if I had gone and told my brother what had happened the State of Mississippi would have been saved the trial of Ouida Keeton and W.M. Carter.
Q.   Then you didn't tell him. Did you tell the Chief of Police?
A.   I told no one.
Q.   There was your mother you say shot down Saturday night, you were back conscious Wednesday morning, and you didn't tell the chief of Police, or the Sheriff anything about it, is that true?
A.   Mother was gone, there was nothing I could do to bring her back and be just where I am today.
Q.   And that is your explanation. Now I will ask you if Wednesday afternoon, subsequent to two o'clock, Mr. Carter didn't stop in front of your residence, coming back from Mobile in his Pontiac?
A.   I don't remember the hour, but it was some time in the afternoon.
Q.   I will ask you if it wasn't in the broad open daylight?
A.   It was in the afternoon.
Q.   I will ask you if when you got toward the front you didn't see him standing on your front steps?
A.   I don't know whether he was on the steps or in the yard.
Q.   You went out there to meet him?
A.   Yes.
Q.   I will ask you if you didn't go out there and say to him, "Mother's gone to New Orleans"?
A.   I made that statement.
Q.   Do you know Mrs. Phil Cook?
A.   I do.
Q.   You have known Mr. Phil Cook twenty years?
A.   Ever since I have been in Laurel.
Q.   And in the presence or hearing of Mrs. Cook you said to Mr. Carter

"Mother's gone to New Orleans?"

A.   Before making that statement to Mr. Carter I had seen the boys across the street out in front.

Q.   The filling station attendants?

A.   Yes, but you didn't have to say "Mother's gone to New Orleans," did you?

A.   If you had had you life threatened as I had, and Mother was gone.

Q.   You went out there in the broad open daylight, about two o'clock in the afternoon, walked out in front with Mr. Carter and got in his car and sat there and talked, didn't you?

A.   I don't recall whether I was in the car or not.

Q.   Sat there and talked to Mr. Carter over an hour right out in the broad open daylight?

A.   I talked to him, I don't know exactly how long.

Q.   You knew he had a friend named Miss Adams in Mobile?

A.   She has been a quest in my home.

Q.   I will ask you didn't you say to him your pipes in the house weren't working and if he didn't go and get a plumber?

A.   The pipe out in the back.

Q.   You asked him to have it fixed, didn't you?

A.   Yes, as customary.

Q.   I will ask you if he didn't get in his car and go up town and come back with a plumber by the name of McLeod and if they didn't walk around by the side of your house and fix that pipe?

A.   They patched the pipe.

Q.   I will ask you if Mr. Mcleod didn't finish that pipe along between four and five o'clock? And then he and Mr. Carter drove off?

A.   They fixed it that afternoon.

Q.   And when the pipe was fixed, Mr. Mcleod and Mr. Carter got in the car and drove off?

A.   That is correct.

Q.   And you never saw Mr. Carter again until you met him in jail in Jackson, Mississippi, to accuse him of the killing of you mother?

A.   That was understood.

Q.   Was it Wednesday or Thursday you went to the beauty parlor to get you hair curled?

A.   I understand it was Thursday.

BY MR. WATKINS:

Q.   You went to the beauty parlor, did you?

A.   I did go to the beauty parlor.

Q.   Now, Miss Ouida, you say you went to the beauty parlor on Thursday afternoon- which beauty parlor did you go to?

221

A.   Mrs. Buntyn's
Q.   Now where did you spend Thursday night?
A.   I spent the balance of that time at my aunt's house.
Q.   You didn't go to Fine's as they call it, and try on a dress during that week?
A.   I don't remember trying on any clothes at all.
Q.   What did you buy in there?
A.   Nothing.
Q.   Did you go in there?
A.   I was in Fine-Brothers.
Q.   And looked around in there?
A.   Yes.
Q.   Any you went back to your aunts' Thursday night, and you remember that, don't you, Ma'am?
A.   That's right.
Q.   Who are your aunts?
A.   Mrs. Richeimer and Miss McKinstry.
Q.   Now Friday morning the Chief of Police came up to see you, didn't he, with Mr. Deavours and some other gentlemen?
A.   Mr. Brown and Mr. Deavours were up there.
Q.   How long have you known Mr. Brown?
A.   Practically all my life.
Q.   All your life- known him as Chief of Police, haven't you?
A.   Yes.
Q.   Now they came and knocked at the door and asked to come in?
A.   I met them at the front door.
Q.   Well, you remember that, don't you?
A.   Yes.
Q.   You let them in, didn't you?
A.   Yes.
Q.   And Chief Brown asked you if he could go through the house, didn't he?
A.   I don't remember.
Q.   Well, he did go through the house, didn't he?
A.   I don't know whether he did at that time or not.
Q.   Well, did he go in the kitchen and look behind the door?
A.   I don't know whether he did or not.
Q.   Well, he said he wanted to see your automobile and you told him where it was?
A.   That is true.
Q.   I'm asking you if Chief Brown and Mr. Deavours asked you where your mother was, and if you didn't say "Mother's gone to New Orleans."
A.   (Determined not to tell him.)

222

Q.   You will not tell me?
A.   (Determined not to tell Chief Brown at that time.

BY THE COURT:
Q.   If you said that you may say yes or no.
A.   Yes.

BY MR. WATKINS:
Q.   That Mr. Carter had killed you mother?
A.   Yes.
Q.   Well, you weren't afraid of anybody then, certainly you had all the police protection you wanted then, didn't you?
A.   There was mighty little to be done then.
Q.   Mighty little then, was it?
A.   Yes.
Q.   Now I will ask you if when Mr. Brown was in the kitchen, if he didn't pick up these four knives?
A.   I don't remember whether he did or not.
Q.   I will ask you if he didn't pick up one of these long brought knives and call your attention to something which looked life human hair down next to the handle?
A.   I don't recall.
Q.   Any don't you know you told him it wasn't human hair you had been cutting some kind of vegetable matter?
A.   No. I was trimming ferns when they came.
Q.   Why, Miss Keeton, when he came there you were down there washing up blood stains in front of the fireplace, weren't you?
A.   Not as I recall, I had already cleaned up the house on Friday morning, and we had had a freeze and there was a great deal dead in the ferns and I was cutting it out.
Q.   Where did you get this particular knife?
A.   They were brought through the W.M. Carter Lumber Company.
Q.   How many years ago?
A.   A number of years ago.
Q.   Do you mean you had the W.M. Carter Lumber Company order the knives?
A.   I ordered the knives.
Q.   How many of them?
A.   These two over here.
Q.   You mean this one and this one?
A.   Yes.
Q.   Your mother was killed in bed. Then what were you painting to cover up? What were blood spots going around that fireplace then?

A.   The bed linens--

Q.   I'm talking about the fireplace--

A.   The pillows mother's head was on and the bed linens and all that was burned there, and a small rug adjoining her bed.

Q.   Who burned them?

A.   I burned them.

Q.   When did you burn them?

A.   Wednesday.

Q.   What time Wednesday?

A.   What time Wednesday?

Q.   Yes.

A.   A little bit after the noon hour.

Q.   You burned what now Ma'am?

A.   The bed linens.

Q.   What else?

A.   Pillows.

Q.   Didn't you also burn your sleeping garments?

A.   I don't remember when those were burned.

Q.   Didn't you tell Mr. Brown that all your sleeping garments you had on were covered with blood and you burned them?

A.   I possibly made that statement.

Q.   You deny that do you?

A.   I don't deny telling him that.

Q.   You deny that when you burned the bed linens you also burned your sleeping garment because it was covered with the blood of your mother?

A.   I won't deny it.

Q.   You won't deny it. Why, Miss Keeton, on Wednesday the blood would have been dry and wouldn't have gotten on the fireplace wouldn't it?

A.   That was just the trouble, it wouldn't come up, it was dry.

Q.   How was that?

A.   It wouldn't come up.

Q.   Why if you took the bed linens off of your mother's bed Wednesday and took them there to that fireplace Wednesday, that blood was dry, wasn't it, ain't that true, Ma'am?

A.   Possibly so.

Q.   You weren't with him. Well they went out there in the ashes, didn't they, in your yard, and they found pieces of human bones, didn't they?

A.   Not in my presence.

Q.   Huh?

A.   Not in my presence.

Q.   But out there in your yard in the ashes they found pieces of human bones, didn't they?

A.   I understand that was done after I was arrested, but I didn't hear anything about that then.

Q.   Found a piece of human skull, didn't they?
A.   I don't know.
Q.   Found pieces of human fingers, didn't they?
A.   I don't know.
Q.   Found pieces of human hair, didn't they?
A.   I don't know.
Q.   You will not deny it?
A.   I have never seen any of those things.
Q.   I will ask you if it isn't true that every time thereafter you made a fire in the fireplace, grease would steam up in the floor up around the fireplace?
A.   I hadn't stayed there, I had stayed up at my aunt's.
Q.   Miss Keeton, when Mr. Brown went up there that Friday morning your hands and wrists were scratched, weren't they? Weren't they?
A.   Possibly so.
Q.   How did you get those scratches and scars?
A.   I had done a great deal of heavy housework.
Q.   When had you done all that heavy housework?
A.   We did all of our housework practically.
Q.   Isn't it a fact that Chief Brown asked you how you got those scars and you told him you did it bringing wood in?
A.   I brought wood in.
Q.   But that isn't where you got those scars?
A.   I don't know where I got the scars.
Q.   Your wrists and hands were scarred, weren't they?
A.   I don't recall any scars, possibly they were.
Q.   Do you remember having any difficulty with them Saturday night Ma'am?
A.   None whatsoever.
Q.   And isn't it true that you left leg was blue from your knee down to your ankle?
A.   There were bruises on both of them.
Q.   Where did you get those bruises?
A.   From the man- I was sitting on the side of the bed, with those sleeping garments of mine on- that they say were burned because the blood on them, that was Mother's blood all right, because I was holding her head--
Q.   All right, I asked you about the bruises--
A.   And while I was sitting there holding her head he kicked me and said "If you don't stop and get up I will do to you what I have done to your mother."
Q.   Was that after the shots were fired?
A.   It was after the shots were fired.
Q.   I thought you said you didn't remember anything after the shots were fired?

A.   I beg your pardon, I said this morning that the man I had always thought was my friend abused me while I was sitting there.

Q.   But you didn't say he kicked you?

A.   I said he abused me. You asked me about the bruises, I wouldn't have told it if you hadn't.

Q.   Well, Miss Keeton, you didn't state this morning that your leg became bruised by reason of his kicking you, did you?

A.   I said he abused me.

Q.   Is that what you meant? That he kicked you?

A.   That is exactly what I meant.

Q.   Did he kick you from your knee down to your shoe?

A.   I had bruises from my knee down.

Q.   Any you say you had bruises on both of your legs?

A.   I don't remember the extent of the bruises now.

Q.   Miss Keeton, did you and your mother have any difficulty that night?

A.   No.

Q.   Miss Keeton, did you take her body in there to that bath tub and put it into the bath tub and cut her body up?

A.   That would have been impossible.

Q.   And you didn't do it? You didn't do it?

A.   I have no- with the shock, I have no knowledge of anything after I was sitting there on her bed, but to take my mother in there, with the weight that she was, that would have been impossible, Mr. Watkins.

Q.   And you didn't do it, If you did you have no recollection of it have you?

A.   I say it would have been impossible.

Q.   And you say your mind went blank just because Mr. Carter said that to you and abused you?

A.   The shock of seeing mother there in that condition is really what brought it on.

Q.   When?

A.   As I was sitting there holding her head, and as I said, the last thing I remembered was sitting there on the bed holding her dead and that is when he kicked me.

Q.   That was Friday- now Miss Keeton, you testified this morning about a lawsuit your mother had with a man named Robinson, is that true?

A.   Yes.

Q.   And they got a judgment against her for $9000.00 didn't they?

A.   Something like that.

Q.   And then It was that your mother took her bonds and her property and put it in your name, didn't she?

A.   That's right.

Q.   And deeded the house to you at that time, did she not?

A. Yes, all transfers were made at that time.

Q. Every transfer was made to you, wasn't it.

A. Yes.

Q. Then at the time of your mother's death there was some twenty or twenty-one thousand dollars in the First National Bank in you savings account which belonged to her that you carried in the name of Ouida Keeton?

A. There were two accounts in the First National Bank.

Q. I am asking you about the one which carried your mother's funds, which you carried in the name of Miss Ouida Keeton, the other account you carried of your own was carried in the name of Miss O. Keeton?

A. Oh, you mean in this bank, that's right.

Q. That represented the balance of all the bonds that your mother had at the time of this judgment, it was converted into money?

A. Represented the sale of the bonds she had at that time.

Q. Nobody had stolen any bonds from her?

A. No.

Q. Nobody had beaten her out of any bonds.?

A. No.

Q. And if your mother wanted any money, she had to get it from you, didn't she?

A. We established a checking account for her so she wouldn't have to be bothered with writing checks.

Q. But you drew all the checks?

A. I beg your pardon the checks from the savings were transferred to a checking account.

Q. And she drew her own?

A. She drew her own checks.

Q. I will ask you then if your mother didn't want that money put back in her name?

A. If she had, it would have been put there.

Q. Ma'am?

A. There had been no mention of that.

Q. There had been no disagreement about that?

A. No.

Q. And you and an account, kept in the name of Miss Ouida Keeton, No. 7374, and you had a balance on January 17, 1932, of $20,000.00 didn't you?

A. I don't remember exactly.

Q. Approximately that- and that account had run down to where at the time of your mother's death it was approximately $2000.00?

A. Correct.

Q. In other words, you had spent the money from approximately $21,000.00 to about $2000.00?

A $6,500.00 of that was invested in Washington.

Q. $6,500.00 was invested with Mr. Grace?

A.   Yes.

Q.   Now the statement you say you made, when did Mr. Carter tell you to make it?

A.   The kidnapping was discussed Wednesday afternoon.

Q.   Oh, that was what he said when he came back, was it?

A.   Wednesday afternoon.

Q.   What did he tell you to say now?

A.   What I tried to say, I don't remember his exact words.

Q.   He told you to say two men came to your house on Sunday, kidnapped you, locked you in the closet, got in you car Monday morning and rode with you to Sandersville?

A.   I was very confused, and as I said , I tried to tell it in exactly the words that Mr. Carter said--

BY MR. RILEY:
We object.

BY MR. COLLINS:
We are trying this man for his life--
We object to that and move that it is excluded.

BY THE COURT:
Let your answer be responsive to the questions Miss Keeton.

BY MR. WATKINS:

Q.   All right, what did Mr. Carter tell you about the kidnapping?

A.   What I tried to tell.

Q.   State now what it was that you told- repeat it now?

A.   About this kidnapping story, making this trip-

Q.   State it like you told it to the officers?

A.   I couldn't do that, it would be utterly impossible.

Q.   Couldn't do it to save your life?

A.   I couldn't state it word for word.

Q.   And you wouldn't try to repeat it- still you say Mr. Carter told you to say that?

A.   I say Mr. Carter told me to tell the kidnapping story, but to repeat it word for word would be utterly impossible.

Q.   Who was to make up the kidnapping story, did he make it up or tell you to make it up?

A.   He made up the kidnapping story.

Q.   Is that the one you told about the bonds and about the kidnapping on Sunday?

A.   I made numerous statements about the kidnapping.

Q.   But I mean did he tell you about the kidnapping on Sunday, locking you up in the closet and going back up there in the car on Monday?

A.   As I said, I don't recall the Sunday part of it.

Q.   Miss Keeton, during the examination in Mr. Deavours' office, didn't you tell Chief Brown that you had left in your home your purse, and that in your home he would find a pistol, and asked him to go and get them?

A.   I recall making the statement, but I don't know whereabouts I made it.

Q.   As a matter of fact, you had left the pistol in your wardrobe, tied up in a handkerchief, wasn't it?

A.   That is not the fact about it.

Q.   All right, where did you leave it?

A.   The pistol was left there in Mother's room.

Q.   How did it get in your wardrobe?

A.   I put it in my wardrobe.

Q.   Sometime during that week?

A.   As I recall it was that Friday morning.

Q.   Friday morning?

A.   Friday morning when I was cleaning up.

Q.   You mean the Friday morning they came there?

A.   As I remember.

Q.   Well, are you sure about that?

A.   Sure enough I will say yes.

Q.   I will ask you if in that statement Chief Brown asked you if this was a premeditated murder and you stated to him that it started last September, do you remember that?

A.   I told him threats were made the latter part of September and on through.

Q.   Then you did tell him that the matter started last September?

A.   The first threat was made the latter part of September.

Q.   And didn't you tell him that Saturday, the 19th, Mr. Carter came to the filling station on the Boulevard, the McRae Filling Station, twice, and it was planned to be done that night?

A.   Threats were renewed that afternoon.

Q.   Did you and him enter into a plan that evening at the filling station that your mother would be killed that night?

A.   Didn't enter into any plan.

Q.   Didn't you tell Mr. Brown that he said to you, "I have got my alibi made, all you have got to do is do like I tell you to." did you make that statement to Mr. Brown as coming from Mr. Carter?

A.   The alibi in detail.

Q.   That he said "I have got my alibi made, all you have to do is to do like I tell you to"?

A.   That is correct.

Q.   That is what Mr. Carter said to you?

A.   Yes.

Q.   When was the first time that you told them about the killing-- that your mother was dead and Mr. Carter killed her, wasn't it Saturday afternoon?

A.   I don't remember when I first told them.

Q.   Well, in none of those statement did you ever say Mr. Carter shot your mother, did you?

A.   I never admitted the hour-- and never admitted how she met her death to the officers until today.

Q.   And you never did state to the officers your mother was shot, that is true, isn't it? Never had admitted it- and didn't' admit in any of those examinations that Mr. Carter shot your mother at all did you?

A.   I told them he killed mother.

Q.   Please answer the question. I said in none of those examinations did you ever state that Mr. Carter shot your mother?

A.   Not to the officers.

Q.   But you never told them Mr. Carter shot your mother, did you?

A.   Told them he killed her, but not how.

Q.   Now in this statement which you have sworn to under date of the 2nd day of February, 1935, I will ask you if you didn't under oath state that about eight or nine o'clock at night Mr. Carter and your mother got into an argument about the proper way to raise children--

A.   I admit the statement as I explained-

Q.   I'm asking you about this- speaking about this time- and that Mr. Carter struck your mother on the head with a poker and hit her after she fell on the floor?

A.   I made that entire statement.

BY THE COURT:

Gentlemen, you have had all day. I want to get through with this trial. Let's work an hour longer.

BY MR. CURRIE:

Judge, I am going to say this- in solicitation- speaking in my own responsibility- I think I am a strong man- entirely well- but it is made apparent that this witness has been subjected to a most grueling cross-examination.

The State of Mississippi,

vs.   No. 577

W. M. Carter.

     This cause this day coming on to be heard upon the petition of the District Attorney, praying for a writ of habeas corpus testificandum, directed to the superintendent of the Mississippi State Insane Asylum, at Whitfield, Mississippi, ordering him to produce one Ouida Keeton before this court on the 19th day of February, 1937, and the court having considered said petition is of the opinion that said Ouida Keeton is a material witness in the cause above named; that her presence before this court is necessary to the proper trial of said cause and the writ as prayed for should be granted.

     It is therefore ordered that the Clerk of this court be and he is hereby directed to issue a writ of habeas corpus testificandum directed to the superintendent or officer in charge of the Mississippi State Insane Asylum, at Whitfield , Mississippi, ordering him to produce before this court on the 19th day of February, 1937, at 9:00 o'clock A. M. one Ouida Keeton, an inmate of said institution as a witness in the case of the State of Mississippi vs. W. M. Carter.

     Ordered this the 18th day of February, A. D., 1937.

                             ....
                                Circuit Judge

231

State of Mississippi,

vs.   No. 577

W. M. Carter.

This cause this day coming on to be heard and it being made to appear to the court that Ouida Keeton, the prosecuting witness against the defendant, has now repudiated her former evidence and states that she is not willing to testify at this time that the defendant was in any way connected with the murder of her mother, Mrs. Daisy Keeton, for whose murder she and the defendant were jointly indicted; and the Supreme Court having, at a former hearing of this cause on appeal, announced her testimony as so unreasonable as to be unworthy of belief and having held the alibi of the defendant to be apparently established by reliable witnesses, and the State after diligent search and inquiry having been unable to find any additional testimony with which to proceed with the prosecution and the cause having been pending for several terms of this court since reversal by the Supreme Court, it is ordered that said cause be nol prossed, and that no further prosecution be had until such time as the State of Mississippi can produce sufficient evidence to secure a new indictment upon which to proceed with the prosecution.

Filed Feb. 26, 1937
F. L. Rummell, clerk
By Julia Johnson D.C.

The following photo is taken from True Crime Magazine in 1935

At slayers' trial, star witness Ouida Keeton attended in a wheelchair.

IN THE CIRCUIT COURT OF THE SECOND JUDICIAL DISTRICT OF JONES COUNTY, MISSISSIPPI.

STATE OF MISSISSIPPI

    V.   NO._____

W. M. CARTER,

    Comes W. M. Carter, defendant in the above-entitled cause, and shows unto the Court that at the last preceding term of the Circuit Court of Jones County, Mississippi, he was convicted of murder and sentenced for life in the state penitentiary; that the said defendant filed a motion for new trial, which was, upon June 29th, 1935, over-ruled by the Circuit Judge; that he desires to appeal said case to the Supreme Court of the State of Mississippi, and for such purpose, files this petition. The said defendant states that he is without means of any kind, and is therefore unable to give bond for costs to accrue in said cause or to make a deposit in cash to cover the costs of said appeal. Wherefore, he prays an appeal with supersedeas, in accordance with the statutes of the State of Mississippi.

                                     _W. M. Carter_____

STATE OF MISSISSIPPI,}
JONES COUNTY.

    Personally came before me, the undersigned officer in and for the aforesaid State and County, the within named W. M. Carter, defendant in the above-entitled cause, who, by me being duly sworn, makes oath that the matters and things stated in the foregoing application for appeal are true as therein stated. The said W. M. Carter states on oath that he is without means of any kind and is financially unable to give bond for costs to accrue on said appeal and to make a bond to cover the same.

                                     _W. M. Carter_____

Sworn to and subscribed before me, this___8___day of July, 1935.

                          T. L. Sumrall, Circuit Clerk
                    By Mrs. L. M. Martin, D.C.

Version two of Daisy Keeton's murder.
She was <u>not</u> struck in the head with the fire poker as the jail cell testimony given to Chief Brown, by Ouida, but the testimony told later and in the trail was that Carter shot Daisy while she was still in bed, three shots to the head. Why would Carter shoot her <u>three</u> times, wouldn't one shot at close range to her head be enough, not to say the noise of three shots echoing throughout the neighborhood in the still of the late hours. I know there was blood on the bed. Ouida's statement of the sight of her mother's <u>head</u> with blood streaming from her nose was to much for her to stand. Plus this version makes it premeditated murder, than the fire poker version of a heated argument ensuing with Carter going into a rage and picking up the poker and striking Daisy in a moment of rage and anger. Of course we will never know for sure how Daisy was killed, because the evidence was burned in the fireplace and the only witnesses to this horrible crime are long since dead. Ouida said Carter told her he had done his part in disposing of his half of her mother's body when she asked "What did you do with the rest of my mother?" A quote that has been used many times since the murder took place.

Carter told her she made a blundering mess disposing of the other half of the body. When he saw her Wednesday after the crime Saturday. He must have been blind not to see the condition Ouida was in after the deed was done. It should have been obvious to him she was in no condition to finish the job put to her alone. If he had really cared for her he would not have expected her to have to do this after being so close to her mother and to leave her alone in the house with her remains, just what was he thinking? If we could have seen what Ouida did all day and all night Sunday we would probably know that complete madness had taken control of her once intelligent mind. She probably walked around in the house talking to herself in a catatonic stupor, totally void of thoughts and her surroundings. She probably talked to her mother as though she was still alive. Not being able to deal with what she and Carter had done to her mother.

Monday morning she dressed totally inappropriate for the weather to go for that final ride in the country. She said she thought she was going to the McKinstry burial grounds. In her demented state she probably knew her mother was dead and was going to bury her in the family cemetery, but because she was unaware of her surroundings she never made it that far. In her words she didn't remember anything after she saw her mother dead. The rest is history.

On May 28, 1935, Ouida was called to testify in the trial of W.M. Carter as co-defendant in the murder of Mrs. Daisy Keeton. She, of course had already been convicted and sentenced to life without parole and sent to Parchman Penitentiary. Her mind seemingly pretty normal other than loss of memory of events following the murder, she calmly answered their endless questions in her testimony. She said that after her sister Eloise moved to New Orleans in August of 1934 that Carter began talking to her about killing her mother, because he could not see her like he wanted. They were having trouble with her mother, because she didn't want Ouida to leave the house and leave her alone and it seems as though Ouida didn't want to leave her alone either. In their love/hate relationship neither one seemed to be able to function for any period of time alone. As I have written before there was some strange bond between them. Ouida was emotionally tied to her mother even with the history of abuse mentally and physically, almost as if they shared the same soul, one could not survive mentally without the other. This proved to be the truth.

In January, 1935 the subject of leaving her mother came up again. Carter wanted Ouida to go to Mobile with him. She said she couldn't leave her mother. Carter then threatened to kill her mother. This is what she testified happened January 19, 1935, when he came by the service station where she worked for her brother-in-law, David McRae. At about 4:00 that afternoon. He came to her house about 6:00 p.m. to bring ice cream and then about 8:00 p.m. he returned for a visit. This is when the story changes. In Ouida's earlier testimony her mother was murdered at this time with the fire poker, but at Carter's trial she gave her third version of the murder. This time after 12:00 a.m. she let Carter in her window and he shot her mother in the head while in her bed. With no altercations before the shots were fired. Ouida said she went into her mothers room and sat on the side of the bed trying to get her to speak to her. Carter began abusing Ouida and threatening the same would happen to her. He said, "Get up or I will do to you just what I did to your mother." She said she went all to pieces and didn't remember anything else. When Ouida saw him next he asked for a ten thousand dollar check for her defense.

I know you think by now that I believe Ouida Keeton was an innocent victim, instead of a conspiring murderess. To a certain extent I do believe this, but I know she did help with the butchering of her mother's body, even if she didn't actually kill her, which I believe she is innocent of that. Even though her rational thoughts were deranged, she did help carry out the dismemberment and burning of the body over a period of many hours, Saturday night and probably all day Sunday, to the point of complete exhaustion. Probably all done in a zombie like state. The final diagnosis of Ouida's mental condition will show she could act violently with no memory of her actions. Her psychosis was being developed in the early years of life up until adulthood, so saying this, you have to decide if you think she was just the instrument used to help with this horrible crime and ultimately the one who paid the price.

Webpages.msh.state.ms.us/tour/tour_directory_09   Mississippi State Hospital,
Whitfield Mississippi.

Admittance to Mississippi State Hospital, April 17, 1936, case # 14,806, Patient Ouida Keeton.

This patient has been of an introvert makeup; has always shown abnormal attachment for her mother. She has been described as having temper-tantrums when a child, following which she would be quite moody, irritable and self absorbed. Her makeup is given as shy, bashful and unsocial. Her family back-ground shows an unstable, irritable makeup in most members of the family. There is no definite history of actual psychosis in the family, however, the entire family shows emotional instability. Psychosis has been characterized by impulsive behavior, periods of mutism. She has shown cera-flexibilitas at times, stares into space for long periods of time and has been out of contact with her surroundings.

The diagnosis in this case seems quite clear-cut- Appears to be malignant in nature and diagnosis offered is Dementia Praecox: Catatonic Type.

The differential diagnosis on Miss Keeton is as follows:

From a longitudinal study of this case, the only other psychosis which might be considered would be Psychosis with Syphilitic Meningo Encephalitis. She shows negative blood Wassermann, therefore, this can be ruled out from a serological examination. The apparent catatonic stupor which she was in could only be approached by hysteria, and even in hysteria it would have been impossible for her to show the cera-flexibilitas, the marked retention of saliva and her impulsive behavior.

There is apparently no precipitating factor in this case except that the abnormal love for her mother apparently turned into hate in her psychotic condition, making it possible for her to show the strong abnormal mental behavior which she has shown.

Patient's entire family was emotionally unstable. She has three Aunts who were described as very nervous and very peculiar. Has one brother who is strongly addicted to alcohol and has been charged with murder, rape and drunkenness(later this charge of rape and murder were dismissed) Her makeup is that of an introvert.

She will be treated institutionally with elimination, hydrotherapy and psychotherapy.

Prognosis in this case is fairly good for remission, however she may have a recurrence at some later date.

Summary of the patient:
White female, age 32 years, Mississippian, No occupation, single, high school education, 3-½ months business college.
Family History:
Patient has one brother who is strongly addicted to alcohol; brother in jail charged with rape, murder and drunkenness. Entire family has been high-tempered and of a nervous make. Three aunts are described as being nervous and very peculiar. Father is described as irritable and very high-tempered. Mother described as very stubborn and very high-tempered. Has two sisters and one brother living, and one brother dead. Since patient's admission to the hospital one brother has been divorced from his wife and her sister has gotten an annulment of her marriage.
Personal History:
Born October 6, 1903, Mississippi. Began talking at age 15 months; walked at age 2 years. She was fearful of dark as a child and was addicted to finger-nail biting. Had severe temper-tantrums and then pout for weeks. As a child had ear trouble, throat trouble and some injury of the spine. At age 15 patient had mumps and her left ear gave her trouble at this time, and she apparently has a total deafness of the left ear which date from the time she had mumps. Began school age and stopped at age 19. Graduated from high school and had 3 1/2 months business college. Was never left back in any grade. Began work at age 21 and continued in the same position until about 1933. Her make up before the onset of psychosis is given as shy, bashful, unsocial, given to day dreaming, she has been suspicious, jealous and sensitive, was quite changeable from cheerful to blue, easily discouraged and at time gloomy. She is very high-tempered and following temper-tantrums would pout for weeks, being very irritable and displaying ugly moods.
Psychosis: Onset and Development:
In January 1934, the first changes noticed was a marked stare and at times silly conversation. She would sit for long periods of time staring into space. This continues until January 1935 when she killed her mother, cut up her body, and went to pieces at this time. She and her mother were quite devoted to each other. Following her mother's death she became mute and inaccessible, and it was impossible to make contact with her. Shows impulsive behavior during this time. At times since this her conversation would appear to be normal. She has lost approximately 50 pounds in weight; has been eating quite poorly and had nervous nausea and vomiting.

On Admission:

Patient was self-absorbed, paid very little attention to her surroundings. Her answer to questions were given in a low monotone consisting of monosyllables. No active hallucinations or delusions could be elicited at this time. Complained of pain in spine, stating that she was quite tired and would like to be left alone so that she could sleep. Her general physical condition was fair on admission. Physical and neurological show height 5'4"; weight 120 pounds; hair streaked with gray; marked discoloration around eyes; appeared somewhat anemic; slight blowing systolic murmur at the apex of the heart which might be attributed to her nervous excited condition. This tends to clear up somewhat when she is quite. Blood pressure 108/64; heart actions regular. Complains of some pain over the spinal column- X-ray of this shows no gross pathology. She is apparently totally deaf in the left ear. Examination shows ear drums normal. She complains of a ringing in her right ear which is irregular in character and comes on several times a week. Neurological examination shows no pathology in reflexes. Urinalysis shows slight trace albumen; occasional hyaline, fine granular casts and occasional pus cells. Blood Wassermann negative. Has 10 teeth missing; 4 broker; slight inflammation of gums. Feces examination negative for parasites.

Subsequent course:

Patient has shown some improvement since admission to the hospital; she has at no time shown any anti-social behavior. She is quite self-absorbed, continues to stare in one spot on the wall for long periods of time and appears to be actively hallucinating at times. She is still well oriented for time, place and person. Her remote memory is still markedly impaired and she shows slight insight into her condition. Her physical condition is somewhat improved. She is now eating regularly and eating solid food; has gained about 2 pounds in weight, and apparently sleeps fairly well at night. Has had only one or two attacks of nausea vomiting since admission to the hospital and this on each time followed interview during which she was questioned for quite a length of time. At the present time she is quite agreeable to the ward routine. She resides in the Hydrotherapy department of the receiving ward where she causes no trouble. She is reclusive and does not mingle with the other patients, and she is quite self-absorbed at times. Still appears to be quite confused, staring into space. She has improved physically and has no physical complaints except of pain in region of spine.

The date is April 17, 1936 and I am still confused. The doctors have told me I killed my own mother and butchered her body. I cannot believe this could be true. How could I do such a horrible thing to my mama, I loved her so very much. I have spent 33 years of my life doing everything she asked of me and I never deserted her. My other siblings left and made a life of their own, but I stayed with her. I can't remember those days that they say it happened. All I remember is that someone told me they were going to kill her and do away with her body. I'm not sure I know who it was. Could it have been Louisa, come back from the dead to get her revenge?

I see my mama with God at her side everyday, she looks so beautiful and happy. Is she really dead or could they be mistaken about who the body parts they found belonged to? Why is it she visits me everyday, if I did murder her. My heart is full of sorrow I don't know how I can live like this. I'm so confused about everything that has happened. Did Will have anything to do with her death. I thought he did when I testified against him, but now I am not sure, nothing is clear to me. I pray for Gods forgiveness if I am indeed guilty in someway of my mama's death.

Admission note: date: April 17, 1936.
Patient was committed to the hospital by Physicians' Certificate from Jones County on April 17, 1936.
On admission this patient was quite self-absorbed, paid no attention to her surroundings, would stare into space and answer question only after repeated urging. Her replies were given in a low monotone and usually consisted of monosyllables. She complained of pain in her back, stated that she was quite tired and wanted to go to sleep. No hallucination or delusions could be elicited at this time. She appeared somewhat confused, was not able to give dates and could not remember how long she had been in different places just prior to hospitalization.
Third day note: April 20, 1936.

Patient is now residing in the Hydrotherapy department on the receiving ward where she is reclusive and does not attempt to mingle with the other patients. She will lie in bed staring at one spot in the wall for long periods of time. She appears to be actively hallucinating, however, it is impossible to elicit any hallucinations or delusions. She states that things are confused and that it seems to her that she imagines things or that she is in a dream-state. States that things are so confused that she cannot remember correctly. She appears to be cooperative; has shown no anti-social behavior; seems to be marked lowering of the emotional tone. She is now eating some better, taking semi-solid food and is no longer bothered with the nervous nausea that she complained of before and after admission.

8th day note: April 25, 1936.

Patient is still residing in the Hydrotherapy department on the receiving service where she is quiet and causes no disturbance. She attempts to cooperate to the best of her ability. She has had one attack of nervous nausea- This was immediately following interview and it is thought that excitement of the interview was the cause of this nervousness. She is now eating solid food and has gained about 2 pounds in weight. Has no complaints except that she still complains of her back hurting. Mentally she is still somewhat confused. Her recent memory appears to be somewhat better; remote memory still impaired. She still appears to be somewhat confused, stating that things are so mixed up in her mind that it is impossible for her to make a correct answer. Still stares into space for long periods of time, is quite self-absorbed and pays very little attention to her surroundings. Still does not mix with the other patients. Still denies any hallucination or delusions, however, states that her confused state, or dream-like state still comes over her at times and that she feels as if she is with her mother and that her mother talks with her.

Three months note: July 17, 1936.

This patient continues to reside in the hydrotherapy department of the receiving ward where she is quiet and agreeable, and causes no trouble. She is somewhat antisocial, sits alone throughout the day, frequently stares to the wall for long periods of time during which she is apparently out of contact with her surroundings. She is eating and sleeping well. She writes long rambling, incoherent letters at frequent intervals.

Dear Sis,   April 10, 1937

I am doing pretty good right now I have gained up to 120 pounds. I am sleeping better. I talked to mama today as I do everyday. She is so beautiful and she seems happy. They have given me a good job here at the library. I think they really needed someone that was educated and intelligent to fill this position. I also help the patients here. There are some really sick people here. You wouldn't believe how some of them act. They must be really crazy. I try to stay to myself as much as I can, because they won't leave me alone. If I sit and stare at the wall for hours they won't bother me.

How is everyone at home? Is Earl still in Jail? I can't believe he did what they say. Did he really rape and murder that girl? Maud I don't know what this world is coming to. My doctor is very nice and handsome too. You know he is in love with me. He is always telling me how beautiful I am. The nurses are jealous. One in particular is mean to me, because she is in love with him and he loves me. They let me cook my own food in the kitchen. You know what a good cook I have always been, but I have a problem about that, these crazy people in here want my food instead of theirs. I must run now, I have so much responsibility here it takes up a lot of my day.

P.S.
Don't they pay people that have a job here? Please find out for me, because I can't make any sense of it.

I Love You Always,
Ouida

Year note: April 17, 1937.
This patient has been residing on the receiving ward since admission to the hospital. She has been kept under close observation. Has periods during which she appears perfectly normal; at other times she has a wild-like stare in her eyes and appears to be actively hallucinating. She still speaks at time of hearing her mother's voice and shows many abnormalities along this line. She is quiet and giving no trouble of any kind. Patient is now working in the library where her work is quite satisfactory, and she seems to be showing slight but steady

improvement.
Progress note: February 11, 1939.
This patient has shown no marked change mentally since she has been under the writer's observation and care. She is very agreeable and cooperative; however, is reclusive and has very little to say to most of the patients; however, is always pleasant and cordial if she comes in contact with them. From our observation, we find that she had days of depression- not crying but apparently in a down cycle. Other times she seems to be of good cheer emotionally. She has been subject to severe headaches but since the removal of her teeth about three months ago, she has not had them as frequently. Her appetite is good- she prepares most all of food herself in the diet kitchen and she sleeps fairly well; however, we are told, by the night supervisor, that, at times, her rest is broken. She is in charge of the Hospital Library under the supervision of the Occupational Therapy Department, seems to enjoy this employment very much and goes about her work very complaisantly. Physically, she is getting along and has gained weight recently, and says that she usually feels well. She receives daily hydrotherapy baths.

Progress note: February 15, 1940.
The physician was called in and Miss Keeton was complaining of fever which she thought was due to a severe cold. We found her to have an upper respiratory infection and a mass in the lower pelvis about the size of a large grape fruit. More careful examination revealed a moveable mass and on vaginal examination we could not tell whether this was a pregnancy or tumorous mass which involved most of the part of the uterus. This information was carried to the superintendent by the ward physician and the superintendent advised that the assistant superintendent be called in for consultation. No definite conclusion has to the diagnosis was arrived.
Progress note: April 15, 1940.
By Dr. Barksdale; it was concluded that it was not a pregnancy but a fibroid tumor. Even though it had increased somewhat in size since the examination in February, he advised surgical removal of the tumor. It did not seem to be interfering with any of the activities of the patient.
Progress note: July 8, 1940.
Patient was rechecked by ward physician and advised the removal of the tumor. Patient bitterly objected to it. She was sent to the superintendent's office by the ward physician. Again after being advised by Dr. Mitchell, she said that she would rather the tumor kill her than go through with the operation.

Sis,   I don't know the
month, 1940
     Please come and get me. They want to cut my
stomach open. I think they want to kill me. Please, please
help me. Can you come? I will kill myself if they try to
torture me by cutting me all to pieces. Mama keeps saying
it won't hurt for long. They won't let me sleep when I want
to. You know how I liked to take naps during the day. How
long do I have to stay here. I don't like this place. What
kind of Hotel makes you do things they want you to do.
They even want me to work here. I am not one of their
employees. This is my vacation I should be able to do
anything I want. I am ready for you to come and pick me
up. I don't like the accommodations here anymore.

                                             Ouida
I have been told it is July 1940. They have come to get me
and take me back to Parchman. I guess because I was
working in the library and doing so much better, they
think I am completely well. I know I am not, but there is
nothing I can do to stop them. I really was enjoying
working again.

Leave note: July 31, 1940.
A traveling sergeant from Parchman Penitentiary came with the order from
Governor Paul B. Johnson, to remove this patient from the insane hospital at
Whitfield to the White Female Camp, Parchman. With the exception of the
tumorous mass that involves the entire pelvis she is considered to be in good
health. She was in a state of mental remission when she left.

Dear Sis,   July,
1940
     I got away from that terrible place. I have arrived at
the same pace I was when I first left home. I think it is in

245

Parchman, Mississippi. Someone said it is a penitentiary. I guess that is right, because I remember someone saying I would have to come here. They think I killed Mama. I tried to tell them someone else did it, but no matter my life is over anyway. I'm sure I will die soon. I have a tumor in my stomach, it doesn't hurt, but I can feel it and it is big. What happened to Earl? Is everyone okay at home? I don't know how long I will have to stay here, but it is better than that other place. You know where I mean. I have to be careful what I say, people are watching me all the time.

Transfer and Development:
Patient depressed, lost interest, refused to work. Superintendent called the Doctor and he excepted the patient. Ouida made statement she had rather die than return to Whitfield.
Now Ouida is transferred back to Whitfield on August 30, 1944 she has a physical examination:
General Appearance:
The patient is a well developed, emaciated white woman, age forty-one years, height 5'4", weight 91 pounds, with brown eyes, and hair turning gray. Skin is pale and dehydrated. The patient looks depressed, but seems clear. There are no noticeable deformities, infirmities, or fractures; no evidence of endocrine disturbance.
Evidence of acute or chronic constitutional disorders.
No important scars. There is a small tumor of the left arm at site of hypodermic injection. There is a large abdominal tumor. The patient is mal-nourished and emaciated.
Nervous System:
The patient was here in 1936, diagnosed, Dementia Praecox, Catatonic Type. Now, there are no areas of numbness or anesthesia. Enunciation is clear and distinct. There is no paralysis.
Sense organs:
Hearing and vision are slightly impaired.
Vaso-motor or Trophic changes:
Patient is dehydrated.
Motor Functions:
Patient has good use of musculature, but she is weak.
Thoracic organs:

Chest is well developed, but very thin, expansion is good. Lungs seem clear and resonant. Heart is normal in size and position, rate 94, slightly irregular, soft systolic murmur. Blood pressure 95/40. No arteriosclerosis.
Digestive system:
Appetite is fair, mouth negative, teeth false, tongue negative, tonsils out, abdomen shows large tumor.
Urinary System:
There is no history of venereal infection; no pregnancy. Menstrual periods are regular, patient is menstruating now. In view of abdominal tumor, a pelvic was done, and a large, hard uttering tumor occupies the whole pelvis and obscures other findings. There is no tenderness. Smear for laboratory. Rectal examination shows external hemorrhoids.

To You, I can't write your name,   1941
You know why
        Somebody needs to help me. This place is dangerous.
Last night some of the women hurt me, I can't say where,
but you know where I mean I have to be careful what I
write, because they all know everything I am doing and
writing. They won't leave me alone. I don't like women
messing with me. It just is not right. I am hurting pretty
bad, I think I am bleeding. They know I am prettier than
them and they don't like it. I do have a boyfriend, one of
the guards is in love with me. I don't mind him touching
me. The other women are jealous I have to go now, because
they are watching.
        From Me

Mental examination, September 5, 1944.
This patient was transferred from the State Penitentiary to this hospital on August 29, 1944. She was a patient from April 17, 1935 to July 31, 1940. At that time the patient was returned to the penitentiary in fair mental condition. She now returns to this hospital in a delusional and somewhat excited state. The full history of the case is herewith appended and I believe the diagnosis is correct.
Diagnosis: Dementia Praecox, Catatonic Phase.

Sis,   August, 1944

I am back at Whitfield. I didn't want to come, but I think I would have died if I stayed any longer at Parchman. I am so tired. I don't have the strength to walk. I am very depressed I think I am going to die soon. I think I am forty one now. They said I only weight ninety one pounds. I know I look very skinny I haven't been this thin since I was a girl. I have to dye my hair, because it is gray now. Maud, what is happening to me? Why has God deserted me? I read the Bible when I am able. What did I do to deserve this kind of life. Why can't I be like you and Eloise? I didn't kill our Mother. I see her everyday, she is alive. If it wasn't for seeing her I would go mad. I am all alone here. Mama never stays, she just comes and goes. I need to sleep now. I will write you later.

                                                    Ouida

Diagnostic Summary; September 14, 1951.
This is a white female patient born in 1903, and admitted to this hospital August 29, 1944, with a history that she would stare into space and at times enter into a silly conversation, this continued until 1935 at which time it is stated that she killed her mother. She has lost approximately 50 pounds in weight and has been eating poorly, has nervous nausea and vomiting. She would have temper tantrums, pout for weeks, suspicious, sensitive and jealous.
Progress note: Cottage 2, February 14, 1956, .
Can tell no difference in the medication she is taking.
Progress note: Cottage 2, May 8, 1956, Dr. Pennington.
At the present time this patient is on Medicine.
She is getting along satisfactorily.
Ward Note: Cottage 2, November 22, 1956, .
This patient was going to the dining room for the noon meal about twelve

o'clock Thanksgiving Day. She suddenly felt faint and told the attendant that she was going to fall; she fell to the ground and had a hard seizure lasting about 5 minutes, with tonic and clonic movements of the extremities. She urinated and defecated in her clothing and became markedly cyanosed. When she returned to the ward her temperature was normal, blood pressure was 100/70. This morning, 11/23/56, it was 120/70, her pulse was regular in rate and rhythm, of good quality. It is considered that this was an epileptic seizure, which is common to catatonic schizophrenics. The patient says that she has had several black-out spells previous to this time. Since these spells are far apart it was thought best not to begin any continuous anti-convulsive medication.

Transfer note: January 29, 1957, to hospital.

This patient was nauseated and vomiting at 6:40 a.m. She was given Emetral at 7:00 a.m. by orders of Miss Young a registered nurse. The medicine was given by Mrs. Long. This patient has been nervous and upset for a considerable period of time. She doesn't like to take medication, in fact she refuses to do so, but recently she had a red area on her forehead, for this she was given Benedryl capsules 1-4 times a day and Benedryl cream to rub on the area. It relieved it, but it did not do away with it entirely. Recently she had a very severe sore throat and cough and coryza, for this she was given Illotycine 1 every four hours for several days and Benedryl capsules 1 q.i.d.. The tear duct in her right eye closed up due to infection and her eye became edemist and red. Hot wet compresses were applied, both eyes were irrigated with boric acid solution and 2 percent argeral was dropped in each eye and Penicillin ophthalmic ointment rubbed on the lids. After several days this relieved the right eye and then the left one became infected. The same treatment was given. On 1/27/57 the patients entire face became a bright red as her forehead had been prior to all of this medication, as she is quite nervous and demanding, it was suggested that she go to the hospital, but she begged off, however, on 1/29/57 the redness continuing she was transferred to the hospital against her protest. She wanted to be sent with the ambulance driver alone without a nurse. She apparently dislikes the idea of an attendant taking her any place, however, this privilege was denied since a woman should always accompany a female patient in any vehicle. She talks in a rather low nervous manner and is quite excitable. It is considered that she is disturbed mentally.

Transfer note: February 7, 1957.

This patient was admitted to the General Hospital on 2/7/57 as per the above note, with evidence of a contact dermatitis about the face, areas of the dorsal of the hand and dorsal of the foot. It was thought this was probably due to hair dye which the patient has admittedly used. However, the story is distorted, she says it has been a period of six months. This is denied by the ward personnel. Because this disease did not respond to routine supportive treatment, the patient was treated with cortisone. Her psychosis was aggravated but soon she returned to her normal state. The lesions disappeared and she was returned to Cottage 2

on 2/7/57.
Ward note: Cottage 2, April 1, 1957.
This patient has had sinus difficulty in her right anthrum hymore. Her face is swollen and edematous. Her right eye is almost closed. She is being given Terroymicin, 1 capsule every four hours, bed rest, forced fluids have been recommended. She continues to receive reserpine 50 mg. t.i.d. Her skin condition has practically cleared up, there is a slight redness just beneath the hair line.
Ward note: December 15, 1957, Cottage 2.
On this day this patient has a running convulsion and ran down the hall and fell. Then she got up and went to her bedroom and fell again when she got inside of the door. She hit the wall and there was a marked discoloration about the left eye and also a cut place on the lid. This was minor and was immediately painted with mythiolate. The patient had difficulty for a couple of days in chewing, although, there seemed to be no fracture of the jaw. The patient was unconscious and she urinated and defecated all over her clothing. Ouida interpreted this incident to me the following morning saying " I slipped on a little piece of paper that was lying on the floor and struck the wall and hit my eye". She is always anxious to have her convulsive seizures attributed to something else. She denies having no insight into her general condition. She is usually nervous several days before having a seizure and this was true this time.
Ward note: November 11, 1959, Cottage 2.
This patient, aged fifty-six years, who carries the diagnosis of Dementia Praecox, Catatonic Type, is a resident of Cottage 2. Patient has adjusted well to the hospital routine. She is quiet, relevant, and coherent. She does not show any evidence of psychosis at this time. She is a good worker. She helps with the other patients. Physical condition is satisfactory. She is on no medication.

Ward Note: September 19, 1960.
This patient, aged fifty-seven years, who carries the diagnosis of Dementia Praecox, Catatonic Type, is a resident of Cottage 2. She has shown no change in her mental or physical condition during the past year. Patient does not appear to be psychotic. She is helpful with the ward work and with errands. Patient's physical condition is satisfactory. She is well nourished. Blood pressure is 120/6. She has a fibroid tumor of the uterus which does not give her any trouble. She is on no medication.
Ward notes: October 5, 1962, Cottage 2.
This patient, aged fifty-eight years, who carried the diagnosis of Dementia Praecox, Catatonic Type, is a resident of Cottage 2. She has shown no change in her mental or physical condition during the past year. Patient does not appear to be psychotic. She is a good worker and helps with the other patients. Physical condition is satisfactory. Blood pressure is 175/60. Recent X-ray of chest was negative. Recent urinalysis was negative. Patient has a fibroid tumor of the

utcrus, but she does not want it to be operated on and the tumor is not causing her any inconvenience.

Ward note: April 2, 1963, W.F. Cottage 2.

This patient, aged sixty years, who carries the diagnosis of Dementia Praecox, Catatonic Type, a resident of Cottage 2. She has shown little change in her mental or physical condition during the past year. Patient does not appear to be psychotic. She is helpful on the ward and runs errands for the other patients and employees. Patient's physical condition is fair. She has a fibroid uterus and refuses to have surgery. She is thin and slightly stooped. Blood pressure is 120/60, weight is 120 pounds. She is on no medication.

Progress note: February 9, 1965, Cottage 2.

This sixty-two year old white woman has been hospitalized here since 1954. She has a diagnosis of Schizophrenic Reaction, Catatonic Type. There is a history that she brutally murdered her mother and she apparently spent time in prison prior to coming to this hospital. She makes a good hospital adjustment, is helpful on the ward, making beds, and helping with other patients. At interview today, she is alert and oriented. She has apparently developed a satisfactory way of handling the guilt about her mother's death in that she completely denies it, stating that she was not guilty and it was done by some strangers. She says that she could not accept a pardon because she was not guilty of the crime in the first. She goes on in a similar grandiose delusional manner. She says, "It is all a big mess and there is a lot involved. She talks about getting letters from J. Edgar Hoover and in the past having asked the F.B.I. to check over the whole case, etc. She will most likely require indefinite institutional care.

Dear Eloise,   1965

I am doing Okay. How is everyone at home? I am working here at Whitfield. They really needed a manager. I see that everything is orderly and on time. I have to help the patients and they are really quite helpless, they can't seem to stay on schedule with the daily routine. I don't know what they would do without me. The nurses have their hands full. OK, yes, I have received a letter from J. Edgar Hoover. He has gotten the FBI to investigate our Mother's murder. We have become good friends thru out correspondence. I'm sure he will get our case solved in no time. Now that someone who knows what they are doing is working on it. I bet you are surprised at what an important person I have become, of course, my good looks helped. I must run now I am needed in administration.

Yours Truly,
Your Sister Ouida

Transfer Note: Cottage 3 to Cottage 5, January 10, 1969.
This patient had an episode of extreme confusion and agitation this morning. She was seen to have fallen in a ditch near Cottage 5 and was brought to that building. She found to be wet and very cold. She was unable to give any reliable history or reason for her behavior because of her disturbed state. She will be allowed to remain on Cottage 5 in the sick room under observation for the present time.

Dear Eloise,   1969
    You have to talk to these people. I am doing perfectly fine, then for no reason they come and get me and take me to a room with all kinds of machines and they put me on a table. Then they put these wires on my head while I am strapped down and so something awful to me. I wish I could tell you what it is, but I keep forgetting what they did. All I know is they have done this to me several times. I know it makes me very tired and weak for the whole day. Why are they doing this to me. Please find out, they won't tell me anything. The Doctor just says it is making me better. Better than what? I am fine. How do they expect me to do my job if they keep doing this to me. Eloise, you have to do something. Please come right away.

Ouida

Transfer Note: Cottage 5 to Cottage 1, January 14, 1969.
This patient continues to be disturbed. She is being transferred to Cottage 1 for close observation and possible shock treatments.

Transfer Note: Cottage 1 to Cottage 3, January 20, 1969.
This patient recently had a confessional episode and either fell or jumped in the lake. She has been on Cottage 1 receiving a brief series of EST. She is now much improved and is being transferred back to her usual cottage.
Transfer note: Cottage 3 to General Hospital, October 7, 1970.
This patient was today transferred from Cottage 3 to the hospital, for further observation and study, because of the presence of rales in both lungs, and because of a very firm mass, the size of a man's hand, in the right lower abdominal quadrant. The patient has lost twelve pounds in the last 65 days, and there has been a noticeable decrease in her energy in the past ten days. She has a very loose productive cough, and I suspect that she is quite a heavy smoker. She does sell cigarettes to other patients, and keeps a good supply on hand at all times, in her locker.
She could offer any explanation as to why she had not made a complaint previously, but her complaint today, that attracted out attention was that she complained to the attendant of having pain in her back. She announced that she had a "disc". The pain is localized as she points out, in the center of the thoracic spine. I note with interest, in a brief scanning of her record, that she had this symptom, or a similar complaint about this pain in her back, thirty years ago. She did remark that she had had this growth in her abdomen for the past thirty years. I very strongly suspected that this was malignant, since she has a loss of energy, a loss of weight, and washed out look, and much paler than she ordinarily is, but on reading the record, I find that she has a fibroid, for which she refused operation a long time ago.
She has a long extensive record in this hospital, to which she was transferred from the Parchman State Penitentiary. She was sent to Parchman, after she had murdered her mother, or after she was convicted of murdering her mother.
The communication with this patient is not as easy as one might expect, because she has always been a pleasant, outgoing type of individual, but I find it quite difficult to get her to commit herself in a clear, distinct manner, or to give an accurate history about her recent illness. She was on no medication at the time of her transfer. She had not been in close contact with any of her relatives, but she does have a couple of nieces, but as far as I know, she has not been visited by these nieces in a long time.
Consulting Physician's Report: November 18, 1970.
I have reviewed this patient's hospital chart. She has a large abdominal mass which is felt to be a calcified fibroid. Her serum creatinine is varied from 2.5 to 3 mgm. Percent. IVP shows bilaterally small kidneys with evidence of chronic pyelonephritis and minimal amount of fullness. There is a 2 cm filling defect in the right renal pelvis which cannot be appreciated as an opacity on the scout film.
Impression:
1.   Mild degree of ureteral obstruction due to compression at the pelvic

brim by the uterine mass;
2.   Filling defect right renal pelvis, possible uric acid calculus, possible papillary neoplasm;
3.   Chronic parenchyma renal disease, probably chronic pyelonephritis, grew out hyperuracemia.
Recommend: I think that the uterine fibroid surgery probably should be done first. This might improve renal functional status by reducing ureteral compression. The right kidney will need to be explored if this filling defect is a persistent finding.
Suggest: After her recovery from the hysterectomy repeat IVP be done. If this is tumor of the renal pelvis, I would be very reluctant to do a right nephrectomy in view of her azotemia. It might be possible to handle with local resection. Keep me posted on her progress.

October 30, 1973,

I have been admitted in the General Hospital. They say I don't have long to live. I know I have some serious physical problems. My health has been poor for some years now and I guess my mental condition is deteriorated as well. Today my mind is pretty clear, so I am writing in my diary, possibly for the last time. I have been keeping a diary since I was a little girl of nine. My Pa bought me my first diary for me in 1912 for my birthday. Education was very important to him. He taught me to read and write at an early age. After I am dead and gone maybe someone will read this and understand what kind of person I really was. I don't know why I became the person I am now. I had some wonderful dreams of a beautiful life. Finding romance and having a beautiful family and being a loving wife and mother.

Why couldn't I have lived like a normal person? I guess I knew early on I was different from everyone else I knew. I have questioned God many times about my fate and why I had to suffer a thousands hells in this life. I think my mother suffered a similar fate. My heart is broken for the way things turned out. My brothers and sisters, I think they loved me too. I know after Ma died they stuck by me until their death. I love them deeply for their devotion. I think it is sad that I have out lived all of them. I only have three nieces left as far as I know.

I loved Ma in a different way. I sometimes think we shared the same soul. I know the moment she took her last breathe, my soul was taken from me forever. I have never been complete since that night. There is a void where my heart used to be. God, please forgive me for my sins against you and my mother. I never meant for things to turn out this way. I have asked for forgiveness many times, I hope God has heard my prayers.

My diary is all I have left to leave behind that is of any importance to me. I hope it will mean something to someone, someday. Worldly treasures don't mean much, when you are about to meet your Savior and be judged by your deeds. I just hope and pray God can see I have tried to live for him in my last years. I'm sure some would say my mind is completely gone and I couldn't possibly have the mental ability to ask for forgiveness, but I do have moments that I am conscious of my need for redemption. I am very weak now, so I will close. I hope I will be able to write again before the end.

Ouida

To Whom It May Concern,   November 1, 1973

I have no family left they are all dead. I am alone now. I don't know who will read my last letter. I am very sick and I am told I will probably die very soon.

If I did something wrong I hope God can forgive me. I don't remember doing anything bad to my Mama. I loved her deeply. I am very confused, because I talk to her all the time I'm sure it is her. Whatever happened along time ago I am sorry. Please, who ever reads this tell God and Mama I am truly sorry. I don't want to go to hell. Louisa is calling to me to join her, but I know where she is and I don't want to go there.

I am very afraid to face death alone, maybe Mama will be here with me at the end. I will have to say farewell and good bye now.

Yours Truly,
Ouida

November 11, 1973

This is my last entry in my diary. I know death is near now. I am so weak I can hardly write, but I want to say my goodbyes and once more ask God for forgiveness. I saw my ma yesterday, she is waiting for me. I have seen my little brother John, he is an angel in heaven. Maud and Eloise have also come to visit me, they are so beautiful, they want me to come home. I thought I would be afraid to face death alone, but now I know I am not alone. They are all waiting for me to come and join them. I know now that God has forgiven me for what I did a long time ago, because I suddenly feel peace and my mind is completely clear. I see God........

DEATH NOTE: NOVEMBER 11, 1973.
This seventy year old white woman was admitted to this institution in 1944 with a diagnosis of Schizophrenia, Paranoid Type. She continued to deteriorate both mentally and physically and three years ago was found to have chronic pyelonephritis. Her renal status continued to deteriorate and she was admitted to the General Hospital on October 30, 1973. She was uremic at that time and continued to deteriorate and aspirated three days prior to her death. She passed away on November 11, 1973 at 2:00 p.m. Immediate cause of death was felt to be aspiration pneumonia. Other significant conditions were felt to be chronic pyelonephritis with uremia. An autopsy was not done.

Now that you have read Ouida Keeton's story how do you feel about this woman? No one has ever written about what her life could have been like. The murder trial has been written about more than once, but has anyone tried to give an account of her life. That is what I have tried to portray here whether it is true or not we will probably never know. From studying about her and her family I have learned a lot. They were very clannish which comes from the Scotch-Irish side of the McKinstry's, her mother's father. The superstitious and peculiar ways of her Grandma Laura who was Creole.

John Keeton was said to have a temper. The whole family was peculiar, high tempered, nervous, stubborn, clannish and as a whole emotionally unstable. Her brother was an alcoholic and was abusive to his wife. They were wealthy people and owned land and property in Laurel, Mississippi, Jasper County, Mississippi and Angie, Louisiana.

We know Ouida lived in an imaginary world all of her life. Was this to escape mental and physical abuse that she suffered by her Mother? We also know she had an abnormal attachment for her Mother that turned to hate and she heard voices. Did Louisa exist and speak to her after death? Were Luke and her two sweethearts real people or a delusion of hers. She was diagnosed with delusional behavior, hallucinating and out of contact with her surroundings. At the time of her admittance to Mississippi State Hospital with the clinical diagnosis: Dementia Praecox: Catatonic Type.

What or who drove her to madness and murder? Was it her mother or was it Carter? Who knows how the human mind thinks when it has been driven over the brink of rational thinking. What pushed Ouida into the depths of hell? What was going thru her brain as she savagely chopped her mother's body into pieces and tried to dispose of it? Burning her Mother's head in the fireplace with the look of shear horror still on her mother's face. How could this seemingly loving person commit such a crime against God and humanity?

Was she responsible for her actions? Did she deserve what she got? All I know is after the verdict of murder with life without parole she was sent to Parchman Prison as a sane woman, but after a year she was transferred to Whitfield Mental Hospital for the criminally insane and she spent the rest of her life there, dying in 1973, at the age of seventy never regaining her sanity!

YOU DECIDE!

INFORMATION ABOUT OUIDA KEETON'S CONDITION:

Technical advise from my niece; Regina Bartran Dixon; who has a Masters Degree in psychology and counseling. She is a licensed mental health counselor, having received her degree at Troy State University in Pensacola, Florida.

Ouida was found to have extremely undeveloped inguinal glands, the whole glandular system was no larger that a pea and stopped developing at about age two. Her thyroid gland was absent. The glands control everything in the human body. They regulate the hormones. Ouida had too much dopamine in her system, causing hallucinations and delusions' layman terms, the over abundance of dopamine is like a person on a "LSD trip" continuously. This chemical is the neurotransmitter in the brain sending messages out. In her case causing insanity; medical term: Catatonia Dementia Praecox, cataleptic type or schizophrenia, but schizophrenia comes from 50% genetic and 50% environment. So, her problem was only half from a medical disorder, the other half was from emotional abuse and traumatic situations suffered in her life.
These problems made Ouida mentally immature and easily controlled. This explains a lot. Her Mother's domination over her and Carter's control of her actions. It is surprising she was so intelligent. Usually a person with this diagnosis would not be able to remember what she learned and would have trouble functioning normally at anytime. Her need for love from a Father figure was understandable. This explains her love for Carter, because she was mentally incapable of feeling sexual pleasure. Lastly and sadly Ouida could have never been able to have children.

August 18, 2010, Interview with Betty Coats Barron, resident of Hattiesburg, Mississippi.

Born in 1930, Betty and her parents, Roy and Ellen Coats rented the Keeton home in 1937, just two years after the murder. The beautiful Keeton home had been divided into two apartments. The Coats lived on the right side of the house where the bedrooms were originally and the murder took place. Betty was a child of seven when they moved in, but her memory is still vivid, as if it were yesterday, of the house and grounds.
The other half of the house was rented as well. The lady next door owned a little café down the street, possibly Cross Street Café. Her daughter, Jean, was a playmate with Betty. There was a carriage house out back, which contained the garage. Upstairs, in what was probably the servants quarters many years ago, was being used for storage. When Betty and Jean went up there, there were trunks of old clothes and boxes of costume jewelry. It was like a treasure

259

hunt going thru the contents of the trunks and the old velvet lined jewelry boxes. The clothes they found were beautiful dresses of silk, satin and lace. Fancy dresses designed for evening wear. The little girls dressed-up in these pretty evening gowns and draped themselves with necklaces of pearls and rhinestones, earbobs that dangled in sparkling splendor, making them look like little princesses. As they danced around pretending to be at a grand ball with an orchestra playing beautiful waltz's. They played for hours in their fantasy world of make believe. I think Ouida would have liked that. Betty remembers how beautiful the old house was. Leaded glass in the front door and transom above and in all the tops of the windows in the front rooms. She especially remembers how finely appointed the kitchen and bathroom was. The kitchen had beautiful cabinets with glass doors for displaying fine China. The counter tops were of fine white veined marble. Large windows flooded the room with natural light. The bathroom she remembers clearly, with it's marble counters and floors, a large footed French tub and a pedestal lavatory. She will never forget the cracks and scratches that were still visible in the tub. The deeper cuts had been patched, but they could still be seen, just the same. Betty remembers baths in that big tub and running her fingers across the crevices on the sides of the tub, as she bathed thinking of what her Mama had told her about an old lady being chopped-up in this same tub. It gave her a creepy feeling each time she took her bath. The whole place had a strange feeling about it. She was too young to understand the true essence of the horrible past of this house. That infamous night on January 19, 1935 when the gruesome murder took place, only two years earlier. Other than Betty's little friend Jean telling her about when they would light the gas heater in the fireplace, grease would bubble up on the hearth, she didn't really see anything else that looked suspicious. After living at the Keeton House for three years they moved to another apartment on Short Avenue and in 1941, just before Pearl Harbor was attacked, moved to Hattiesburg and has lived there until present day. She is now eighty years old and a fine Southern lady.

September 13, 2010, Interview with retired Baptist Pastor, Robert Bullock, now living in Ellisville, Mississippi.

Rev. Bullock was Pastor of the Calvary Baptist Church in Picayune, Mississippi, from 1969 to 1975. As a small child he had heard about the murder trial of Ouida Keeton in 1935. He still remembers how everyone was talking about the gruesome crime. As he grew older the memories of this beautiful murderess stayed on his mind. When he became a preacher, he prayed for her salvation, only to be left with the uncertainty if she had mind enough to ask for forgiveness. It weighted heavy on his heart. The long awaited answer to his troubled prayers were put to rest in November, 1973, when he attended the sad funeral of a little old lady being sent to her final destination on this earth. As he entered McDonald's Funeral Home in Picayune, Mississippi, a place he knew well from the many funeral services he had performed there through the years, as pastor at the nearby Baptist Church. He had seen so many dear souls in their satin lined caskets, no longer feeling the sorrows and pain of this earth. He knew most would be with their Savior, but for some it was uncertain of their salvation and if they were with our Lord, Jesus Christ. On this cold November day he would finally see the woman who had haunted his thoughts from the past. It was Ouida Keeton, the once beautiful woman who had killed her mother. As he approached the casket he noticed a lady standing alone in the room, this lady was Ouida's niece, one of only a few survivors of the Keeton family. There was no one else at the funeral. As he looked in the casket he was surprised to see how delicate and tiny she was. Her hair was completely gray and she was dressed in a pretty gray suit. He could still see a gracefully aged beauty lying there, but what impressed him most was the look of complete peace on her lovely face. He watched as they closed the lid forever on Ouida's coffin; he was the last person to see her in this world.

His questions and prayers were answered at last. She was forgiven by our merciful and forgiving Savior. He left the funeral home knowing that a burden had been lifted off of his heart that had been there for many, many years. He also knew after seeing her tiny frame that she could not have done this awful crime alone.

Robert Bullock retired after 51 years of service in the Lord's work. Now at 80 years old he has lead a full and fruitful life and now he is spending his golden years with his loving family, they reminisce of times long ago of cherished memories that will never be forgotten.

I want to thank Reverend Bullock very much for this interview. It has finally brought resolve to my own troubled thoughts.

I want to write one last thing about Ouida Keeton; at the beginning I wanted to write about this beautiful young woman, who became famous, because of the brutal murder of her mother and **why** she did it. I did not know what an effect it would have on me as I got deeper into my research of her life. She haunted my soul. I could not get her off my mind. I thought of nothing else for months.

With the knowledge of mental illness in my own family, in the early 1900's, where a beautiful great aunt lost her mind and could not be helped, because of medieval techniques being used 100 years ago. Seeing "Rain Tree County", with Elizabeth Taylor, for the thirtieth time, finally was clear to me, "Street Car Named Desire", with Vivian Leigh was no longer a mystery.

Ouida has opened a world of understanding of mental illness. I got more emotionally involved in her life than I ever meant to. If only a few who read this book can have empathy for this poor girl, it will be worth my efforts to have written it. Mental illness is a tragic disease that many suffer from; Schizophrenia is probably one of the worse. I think Ouida Keeton's story is a perfect example of our society's ignorance of the effects and outcome of this terrible illness.

Made in the USA
Charleston, SC
01 March 2011